For Helena

ACKNOWLEDGMENTS

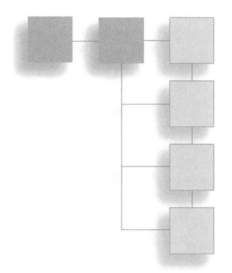

I would like to thank my friend and colleague Karyn Jimenez-Elliott for helping with graphics and design for the prototype of this book and its cover; my friend and colleague Thomas H. Calabrese, Ph.D., for inspiring me to get started on this project; and especially James F. Brennan, Ph.D., for countless years of personal, academic, and professional guidance.

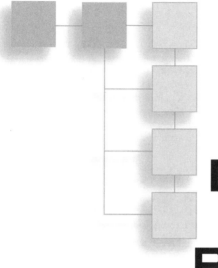

ANDROID™
APPLICATION
DEVELOPMENT
FOR JAVA®
PROGRAMMERS

JAMES C. SHEUSI

Course Technology PTR
A part of Cengage Learning

COURS
CENGAG

Australia • Brazil • Japan • Korea • Mexico • Singapore • Spain • United Kingdom • United States

COURSE TECHNOLOGY
CENGAGE Learning®

Android™ Application Development for Java® Programmers
James C. Sheusi

Publisher and General Manager, Course Technology PTR:
Stacy L. Hiquet

Associate Director of Marketing:
Sarah Panella

Manager of Editorial Services:
Heather Talbot

Senior Marketing Manager:
Mark Hughes

Senior Acquisitions Editor:
Mitzi Koontz

Project/Copy Editor: Karen A. Gill

Technical Reviewer: Jeffrey Tagen

Interior Layout Tech:
MPS Limited, a Macmillan Company

Cover Designers: Karyn Jimenez-Elliott and Mike Tanamachi

Indexer: Sharon Shock

Proofreader: Sue Boshers

For product information and technology assistance, contact us at **Cengage Learning Customer & Sales Support, 1-800-354-9706.**

For permission to use material from this text or product, submit all requests online at **www.cengage.com/permissions.**

Further permissions questions can be emailed to **permissionrequest@cengage.com.**

Library of Congress Control Number: 2011945858

ISBN-13: 978-1-133-59354-6

ISBN-10: 1-133-59354-2

Course Technology, a part of Cengage Learning
20 Channel Center Street
Boston, MA 02210
USA

Cengage Learning is a leading provider of customized learning solutions with office locations around the globe, including Singapore, the United Kingdom, Australia, Mexico, Brazil, and Japan. Locate your local office at: **international.cengage.com/region.**

Cengage Learning products are represented in Canada by Nelson Education, Ltd.

For your lifelong learning solutions, visit **courseptr.com.**

Visit our corporate website at **cengage.com.**

Printed in the United States of America
1 2 3 4 5 6 7 14 13 12

ABOUT THE AUTHOR

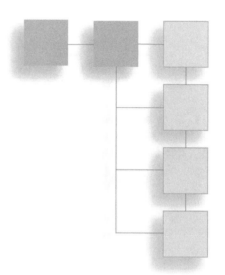

James C. Sheusi copyrighted and sold his first application for the real estate sales industry in 1984 and has developed applications for small businesses for more than 25 years. He is an associate professor and currently chair of the Department of Computer and Information Science in the School of Technology at Johnson and Wales University in Providence, Rhode Island. He resides with his wife in Bristol, Rhode Island.

Contents

PREFACE

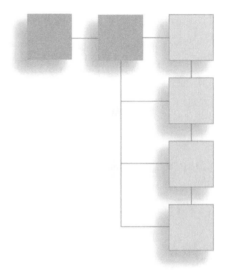

We are witnessing an explosion in the use of handheld mobile devices worldwide. Recent polls have shown that many people own and use more than one mobile device, and some use as many as three or four. Smart phones, tablets, and handheld game devices are ubiquitous. The Android operating system (OS)—an open-source OS with Linux at its core—is an ever-more-popular OS on these devices.

In September 2011, *Computerworld* magazine's website predicted that the Android OS would claim 39 percent of the global market this year. In the first two weeks of October 2011, India announced its intention to subsidize the purchase of tablet devices targeting students, reducing the price about $35. The devices will run the Android OS. In the same period, Bangladesh unveiled the Doel, a netbook set to sell for about $130, and an ambitious plan to have all its citizens digitally connected by 2021. Both the Indian tablet and the Doel will run the Android OS.

Currently, more than 40 different mobile phones run the Android OS from more than 10 different manufacturers. The potential market for mobile applications based on the Android market is staggering. You have come to the right place.

This book is a tutorial for programming Android applications. The examples presented are created using the Eclipse integrated development environment (IDE) with the J2SE, Java Standard Edition, and the Android Development Kit (ADK) added in.

Android Application Development for Java Programmers is intended to be a tutorial, not a reference manual. It is a quick-start for sparking interest in Android application programming. This book provides enough detail that a newcomer to Android programming can create a useful and, indeed, marketable application. However, each section covers only the surface of a topic; there is plenty of room for outside research. Java and Android are extremely well-covered topics on the Internet. You need only to search class names, method names, or key questions to receive further guidance. Simply add the word *tutorial* or *example* to your search query, and you will find plenty of what you are looking for.

This book is meant for programmers familiar with Object Oriented Programming (OOP) principles, and preferably with Java programming experience. If you are familiar with C++ or C#, you will be able to follow the examples well enough to make the book a worthwhile read. Familiarity with the Eclipse IDE is ideal but not necessary. This book covers the basic install of the Java Development Kit (JDK), the ADK, and the Eclipse IDE. Configuration of the IDE is covered as the steps become necessary.

Because the ADK contains the necessary software to generate emulators for Android devices such as smart phones and tablets, you need not possess an actual device to develop and test an application. An emulator is a program that produces a screen display and the functionality of a handheld device on your development computer. Using the emulator, you can fine-tune the look of your application and test most of its features. Of course, the development experience will be much more rewarding if you can actually carry around your creations and use them as they are intended.

Early on in the text, you are introduced to each section and file type developed for a particular application. Eclipse will generate most of these necessary folders, sub-folders, and files at the onset of a new project. For any file that the developer needs to create or modify, the actual code for the example is printed in the book.

Each example in this tutorial is functional and usable. The user can copy the screen designs in the form of XML files from one application to others where the same configuration is appropriate. The same is true with subclasses found in examples—especially inline classes. The chapters are arranged in a way that concepts introduced in the early chapters are used throughout the balance of the book. For example, screen arrangements and user controls are introduced early on because user control of applications is essential. Gradually, built-in device features such as the GPS system, file storage, and access to networks and the Internet will be added to applications. The reader should use her imagination as she reads the book to convert the principles presented into useful, appealing applications. There is plenty of room in the marketplace. Good luck and enjoy!

INTRODUCTION

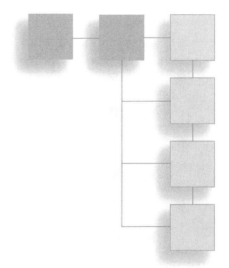

You could argue that the success of the Microsoft Windows OS on the desktop, somewhere over 90 percent of all desktops, is attributable to Microsoft being at the right place at the right time. The rapid evolution and popularity of the personal computer, the rapid advance of CPU technology, and the standardization of PC architecture based on the IBM PC-AT gave Microsoft a market on which to thrive. This is not to say that Microsoft doesn't deserve credit for its success in its own right or that it didn't contribute to the success of the personal computer industry.

The same could be said for the rapid advance in technology and popularity of the smart phone and the evolution of the Android OS. In three short years, Android has become the most popular OS on mobile phones in the United States. In the spring of 2011, a Nielsen survey concluded that Android controlled 36 percent of the market, followed by Apple iOS at 26 percent (Feb-Apr 2011 Nielsen Mobile Insights, National). Estimates are that by the end of 2012, Android will control 50 percent of the global smart phone market, the other 50 percent being divided among all other systems. In February 2010, CBS reported that the worldwide number of mobile phone subscriptions was 4.6 billion, and that was expected to grow to 5 billion during 2010. 2011 estimates are 5.6 billion mobile subscriptions worldwide, 77 percent of the population, with the largest growth in China and India. So, what is Android, and where did it come from?

In August 2005, *Business Week* reported that Google acquired Android, Inc., a 22-month-old start-up, which signaled Google's push into the wireless market. In 2007, Google and several other industry giants such as Motorola, Toshiba, Texas Instruments, and T-Mobile, just to name a few, formed the Open Handset Alliance.

The alliance members released a significant amount of intellectual property into open source and released the Android platform.

In September 2008, T-Mobile released the G1, the first smart phone based on Android. It ran Android 1.0, the world's first open-source mobile OS. In April 2009, Android 1.6 added Google Maps. That same year Motorola released the Droid mobile device. The next significant release was Android 2.2, nicknamed Froyo (short for Frozen Yogurt), which offered an OS tune-up for speed, USB tethering for WiFi hot spots, and support for Adobe Flash 10.1 for watching videos on the built-in browser. In 2010, Motorola released the Backflip and the Droid X, and T-Mobile released the G2. In February 2011, Android released 3.0, the made-for-tablet installment. This brief history mentions just a few Android devices; today there are dozens, and the number is steadily increasing.

The Android platform, based on the Linux OS, is designed to be a general-purpose handheld computing platform. The Linux core controls the mobile device's memory, internal devices, and processes. The Android libraries control telephony, video, graphics, and the user interface. Like any Linux system, the Android OS is a multiuser system in which each application is treated as a different user with a unique user ID. The OS sets permissions on files based on the application's ID so that applications have access to the necessary files.

The Android software development kit (SDK) supports most of the Java Standard Edition. However, Android replaces the Java abstract windowing toolkit (AWT) and Swing packages with its own user interface (UI) framework. The popularity of the Java programming language, along with the extensive class library associated with the ADK, makes it an attractive development platform. As you might expect as a Java programmer, each application runs on its own Java virtual machine (JVM). However, Android supplies its own optimized JVM called the Dalvik virtual machine.

Android applications are composed of one or more of four types of core components. These are activities, the base of all of the examples in this book; services; content providers; and broadcast receivers. Applications can request services from the device's built-in components, such as the camera and networking components, but requests for these services are added to a "manifest file" at application design and development time. The manifest file is referred to frequently throughout the book. At application install time, the user of the device will respond to requests for services listed in the manifest, either granting or denying the request.

- **Activity**—Represents a single screen and user interface. During application development, an activity is written as a single Java class, with the application's main class extending the Android development kit's `Activity` class. Although activities are independent of one another, they are allowed to work together with one activity initiating another.

- **Service**—A process that runs in the background to perform long-term operations or work for remote processes, not unlike daemons on Linux-based computers or services on Windows-based computers. Services do not provide a user interface. A service, for example, might be used to download data in the background, allowing the user of an application (activity) to interact with that application without delay. The developer creates a service as a subclass of the Android `Service` class.

- **Content provider**—Manages persistent data on the device or external sources such as the web or cloud, or any other system the application has access to. You can think of content providers as the file managers for the system. For instance, Android devices have an on-board SQLite database management system to provide organized persistent data storage. Another example is the device's contact list, which applications can access if they have permission.

- **Broadcast receiver**—A component that responds to system conditions such as low battery or the screen being turned off. You can use broadcast receivers to initiate a response from a running application, such as if a picture has been taken. A broadcast receiver that a developer writes is implemented as a subclass of the Android `BroadcastReceiver` class.

A unique benefit of the Android system design is that one application can start another application's components, whether written by the developer or a third party or built into the system. For instance, a developer can write an application that uses the device's phone dialer, and it will appear that the phone was built into the developer's own application. Because each of the application types listed runs as a separate process with its own file permissions, one activity requests access to another through an `Intent`. The way the `Intents` will respond to activities is determined at design time by employing "`Intent` filters" that are set in the application's manifest file.

The relative ease of programming in Java, coupled with the cooperative features of the Android OS and the gargantuan user base of Android devices, creates an attractive opportunity to earn income from application development. Along with the "official" Android market, http://market.android.com, there are many other Android markets on which to post your creations. At the time of this writing, the cost to belong to market.android.com is $25, and the developer is allowed unlimited postings. Vendors are given a page to add new applications, post upgraded versions, view download statistics, and so on. Developers can post on many markets free of charge.

Caution

Unlike other platforms, Android applications can be distributed and installed through direct-connect to the computer the application was developed on or even as an email attachment. Details on application signing, publishing, and distribution are given in Chapter 11, "Publishing Your Application." Developers can earn from their applications either by charging directly for the application or by offering ad space on the application. For example, Google offers www.admob.com as a starting point; developers receive instructions on how to include ads on the screen, the necessary code to be downloaded and added to the application, and the ability to create their own ads for their own business. Like the market sites, the developer is given a page on which to view income reports. Two other such mobile ad networks are Jumptap and Mojiva. You can find a comprehensive listing of these at http://mobithinking.com/mobile-ad-network-guide.

In conclusion, the array of features contained in the Android OS, along with the rich development set offered by both the Java and Android development kits, offers the developer mobile computing solutions and an array of distribution channels and options to allow their deployment. You can find complete documentation of the ADK at http://developer.android.com. The packages, classes, and interfaces are described in standard java-doc style under the Reference tab on the web pages.

CONVENTIONS USED IN THIS TUTORIAL

To make this book easier to read, special conventions are employed throughout.

Italic is used to indicate new terms.

`Monospace type` is used to indicate blocks of code, commands to be entered at a terminal screen, menu paths, controls, file and directory names, extensions, parameters, objects, classes, tags, methods, and variables.

WHAT YOU'LL FIND IN THIS BOOK

Here's what you'll find throughout the pages of this book:

- A guide to installing and configuring an Android development environment on your personal computer.

- A guide to configuring an Android device emulator on your personal computer and illustrations of running applications on the emulator.

- All the code necessary to create several simple applications to demonstrate the capabilities of an Android mobile device.

- A guide to publishing an Android mobile application.

- Explanations of the methodologies used in the examples, as well as descriptions of the classes and their methods used in the examples.

- Follow-up exercises and recommendations for further study as well as many outside references for clarification of principles and techniques used in the book.

WHO THIS BOOK IS FOR

This book is an ideal, quick-start tutorial for anyone interested in developing Android mobile device applications, from the student or hobbyist familiar with Java, to the experienced programmer wanting to enter the mobile device application market. Because the Android development software provides an emulator program, the reader doesn't need to own an Android mobile device to take advantage of this book. Although the code presented in the book can be used to produce complete running applications, the goal is to inspire the reader to bring his own mobile application ideas to reality in a short time.

HOW THIS BOOK IS ORGANIZED

The book is organized in a logical, evolutionary manner starting with configuration of the development environment and ending with two comprehensive projects. The beginning chapters cover basic application components and configuration of the Android emulator and basic user interface design, whereas later chapters cover how to accomplish more involved areas such as use of GPS, graphics, networking, and databases. In most chapters the reader will find the following:

- An introduction to the concept or technique to be covered

- A description of the example application presented to demonstrate the concept

- All the coding necessary to produce a running application to demonstrate the chapter's topic

- Recommendations for reader follow-up to extend the reader's knowledge of key points in the chapter

- A list and description of the Java classes highlighted in the chapter

- Space for the reader to record notes and research on the chapter's topics

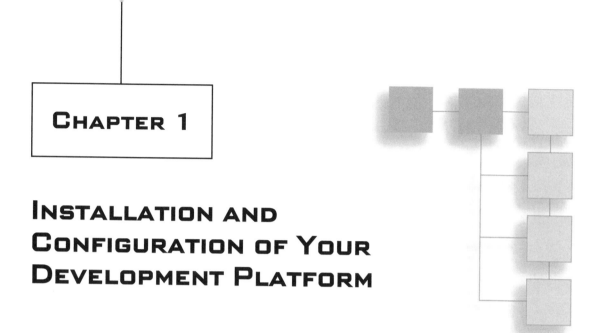

CHAPTER 1

INSTALLATION AND CONFIGURATION OF YOUR DEVELOPMENT PLATFORM

INSTALLING ECLIPSE AND JAVA

If you are already developing Java applications, chances are that you are using the Eclipse integrated development environment (IDE), and of course the Java Development Kit (JDK), and you are using JDK5 or above and most likely the J2SE or Standard Edition. If this is the case, you can skip down to the later section titled "Installing the Android Development Kit." On the other hand, if you are starting from scratch, Eclipse is available from www.eclipse.org, and the JDK is available from www.oracle.com/technetwork/java/javase/downloads/index.html. The current version of the Java Standard Edition is version 7.

In my experience, it is better to download and install the JDK first. There are two possible downloads: the JDK and the JRE. The JDK is the development software, and the JRE is simply the "run-time environment," a piece of software required by an operating system to host a Java application. Be sure you download and install the JDK. It contains and installs a copy of the JRE, so there is no need to install them separately. You should also note that Eclipse, Java, and Android development software are available for the Linux and Mac OSs, although they are not directly addressed here. After the JDK installs, you will want to set its location in your computer system's PATH variable. You can consult references on how to do this on the Internet, but if you are using Windows 7 as I am, you can use the following steps:

1. Click the Start button. Then right-click on Computer on the right side of the Start menu and choose Properties. You will see a new window, and the left side will look like Figure 1.1.

1

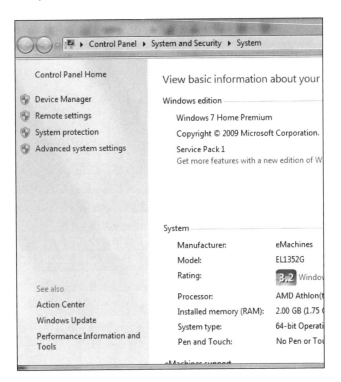

Figure 1.1
Windows 7 System Settings panel.

2. Choose Advanced System Settings on the left. You will see another new window like Figure 1.2.

3. If it isn't selected already, select the Advanced tab at the top. Then click the Environment Variables button at the bottom-right. You will see the window shown in Figure 1.3.

4. In the bottom System Variables area, select Path from the list of variables, and click the Edit button. At the end of that line, insert a semicolon (;) followed by the path to your installed JDK, probably a line similar to the following:

```
c:\program files\java\jdk1.6.0_24\bin\
```

5. Finally, click OK and work your way out of the windows.

Go ahead and install Eclipse. You can download it at www.eclipse.org. The Eclipse website offers documentation to help you with the install, but it is pretty straightforward. The Eclipse installation should use the system's path variable to find JDK. If you haven't updated your version of Eclipse lately, be aware that Android development will need versions Europa or newer. At the time of this writing, the current version is Indigo. Development used in this tutorial was done on Eclipse Galileo.

Figure 1.2
Windows 7 System Properties panel.

Figure 1.3
Windows 7 Environment Variables panel.

You should note that Eclipse does not install like most Windows software installs. It comes as a ZIP file that can be placed anywhere on the system and unzipped. I recommend that you create a folder in the Program Files folder on a Windows system called Eclipse or something equally appropriate and unzip the ZIP file there. You might also want to create a shortcut for the Eclipse start icon and place it on your desktop.

When you select the New menu and choose Project, if you can start Eclipse and you see Java Project as a choice, so far so good. If that doesn't happen for you, go back and check the documentation for the Eclipse and Java installations. Above all, be patient.

INSTALLING THE ANDROID DEVELOPMENT KIT

Finally, you can begin to install the Android Development Kit (ADK). There are actually two steps to getting Android configured. First, you need the kit; then you need to configure Eclipse. You can download the ADK at http://developer.android. com/sdk. Once you have it installed, you need to make a change to your PATH environment variable similar to what you did earlier. You will follow the same steps and add something like the following to the path: `c:\program files (x86)\android\` `android-sdk\tools\`. Don't forget to separate entries with a semicolon.

To configure the Eclipse plug-in for Android, start Eclipse and select Install New Software from the Help menu. You will see the screen shown in Figure 1.4.

In the Work With field, enter the following website: http://dl-ssl.google.com/android/ eclipse/. After clicking Add and waiting a moment, a Developer Tools line appears below. Put a check in the box that appears in the screen below, click Next, and follow the prompts to the end of the process. You need to agree to all the licenses to get to the Finish button.

Caution

You must be running Eclipse as an administrator to install plug-ins. For a typical configuration, the steps in the previous paragraph will fail unless you right-click Eclipse and choose Run as Administrator. Otherwise, you get an unhelpful error about `Missing requirement: Shared Plugin`.

Testing the Android installation is similar to testing the Java installation. Again, select the File menu on Eclipse, select New, Project, and you should see Android Project as a choice. If it is there, you should be good to go. If not, check your steps and look for some online troubleshooting help. There is no lack of documentation on the Internet for Eclipse, Java, and Android. Just use your favorite search engine.

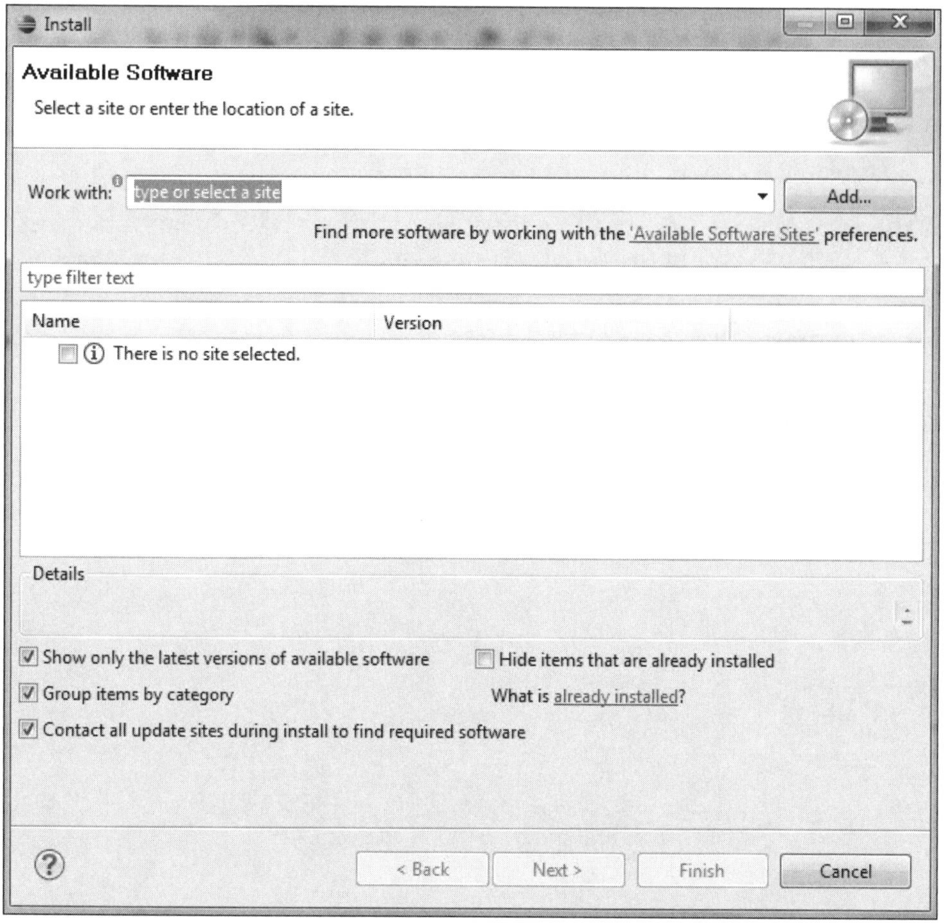

Figure 1.4
Eclipse Install New Software panel.

Indeed, if you ever run into a problem with part of a project you see in this tutorial or attempt on your own, you can rest assured many other developers have run into the same problem and are more than likely to have posted solutions on the Internet. The following list contains some websites I have found useful:

http://download.oracle.com/javase	Documentation on J2SE
http://developer.android.com	Documentation on the ADK
www.dreamincode.net	General programming help for many development languages
www.stackoverflow.com	Solutions to many common programming problems offered by other developers.

Follow-Up

1. Install and configure the components needed to build your Android application development environment.

2. Review the websites listed at the end of this chapter.

3. Research the sequence of Android OS versions and their added features to help you target the appropriate levels in your applications.

Reader's Notes

CHAPTER 2

STARTING AN ANDROID APPLICATION PROJECT

ANDROID APPLICATIONS COMPONENTS

Let's assume at this point that you have correctly configured Eclipse with Java and the Android Development Kit (ADK). It's time to write the first application. If you have used Eclipse before, you know how to start a project. If not, here's what you need to know about projects. Eclipse creates a directory, or folder, to store your programming projects called Workspace. When Eclipse is installed, the installer is prompted for the desired location for this directory. After installation, Eclipse allows for the creation of new Workspace directories and allows you to change Workspace directories each time you open Eclipse.

Any time you start a new project, Eclipse prompts for a project name and creates a subdirectory (subfolder) in the Workspace directory for the project using the chosen project name for the subdirectory name. From here on, the terms *directory* and *folder*, and the terms *subdirectory* and *subfolder*, may be used interchangeably.

Inside the project directory, Eclipse creates several subdirectories for specific purposes; those will be discussed in detail later in the chapter. Although Eclipse organizes these subdirectories on its own and the project file and directory structure doesn't determine the functionality of the final application, you should preserve the file and directory structure because Eclipse uses file paths in the assembly of the project's components. This will be explained and illustrated more clearly later in the chapter as well.

On the Eclipse desktop, select File, New, Project. You are presented with a new dialog box. Select Android Project under the Android heading, and then select Next. You will see the dialog box in Figure 2.1.

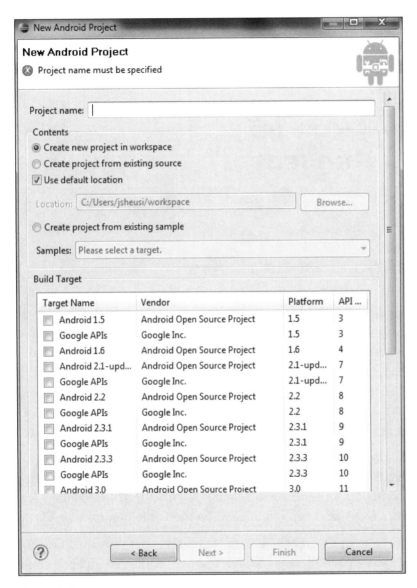

Figure 2.1
Eclipse New Android Project panel.

Choose a project name, such as Project_1. Notice the check box labeled Use Default Location. It is checked and contains a path with "workspace" as the final directory in the path. This is what I referred to earlier; you can leave it as is. Next, the Build Target area refers to the version of the Android operating system (OS) you want your application to be used on. The lower the application programming interface (API) you choose, the more inclusive you will be of devices that will run your application. On the other hand, the lower the number you choose, the fewer features of devices and advances in the Android platform your application will be able to take advantage of. Table 2.1 shows the complete list of versions and corresponding APIs at the time of this writing. For basic applications such as our first application here, you can choose platform 1.5 at the top of the list.

Table 2.1   Android Versions, API Levels, and Code Names

Platform Version	API Level	VERSION_CODE
Android 3.2	13	HONEYCOMB_MR2
Android 3.1.x	12	HONEYCOMB_MR1
Android 3.0.x	11	HONEYCOMB
Android 2.3.4 Android 2.3.3	10	GINGERBREAD_MR1
Android 2.3.2 Android 2.3.1 Android 2.3	9	GINGERBREAD
Android 2.2.x	8	FROYO
Android 2.1.x	7	ECLAIR_MR1
Android 2.0.1	6	ECLAIR_0_1
Android 2.0	5	ECLAIR
Android 1.6	4	DONUT
Android 1.5	3	CUPCAKE
Android 1.1	2	BASE_1_
Android 1.0	1	BASE

Source: http://developer.android.com/guide/appendix/api-levels.html

Figure 2.2 shows the bottom half of the dialog box, which may not show immediately because of your monitor's resolution settings.

Next, you need to choose an application name. Android device owners who download your application will see this name and identify the application on their device by this name, so make it plain English, such as Tip Calculator.

Figure 2.2
Bottom portion of Eclipse New Android Project panel.

The Package Name is a little more complicated and refers to the Java structure referred to as a package. Simply put, a *package* is a related set of classes. Your project could contain many classes, related to each other by a single purpose: to provide the functionality of your Android app. All the package names in the Android system must be unique. To be sure whatever you are adding will not coincidentally match anything else, a domain-style naming system is used. The Java convention for naming packages is sort of a web domain name backward, such as com.sheusi.TipCalculator. You should note that reverse-domain naming is the convention here. You need not own a domain name; you can just make one up. (You can learn more about package naming at http://download.oracle.com/javase/tutorial/java/package/namingpkgs.html.)

The activity name is actually the class name for the primary Java class of your project, so you must follow the Java class naming conventions; for instance, don't include spaces in the name. Otherwise, it could be any name you want, but it should be consistent with the rest of the project, such as TipCalc. Just as all Java programs are subclasses of the Java class called Object, all Android applications are subclasses of the Activity class, or subclasses of some subclass of the Activity class. An example we will see later is the MapActivity class, which is a subclass of the Activity class. The full name for your Activity class will be the package name plus the activity name, such as com.sheusi.TipCalculator.TipCalc. An old but useful guide to naming Java files as well as other Java programming best practices is the document "Java Code Conventions," found and downloaded at www.oracle.com/technetwork/java/codeconventions-150003.pdf.

You need to enter an integer to indicate the minimum SDK version for your project. Entry of this value determines which versions of the Android OSs on devices that ultimately will want to download your application will be compatible, and which features your application will be able to use. You can discover more details on the following website: http://developer.android.com/guide/developing/projects/projects-eclipse.html.

If you are unsure, simply use the number listed under the API column corresponding to the Target Name you chose in the Build Target window. The lowest usable value is 1.

After you click the Finish button, Eclipse creates an empty project framework for you. Eclipse is a powerful, versatile development environment that can be complicated and intimidating. It is easy to click the wrong place with the mouse and change the appearance of the whole editor. If nothing else, it takes practice. Figure 2.3 is an illustration of the entire Eclipse screen with the essential areas labeled. If any of these accidently "disappear" on you, you can probably restore them by choosing Window on the menu bar, choosing Show View, and finally choosing the panel you want to restore. If you accidentally minimize the editor screen, look for an icon on the right side of the screen displaying a pencil on a piece of paper. Click this to restore the editor.

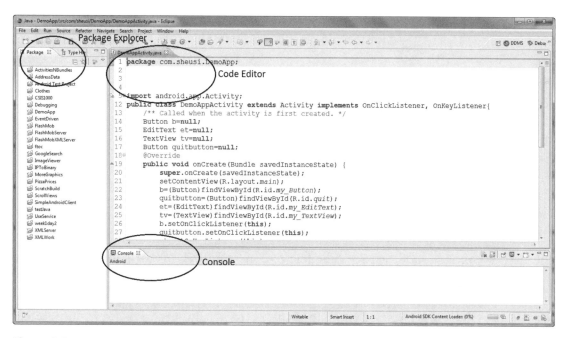

Figure 2.3
Eclipse IDE screen.

The right side of the screen is the editor space. If you are familiar with Eclipse, you will recognize this. On the left side is the Package Explorer window. You will find a list for all the projects in your workspace as described earlier. If you click on your newly created project, you see a breakdown of the components of the project Eclipse created. It's a combination of directories, subdirectories, and files. As mentioned before, their correct organization is essential to a successful project build, so you should leave them organized as they are, although you will be adding files as the project goes on. The breakdown should look like Figure 2.4.

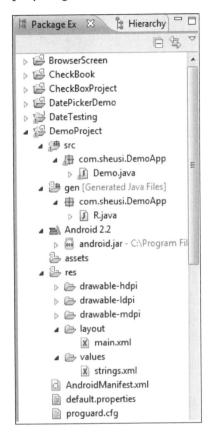

Figure 2.4
Eclipse Package Explorer.

The first listing is a subdirectory called src. This subdirectory or subfolder contains all the source code for the class(es) you intend to create for your application. You should recognize the package name that you used in the dialog box in the first level below the src icon, and the activity name you chose with the .java extension added. This is the primary class of the application.

Next is the directory named gen. The primary file here is called R.java, and it is created based on your configuration of the main.xml and strings.xml at a minimum. You can read this file; it looks like any other Java class, but as Eclipse warns, you do not modify it. It will take care of itself as you modify other components of the project.

The next component is a collection of API files based on the version you chose in the dialog box in the beginning. It will be numbered based on your choice—2.2 in this case—and the number can be different for different projects. You will likely not need to deal with this section of the project.

Following that is a directory called res, which is short for resources. It contains folders whose names begin with drawable; these contain graphics files such as the launch icons for the application. If you intend to use a launch icon other than the standard Android "robot" icon, you need to put a graphic of a specified size and type in each of these folders. You will find more on that topic later in the book. The layout and values subdirectories under res contain XML files. The layout directory contains XML files that configure the screens of the application. The values folder contains values for text strings and a couple of other data types you might use in your application. Assignments can be made here in the XML file, and they will be available throughout the coded application. These XML files together allow you to design the whole user interface without having to write a single line of Java code.

Finally, we come to the AndroidManifest.xml file. This file can be viewed as the "instruction book" the target device uses to run the application. It contains things like permissions to use features on the device such as the GPS system, references to the files that should be included when the application is bundled up for deployment (hence the inclusion of the word *manifest* in the filename), version and revision numbers, API information, and so on. This file is important to the application, and you should take care to construct it correctly. Following is a basic manifest file. It belongs to one of the tutorials found in Chapter 9, "Text Files, Data Tables, and XML."

```xml
<?xml version="1.0" encoding="utf-8"?>
<manifest xmlns:android="http://schemas.android.com/apk/res/android"
    package="com.sheusi.CheckBook"
    android:versionCode="1"
    android:versionName="1.0">
    <uses-sdk android:minSdkVersion="8" />

    <application android:icon="@drawable/icon" android:label="@string/app_name">
        <activity android:name=".CheckBook"
                android:label="@string/app_name">
            <intent-filter>
                <action android:name="android.intent.action.MAIN" />
                <category android:name="android.intent.category.LAUNCHER" />
            </intent-filter>
        </activity>

    </application>
</manifest>
```

Under the manifest tag is the package name, which is set at the beginning of the project. There's also a version code; it's a numeric value only, and it's used internally to be sure that subsequent installs of the same application are newer versions. Finally, the version name is the version information that the user will see, and it is used only for this purpose.

The <uses-sdk> can contain more than one specification. The minSdkVersion specification shown here prevents devices with a lower API than you specify from installing your application. The platform version and the corresponding API level numbers are on the screen when you are configuring the project. Review Figure 2.2. You should always add this specification. If you don't, it defaults to 1, and you run the risk of having your application crash if the device has too low an API. The other specifications you can add under this tag are targetSdkVersion and maxSdkVersion. The first of these has an obvious meaning. The second, however, is important to understand. When you specify a maxSdkVersion, devices that have a higher version installed don't install your application. But it is trickier than that. If a device has an OS version lower than the maximum you specify, it downloads and installs your application. However, as the device installs OS upgrades, it revalidates all the applications on it. Once an OS upgrade surpasses your maximum specification, the device does not revalidate your application, and it is no longer visible on the device. Essentially, it is deleted. It is recommended that you never use the maxSdkVersion setting in your manifest file.

Inside the <application> tag, the parameter android:icon represents the graphic to be used as the launch icon on the device. You will want to make this your own; instructions for how to do this are discussed in Chapter 11, "Publishing Your Application." The android:label parameter is the name you gave the application when you started the project. Inside the <activity> tag, the first parameter, android:name, is the activity name you specified in the project setup. This will be the name of the Java class file that extends the Activity class, which is the main Java file in your application. The android:label parameter is the same as the previous android:label.

Finally, inside the <intent-filter> tag, the parameter android:name is set to .MAIN. It is an action built into the Android Intent class that instructs the device to open this application to the home screen. The second android.name parameter, set to .LAUNCHER, defines the starting point. You can find more on the Intent class at http://developer.android.com/reference/android/content/Intent.html.

All the sections of the application discussed here work with each other and actually modify each other through Eclipse. An example mentioned earlier is that the contents of the `main.xml` and `strings.xml` files determine the content of the `R.java` class. Another example, although done manually, is that the names of the graphics files that launch the application on the target device must be reflected in the `AndroidManifest.xml` file. XML files created to configure additional screens must also be specified in the `AndroidManifest.xml` file.

All this configuration and organization can seem overwhelming now, but Eclipse handles much of it on its own. Any steps that must be done manually are addressed as they become necessary. For now, let's get back to our first application.

Double-click the `res` folder to expose the `layout` and `values` folders. Double-click each of those folders to expose the `main.xml` and `strings.xml` files, respectively. Double-click each of those to load them into the editor space. Multiple files can be loaded into the editor space, each file having its own tab. Look at the `main.xml` file first. It has two possible views—the graphical layout and the plain text—referred to at the bottom of the editor as Graphical Layout and `main.xml`, respectively. You can design a screen in graphical mode using drag and drop, but I find it more useful to do this in text mode. You may find it helpful to review some XML tutorials in text or on the Internet, but you can be confident that Eclipse will take care of most of the work for you and indicate any errors you make as you go along.

You are free to try either mode and see how changing one automatically changes the other, but for now examine the text mode, `main.xml`. Eclipse starts all projects with a basic `LinearLayout` framework and a `TextView` control with a `Hello, World` greeting in it. Note the line of code in the `TextView` area:

```
android:text="@string/hello"
```

The statement assigns the contents of the `TextView` control. You could assign a text string here like this:

```
android:text="Hello from Jim"
```

but as seen earlier, Eclipse sets up a file to store all string assignments in the same place in a file called `strings.xml`. You should have `strings.xml` loaded in the editor by now. Click on its tab to expose its contents. Note the following lines:

```
<string name="hello">Hello World, Demo!</string>
<string name="app_name">DemoApp</string>
```

The first creates a string variable called `name` and assigns it the value `Hello World, Demo!`. The next creates a variable called `app_name` and assigns it the value `DemoApp`. (Note that `Demo` and `DemoApp` were some of the values we entered when we started the application and filled in the original dialog box.)

Again, looking at the line from `main.xml`, you will see that `@string` refers to a string in the `strings.xml` file, and `/hello` refers to the particular string variable by name. Hence, we are loading that `TextView` with `Hello World, Demo!` when the application starts. We will see if this actually happens shortly.

For now, go back to the Package Explorer on the left side of Eclipse, and select the `src` folder. Double-click all the subfolders until you reach `Demo.java`. (At this point, there should be only one `.java` file, and it will have whatever name you gave it when you filled out the large dialog box at the beginning of the project.) Double-click that filename to open it in the editor space. Eclipse produces some common Java code automatically for you. Notice the following line:

```
setContentView(R.layout.main);
```

As you can probably guess by now, the word `main` refers to the `main.xml` file. But where does `R.layout.` come from? Go back to the Package Explorer, and double-click the `gen` folder. Double-click the package icon, and you see a file named `R.java`. Double-click the file, and it appears in the editor space. As stated at the beginning of the chapter, this is a Java class created by Eclipse to represent all the objects created by the various XML files in the project. If you are familiar with Java, you know that `R.layout.main` refers to a variable called `main` belonging to an inner class, `layout` of the class, `R`. You should begin to see how all the folders and files Eclipse creates are essential, and their locations and structures must be preserved for an application to come together correctly.

Open the `Demo.java` file again in the editor by double-clicking its tab. Refer to Figure 2.5. Note that there may be code in this illustration that is not on your editor. That isn't important at this point.

Notice the icon that is a green circle with an arrowhead pointing right in it. Double-click that icon. You are asked how to run the project; choose Android Project. This starts the default emulator of an Android device and then loads and starts your application. This may take a few minutes, so be patient. Below the editor area of the Eclipse workspace is an area labeled Console. As the emulator loads and your application loads in it, you see the status of the loads in that area. Finally, you see a screen similar to Figure 2.6.

The left side represents the screen of the Android device. Note that the application is labeled DemoApp, and the text on the screen says `Hello World, Demo!`. These texts were predefined in the file `strings.xml`. Because the emulator takes some time to load, you can minimize it to get it out of the way for the time being.

In the editor, go back to `strings.xml`. Try changing the values of those strings; choose whatever you like to replace the terms `DemoApp` and `Hello World, Demo!`.

```
1  package com.sheusi.DemoApp;
2
3  import android.app.Activity;
9  public class Demo extends Activity implements OnClickListener{
10     /** Called when the activity is first created. */
11     Button b=null;
12     EditText et=null;
13     TextView tv=null;
14     Button quitbutton=null;
15     @Override
16     public void onCreate(Bundle savedInstanceState) {
17         super.onCreate(savedInstanceState);
18         setContentView(R.layout.main);
19         b=(Button)findViewById(R.id.my_Button);
20         quitbutton=(Button)findViewById(R.id.quit);
21         et=(EditText)findViewById(R.id.my_EditText);
22         tv=(TextView)findViewById(R.id.my_TextView);
23         b.setOnClickListener(this);
24         quitbutton.setOnClickListener(this);
25     }
26     public void onClick(View v){
```

Figure 2.5
Eclipse Editor panel.

Figure 2.6
Running emulator screen.

The only caution here is that the string values must conform to what Java permits. For example, certain punctuation must be preceded by the escape character, \.

When you want to restart the application, you should have the Demo.java file showing in the editor; just double-click its tab at the top of the editor space as shown in Figure 2.5. Then click the green icon again and restore the minimized emulator screen. In a moment, the application should restart in the emulator, reflecting your text changes.

A reminder about the R.java file: There is a warning at the top of this file not to change it. Heed that warning. This file is automatically regenerated any time you add components to the main.xml file, create new entries in strings.xml, add graphics to the application, and so on. You should never need to modify R.java.

Let's stop a minute and take a breath. Most of us programmers are used to starting off with the basic "Hello, world!" console application, using a single simple source code file similar to the following Java file:

```java
public class hello{

  public static void main(String args[]){
   System.out.println("Hello, world!");
  }
}
```

For Android application development, we have XML files, Java files we never wrote and shouldn't touch, manifest files, and so on. How did it ever get this complicated? Well, actually, it isn't. Take a look at the following source code:

```java
package com.sheusi.HandCodedHello;

import android.app.Activity;
import android.os.Bundle;
import android.widget.*;
import android.content.Context;
public class HandCodedHello extends Activity {
   /** Called when the activity is first created. */
Context myContext=null;
TextView myTextView=null;
LinearLayout myLayout=null;
   @Override
   public void onCreate(Bundle savedInstanceState) {
     super.onCreate(savedInstanceState);
     //setContentView(R.layout.main);
     //no generated files in this program!
   myContext=this.getApplicationContext();
   myLayout= new LinearLayout(myContext);
   myLayout.setOrientation(LinearLayout.VERTICAL);
   this.setContentView(myLayout);
   myTextView=new TextView(myContext);
   myTextView.setText("Hello,world from Jim!");
```

```
        myLayout.addView(myTextView);
    }
}
```

It is a hand-coded version of Hello, world! for the Android. Compare that to the source code that follows, which uses the generated layout files:

```
package com.sheusi.HandCodedHello;

import android.app.Activity;
import android.os.Bundle;
public class HandCodedHello extends Activity {
    /** Called when the activity is first created. */ @Override
    public void onCreate(Bundle savedInstanceState) {
        super.onCreate(savedInstanceState);
        setContentView(R.layout.main);

    }
}
```

The second code takes advantage of the generated layout files, namely main.xml and R.java. Notice that there are about 50% fewer lines of code, and to be honest, formatting the screen in the main.xml file is much simpler than trying to format the screen in the Java code. The previous example barely gets by with a minimum of screen formatting.

Does this mean that you will never want to create a layout or control object in your Java code? No. You may encounter occasions where you want to dynamically add screen components or reformat them based on what is happening in your application at run-time. For example, you may want to change the font color of a text entry after an error check is done, or you may want to add text fields to collect data under certain conditions. You are more likely to use a combination of both XML formatting and design in the Java code. It pays to know how to do both.

Table 2.2 illustrates just a handful of the formatting attributes for the TextView widget that you can use in XML and their corresponding methods used in Java code. There are dozens!

Once you learn to use the main.xml file and to make your own XML files for other purposes, you will be happy they exist. They just take getting used to.

DEBUGGING WITH ECLIPSE

One of the biggest benefits to using an integrated development environment (IDE) such as Eclipse over using a simple editor to write source code is the extensive error detection and debugging facilities included in the IDE. The common errors that

Table 2.2 XML Attributes and Associated Class Methods

XML Attribute	TextView Class Method
android:height	setHeight(int)
android:lines	setHeight(int)
android:maxLines	setMaxLines(int)
android:text	setText(CharSequence,TextView.BufferType)
android:textColor	setTextColor(int)

occur in application development fall into one of three common categories: syntax, logic, and run-time. The second type, the logic error, is essentially impossible for the IDE to detect and diagnose because these errors are flaws in the approach to solving the problem that the application is meant to do. Some causes are incorrect formulas, complex decision structures that are designed incorrectly, and misapplication of essential values. For example, consider the following method to convert Fahrenheit to Celsius:

```
public double FtoC(double f){
return 5.0 / 9.0 * f - 32;
}
```

Syntactically, this method is okay, and the application it is part of will work quite nicely. However, the value produced when the method is called will not be what the programmer expects. The reason is the missing parentheses. The method that follows is correct.

```
public double FtoC(double f){
return 5.0 / 9.0 * (f - 32);
}
```

The IDE cannot second-guess your intentions; therefore, it cannot help you with this kind of error. The others are different. Take syntax errors, for example. These errors can include missing or incorrectly matching curly braces in code, missing semicolons at the end of a line, incorrect uppercase or lowercase letters, and so on. In other words, they're what we could call "spelling and grammar." These errors could also be use of classes without including the correct import statements, mistakes in variable scope, and other language-based errors. Here, the IDE will generally highlight mistakes right on the editor screen and not let you run the application on the screen or in the editor. In fact, these are the most obvious and easiest errors to fix. Figure 2.7 is a screenshot with an Eclipse error indicator to the left of the code lines.

```
11              System.out.println(convert(d));
12        }
13⊝       public static double convert(double f){
⊗14           return 5.0/9.0 (f-32)
15        }
16 }
17
```

Figure 2.7
Error markers in the Eclipse editor.

The error, indicated by a red circle, indicates a missing semicolon at the end of the line, a *punctuation* error, so to speak. If you spot one of these and you don't immediately know what the problem is, hold the mouse pointer over the red circle (or square, in the case of certain errors) a moment, and an explanation of the error appears.

The last type of error, the run-time error, can be the most frustrating. That is because this error occurs when the application is running, and there is no indication at compile time that anything is wrong. A run-time error turns up in the emulator when the application is running and generally looks like Figure 2.8.

Figure 2.8
A run-time error indication in the emulator.

What's more, due to the nature of run-time errors, they don't occur every time the application runs. Unlike syntax errors, when run-time errors occur, the emulator gives no explanation. Frustrating, indeed! This is where the Debug perspective in Eclipse is the biggest help.

The error in Figure 2.8 is the result of the following application code:

```java
package com.sheusi.Debugging;

import android.app.Activity;
import android.os.Bundle;

public class DebuggingActivity extends Activity {
    /** Called when the activity is first created. */
    @Override
    public void onCreate(Bundle savedInstanceState) {
        super.onCreate(savedInstanceState);
        setContentView(R.layout.main);
        int bogus[]=new int[5];

        for(int ct=0;ct<=5;++ct){
        bogus[ct]=ct;
        }

    }
}
```

Close examination reveals that we are outrunning the array of integers, which causes an unchecked Java exception: `ArrayIndexOutOfBounds Exception`. Java programmers are familiar with exception handling. To look at the Debug perspective in Eclipse, choose View Perspective under the Window menu, and choose Debug. You will see a screen similar to Figure 2.9.

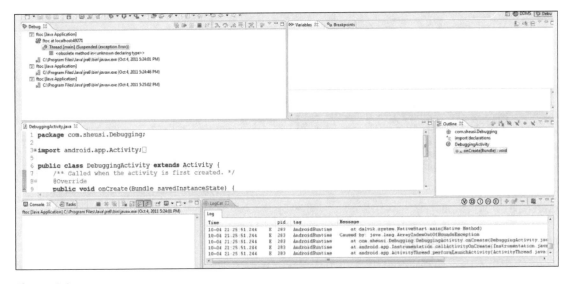

Figure 2.9
Eclipse Debug perspective.

In the lower-right corner is a panel with a tab marked LogCat. This is the first place to check for the source of the error. Any text in red is what you should examine. Look at the close-up in Figure 2.10.

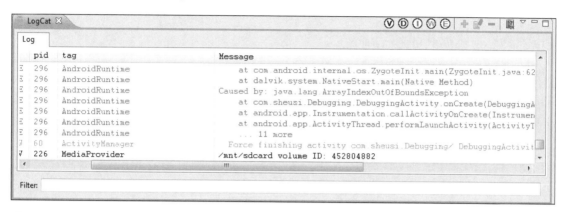

Figure 2.10
Eclipse LogCat panel.

Notice the line `Caused by: java.lang.ArrayIndexOutOfBoundsException`. Here is our problem. Now we know what to look for in our code to correct the problem. Let's go back and fix the problem with a try-catch block. In the catch portion, we will print some diagnostics. Notice that we cannot use the typical `printStackTrace( )` on a mobile application to help us. Instead, we can use the logger. Notice the changes in the following code:

```
package com.sheusi.Debugging;

import android.app.Activity;
import android.os.Bundle;
import android.util.Log;
public class DebuggingActivity extends Activity {
   /** Called when the activity is first created. */
   @Override
   public void onCreate(Bundle savedInstanceState) {
      super.onCreate(savedInstanceState);
      setContentView(R.layout.main);
      int bogus[]=new int[5];
      try{
      for(int ct=0;ct<=5;++ct){
      bogus[ct]=ct;
      }
      }catch(ArrayIndexOutOfBoundsException aioe){
      String err;
      if(aioe.getMessage()==null)
```

```
        err="Outran Array";
    else
        err=aioe.getMessage();
    Log.i("Error Here",err);
    }
  }
}
```

Notice that we added a try-catch block, a `Log` statement, and an additional import statement to include the android `Log` class on our namespace. The try-catch block allows the application to run, but if we take another look at the debug screen, we find the `LogCat` section shown in Figure 2.11.

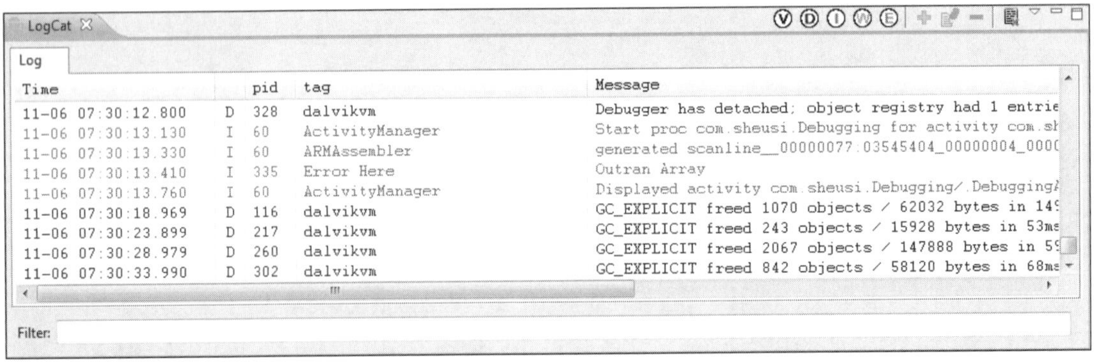

Figure 2.11
Eclipse LogCat panel showing user Log messages.

Under Tag, we see `Error Here`, which was the tag specified as the first argument in the `Log.i ( )` method call and the message we specified. If the exception had a message to print, it would have appeared in place of `Outran Array`. We can use the `Log` class methods in place of the traditional `printStackTrace( )`. The I to the left of the Pid column indicates that this is an INFO, or informational message. This is specified by the use of the `.i( )` method in the `Log` class. Other common choices are D for DEBUG, E for ERROR, and W for WARNING.

We can also use the Eclipse debugger to check the values of variables at run-time by setting breakpoints in our code. In fact, the use of breakpoints to check values is useful during application design and testing and need not involve errors. For instance, you may want to check intermittent values during execution of a loop, or values of variables during calculation of a complex formula. To set a breakpoint, just double-click on the line number (or the left margin if you are not using line numbers) next to the line you would like execution to pause at. Next, switch to the debug perspective, and start the application by using the green bug icon instead of the green circle icon at the top of the screen.

When execution reaches the line where you set the breakpoint, that line becomes highlighted in the code screen, and the variables and corresponding values appear one by one under the Variables tab on the upper right. In the example, the breakpoint was set at line 87. See Figure 2.12.

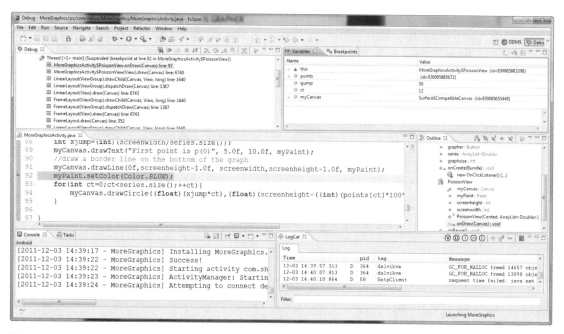

Figure 2.12
Eclipse debug screen showing a breakpoint.

Keep in mind that Android applications are event driven, so you may need to bring up the emulator and perform the necessary actions on it for the debugger to reach the breakpoint, such as clicking a button onscreen. If you want execution to continue beyond the breakpoint, you can use the following function keys to obtain the corresponding results.

F5	Execution resumes at the next step. If the next step is a method call, the debugger jumps to that method.
F6	Execution runs the method, but the debugger does not step through the method.
F7	Execution runs the method, but the debugger steps through it.
F8	Execution continues until the next breakpoint is encountered.

You can find more comprehensive guides to the use of the Eclipse debugger on the Internet. One example in particular is a series of videos and a companion PDF called

"Eclipse and Java: Using the Debugger Companion Tutorial Document" by Mark Dexter. You can find them at http://eclipsetutorial.sourceforge.net.

FOLLOW-UP

1. Research and practice constructing XML files. Learn the key components.

2. Fill in the following chart of the versions of the Android OS and the corresponding API levels. Research the improvements and key features for each release.

3. Study and practice the Eclipse Debugger.

Android Platform Number	API Level	Added Features and Improvements

KEY CLASSES USED IN THIS CHAPTER

Activity

Class   Activity

Package   android.app

Extends   Android.view.ContextThemeWrapper

An activity is generally a single-purpose screen and user interface. The activity takes care of creating the window on which the application designer places controls that allow the user to interact with the activity.

Figure 2.13 shows detail of a running activity's different states and the methods that respond to the states. In this chapter we find the onCreate( ) method, which

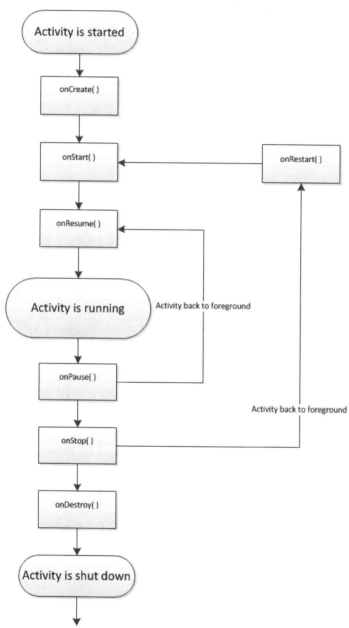

Figure 2.13
Simple Activity class state chart.

responds to the start of the application. Most of the screen configuration, initialization of variables, and design of event listeners take place in the onCreate( ) method.

Other commonly used methods:

onStart( )   Called when the activity becomes visible to the user.

onResume( ) Called when the activity starts interacting with the user.

onPause( )   Called when the application/system resumes a previous activity. It is typically used to commit data to persistent storage.

onStop( )   Called when the activity is no longer visible to the user. Could be called when a new activity is being started or an existing one is brought to the front of this one.

READER'S NOTES

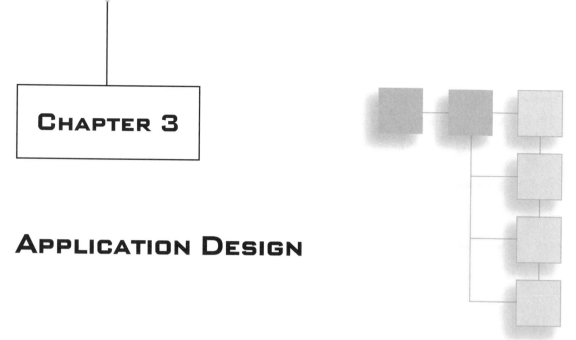

CHAPTER 3

APPLICATION DESIGN

Model-View-Controller (MVC) is a graphical user interface (GUI) application paradigm that has recently taken hold. The concept involves the developer considering three main areas when developing an application. These areas can be kept as independent as possible. The model, loosely analogous to the process in the traditional Input-Process-Output (IPO) model, represents what the application does and the coding behind what it is intended to do. The view, analogous to the output in the IPO model, is concerned with rendering the results on the display. The controller, analogous to the input in the IPO model, deals with how the user will interact with the application, including mouse movements, button clicks, and so on.

When developing Android applications, we can easily isolate the view from the model and controller components. The view or layout of components is written in XML format in the main.xml file. Once the programmer determines which controls are necessary for the application, such as lists, text fields, buttons, and so on, he can plan and code their arrangement, size, labels, fonts, and colors in the main.xml file. Indeed, after the application is written, should the programmer decide he does not like the user interface's aesthetics, he can make changes without altering the Java classes and methods that produce the model and controller components of the MVC model. For instance, would two input fields work better side by side, or one atop the other? The programmer can try both arrangements by altering the main.xml file only without having to find their references in Java code and making changes there. In the sections that follow, we will look at how the main.xml file works. But before we get into that, Table 3.1 offers a quick refresher on the rules and syntax of XML files.

Table 3.1 Key XML Structure Elements

`<some_element></some_element>` or `<some_element />`	Empty element
`<some_element>`	Opening tag
`</some_element>`	Closing tag
`some_attribute = "some value"`	Attribute
`some_attribute`	Name of the attribute
`"some value"`	Value of the attribute
`<!-- comment -->`	Comment

Following are the rules for XML files:

1. All XML elements must have opening and closing tags.

2. XML tags are case sensitive.

3. XML elements must be properly nested.

```
ex.
<tag1>
   <tag2>
   </tag2>
</tag1>
```

4. XML documents must have a root element. A single tag pair must surround all other elements of the document. This is the root element.

5. XML attribute values must be quoted using either single or double quotes.

THE SCREEN LAYOUT AND THE MAIN.XML FILE

As you have seen already, Eclipse creates a functional application as soon as you create a new project; you don't have to do anything. You have also seen that the screen configuration is controlled by the `main.xml` file that Eclipse generates. Take a moment to study the Eclipse-generated `main.xml` file here:

```
<?xml version="1.0" encoding="utf-8"?>
<LinearLayout xmlns:android="http://schemas.android.com/apk/res/android"
   android:orientation="vertical"
   android:layout_width="fill_parent"
   android:layout_height="fill_parent"
   >
```

```
<TextView
    android:layout_width="fill_parent"
    android:layout_height="wrap_content"
    android:text="@string/hello"
    />
</LinearLayout>
```

Normally, Java programmers don't encounter XML files, so let's take a minute to look at how they are configured. XML files are composed of units called *elements* with opening and closing tags. The opening tag consists of a tag name surrounded by right and left arrows (less-than and greater-than signs, respectively) such as `<some_element>`. The closing tag is the same name, but with a slash mark / in front of the tag name, such as `</some_element>`. To be usable, the XML file must be perfectly formed; in other words, all the tags have to be perfectly matched. Occasionally you will see a shortcut used where an element is included in one tag, ending with `/>`. For example:

```
<TextView
    android:layout_width="fill_parent"
    android:layout_height="wrap_content"
    android:text="@string/hello"
    />
```

would be functionally equivalent to

```
<TextView
    android:layout_width="fill_parent"
    android:layout_height="wrap_content"
    android:text="@string/hello">
    </TextView>
```

For more on XML files, please review some outside references, such as those found at www.w3schools.com/xml/ and www.xmlfiles.com/xml/.

The `LinearLayout` class is indeed a Java class found in the Android software development kit (SDK). It is one of many subclasses of the `ViewGroup` class. The attributes that are set in the XML file, namely `orientation`, `layout_width`, and `layout_length`, can be set in Java code by using methods that belong to the `LinearLayout` class, one or more of the classes in its hierarchy, or one or more of the inner classes in the hierarchy. Using the `main.xml` file, we can separate form from functionality and design our user interface without writing a line of Java code.

The outermost `LinearLayout` object normally represents the whole screen in an application, similar to the way a `Frame` class represents the application window in a PC Java application. Note that the two attributes, `layout_width` and layout_height, are set to fill_parent. These two settings together cause LinearLayout to occupy the whole screen, filling all the way across and all the way down. The orientation attribute set to Vertical means that objects are added top to bottom. Try this little experiment.

Using copy and paste, take this portion of code and duplicate it:

```
<TextView
    android:layout_width="fill_parent"
    android:layout_height="wrap_content"
    android:text="@string/hello"
    />
```

in such a way that your main.xml looks like this:

```
<?xml version="1.0" encoding="utf-8"?>
<LinearLayout xmlns:android="http://schemas.android.com/apk/res/android"
    android:orientation="vertical"
    android:layout_width="fill_parent"
    android:layout_height="fill_parent"
    >
<TextView
    android:layout_width="fill_parent"
    android:layout_height="wrap_content"
    android:text="@string/hello"
    />
<TextView
    android:layout_width="fill_parent"
    android:layout_height="wrap_content"
    android:text="@string/hello"
    />
</LinearLayout>
```

Rerun the application as you did in the first chapter. Remember to put the .java file on the editor screen to make the application start correctly. Your application running in the emulator should look Figure 3.1.

Your text may be different, but you should see that the two lines come one below the other, or in Vertical orientation. This is what the orientation attribute in the LinearLayout section of main.xml specifies. Now change the word, vertical to horizontal. As you might guess, the two lines of text should show side by side, rather than top and bottom. But hold on a moment! Remember that the parameter for the TextView objects' widths is set to fill-parent. This means that each is set to occupy the full width of the screen, hence *fill* the parent. If you ran the application at this point, you would only see one TextView object on the screen,

Figure 3.1
Emulator display of two TextView objects.

because it is set to fill the screen completely from left to right. So before we run the application, let's change the horizontal property for both TextViews to wrap-content. Your main.xml file should look like the following example:

```
<?xml version="1.0" encoding="utf-8"?>
<LinearLayout xmlns:android="http://schemas.android.com/apk/res/android"
    android:orientation="horizontal"
    android:layout_width="fill_parent"
    android:layout_height="fill_parent"
    >
<TextView
    android:layout_width="wrap_content"
    android:layout_height="wrap_content"
    android:text="@string/hello"
    />
<TextView
    android:layout_width="wrap_content"
    android:layout_height="wrap_content"
    android:text="@string/hello"
    />
</LinearLayout>
```

Now rerun the application. You should see a screen like Figure 3.2.

This exercise gives you an idea of how Android application screens are constructed; again, we never wrote a line of Java code.

Figure 3.2
Emulator shows two TextViews, arranged horizontally.

Java programmers are familiar with the different layouts used in `Frames`, such as the `BorderLayout` and `FlowLayout`. The "layouts" for Android applications vary in a similar manner. Some of the other `Layout` classes that are also subclasses of the `ViewGroup` class are `FrameLayout`, `AbsoluteLayout`, `TableLayout`, and `RelativeLayout`. The `AbsoluteLayout` allows the programmer to specify the exact x,y coordinates of the components on the screen, but it is of limited use because it doesn't adjust for variations in the screen resolution of multiple target devices. On the other hand, if the programmer is writing for only one type of device, say for a specific client, it may be useful. The `FrameLayout` layers multiple controls one on top of the other. This layout might be useful for graphics in an application. To get a quick idea of how the `FrameLayout` responds to text controls such as the `Text-View` control, modify your `main.xml` file to look like this:

```
<?xml version="1.0" encoding="utf-8"?>
<FrameLayout xmlns:android="http://schemas.android.com/apk/res/android"
    android:orientation="horizontal"
    android:layout_width="fill_parent"
    android:layout_height="fill_parent"
    >
<TextView
    android:layout_width="wrap_content"
    android:layout_height="wrap_content"
    android:text="@string/hello"
```

```
                />
                <TextView
                    android:layout_width="fill_parent"
                    android:layout_height="wrap_content"
                    android:text="Text View number two"
                />
                <TextView
                    android:layout_width="fill_parent"
                    android:layout_height="wrap_content"
                    android:text="Text View number three"
                />
            </FrameLayout>
```

Then restart your application. You should see three text strings layered on top of one another.

The RelativeLayout allows the programmer to position controls such as buttons on the screen relative to each other, such as above or below. To try a RelativeLayout, modify your main.xml to look like the following, and then restart your application:

```
<?xml version="1.0" encoding="utf-8"?>
<RelativeLayout xmlns:android="http://schemas.android.com/apk/res/android"
    android:orientation="horizontal"
    android:layout_width="fill_parent"
    android:layout_height="fill_parent"
    >
<TextView
    android:id="@+id/centertext"
    android:layout_width="wrap_content"
    android:layout_height="wrap_content"
    android:text="@string/hello"
    android:layout_centerHorizontal="true"
    android:layout_centerVertical="true"
    />
    <TextView
    android:layout_width="fill_parent"
    android:layout_height="wrap_content"
    android:text="Text View number two"
    android:layout_above="@id/centertext"
    />
    <TextView
    android:layout_width="fill_parent"
    android:layout_height="wrap_content"
    android:text="Text View number three"
    android:layout_below="@id/centertext"
```

```
    />
</RelativeLayout>
```

Notice that the second and third TextViews appear at the top and bottom, respectively. Look carefully at this main.xml file. See the introduction of the android:id attribute for the first TextView.

```
android:id="@+id/centertext"
```

This is required because the other two TextView objects need to refer to the position of the first and need a way to identify it. The programmer can choose any ID for the control; it's a good idea to choose a short name that identifies the control. Later we will learn how this ID is also used to identify a control in the Java code for the application. The coding @+id/ probably looks strange even to the Java programmer. In Chapter 2, "Starting an Android Application Project," we discussed the R.java Java file generated by Eclipse. This file will contain several inner classes. One such inner class is called id. This prefix on the id name causes the actual identification value to be entered in that inner class. Take a look at the R.java file by double-clicking the R.java entry in the Package Explorer window on the left side of the Eclipse Screen (it's in the gen folder), and it opens in the editor. You will see the entry centertext in the id inner class.

Finally, the TableLayout is similar in appearance to the Java Frame's GridLayout, but it is configured quite differently. Within the TableLayout, the programmer makes one or more TableRow entries. Controls are placed inside the TableRow and appear in the order in which they are entered into the XML file. Columns are created as entries are made; however, to skip a column, the programmer can make a zero-based column specification. If only one row is specified, no gap appears between columns, even if there is a gap specified in the column indexes. However, if multiple rows are used, gaps appear where column index values are skipped. The column index is specified by the android:layout_column attribute (android:layout_column="1").

Modify your main.xml file to match the following. Note that several lines necessary for the RelativeLayout have been removed:

```
<?xml version="1.0" encoding="utf-8"?>
<TableLayout xmlns:android="http://schemas.android.com/apk/res/android"
    android:orientation="horizontal"
    android:layout_width="fill_parent"
    android:layout_height="fill_parent"
    >
<TableRow>
<TextView
```

```
    android:layout_width="wrap_content"
    android:layout_height="wrap_content"
    android:text="Column 1"
    android:layout_column="0"
    />
    <TextView
    android:layout_width="fill_parent"
    android:layout_height="wrap_content"
    android:text="Column 2"
    android:layout_column="1"
    />
    <TextView
    android:layout_width="fill_parent"
    android:layout_height="wrap_content"
    android:text="Column 3"
    android:layout_column="3"
    />
    </TableRow>
<TableRow>
<TextView
    android:layout_width="wrap_content"
    android:layout_height="wrap_content"
    android:text="Column 1"
    android:layout_column="0"
    />
    <TextView
    android:layout_width="fill_parent"
    android:layout_height="wrap_content"
    android:text="Column 2"
    android:layout_column="2"
    />
    <TextView
    android:layout_width="fill_parent"
    android:layout_height="wrap_content"
    android:text="Column 3"
    android:layout_column="4"
    />
    </TableRow>
</TableLayout>
```

When you rerun the application, your emulator should look like Figure 3.3.

Remember, we are actually using *five* columns, indexed zero through four (0,1,2,3,4), and they are specified by the attribute `android:layout_column`. They have nothing to do with the attribute `android:text`, although we are using the word `Column` in the text.

Figure 3.3
Emulator image showing rows and columns.

It is quite common in Java applications for the personal computer to embed one container in another, such as filling a frame with panels. Likewise, it is common for the Android programmer to put one layout manager inside another to achieve a desired screen layout. Look carefully at the following example. You will notice that the outermost layout is a `LinearLayout`, and it contains two `TableLayouts`. Each of the `TableLayouts` contains a single row, with several `TextViews` included in the row. A programmer might do this to produce rows with differing numbers of columns, or maybe two groups with rows and columns, but containing some other object or layout of many objects in the middle. Take a minute to study the example:

```xml
<?xml version="1.0" encoding="utf-8"?>
<LinearLayout xmlns:android="http://schemas.android.com/apk/res/android"
   android:orientation="vertical"
   android:layout_width="fill_parent"
   android:layout_height="fill_parent"
   >
<TableLayout
android:background="#0000ff"
android:layout_width="fill_parent"
android:layout_height="wrap_content"
>
<TableRow>
<TextView

   android:layout_width="wrap_content"
   android:layout_height="wrap_content"
```

```
    android:text="Column 1"
    android:layout_column="0"
    />
    <TextView
    android:layout_width="wrap_content"
    android:layout_height="wrap_content"
    android:text="Column 2"
    android:layout_column="1"
    />
    <TextView
    android:layout_width="wrap_content"
    android:layout_height="wrap_content"
    android:text="Column 3"
    android:layout_column="3"
    />
    </TableRow>
</TableLayout>
<TableLayout
  android:background="#ff0000"
android:layout_width="fill_parent"
    android:layout_height="wrap_content">
    <TableRow>

    <TextView

    android:layout_width="wrap_content"
    android:layout_height="wrap_content"
    android:text="Column 1"
    android:layout_column="0"
    />
    <TextView
    android:layout_width="wrap_content"
    android:layout_height="wrap_content"
    android:text="Column 2"
    android:layout_column="2"
    />
    <TextView
    android:layout_width="wrap_content"
    android:layout_height="wrap_content"
    android:text="Column 3"
    android:layout_column="4"
    />
    </TableRow>
</TableLayout>
</LinearLayout>
```

First, notice that the orientation attribute in the LinearLayout is changed to vertical. This causes the multiple embedded layouts to be stacked top to bottom instead of left to right. If the orientation value is left as horizontal, the Linear-Layout would attempt to place the embedded TableLayouts side by side, which is not the intent here. Second, notice that we added background attributes to the TableLayouts; in this case, we set them to a color. The first one is solid blue (#0000FF) and the second is solid red (#FF0000). If you have created colors in Java code or HTML, you know how these values work. If not, what follows is a quick lesson.

Colors are made of three component values: one for red, one for green, and one for blue. Each component can have a value ranging from 0 to 255. The values are specified in hexadecimal, or base-16. The hexadecimal values and their decimal equivalents are specified in Table 3.2.

Table 3.2 Hexadecimal Values and Their Decimal Equivalents

Hex Value	Decimal Equivalent
0	0
1	1
2	2
3	3
4	4
5	5
6	6
7	7
8	8
9	9
A	10
B	11
C	12
D	13
E	14
F	15

The hexadecimal equivalent for 255 is FF (15*16 + 15).

Next to the pound sign (#) are three pairs of hex values, one for each color. So in our sample values, #FF0000 gives the maximum value for red (FF or 255), and zero for both green and blue. This yields the brightest, purest red. Likewise, #0000FF gives us the brightest, purest blue. All zeroes give us black, and all Fs give us white. In any case, where we use the same value for each red, green, and blue, we have a shade of gray. The higher the numbers, the lighter the shade. Combinations yield different colors. Table 3.3 shows some combinations for common colors.

Table 3.3   RGB Values in Hexadecimal and Their Color Name Equivalents

RGB Value	Corresponding Color
#FFFF00	Yellow
#FF00FF	Magenta
#00FFFF	Cyan
#FFA500	Orange
#A0522D	Sienna

We added colors here so you could see where one TableLayout ends and the other begins. There are several ways to add background colors to Android controls and layouts. The one used here is crude, but it is simple and does the trick. Load this as your main.xml file and restart your application. Figure 3.4 shows what you should get in your emulator.

Pay particular attention to two attributes in any of the layouts—android: layout_width and android:layout_height—and their typical settings: either fill_parent or wrap_content. These two settings can lead to plenty of frustration when building a screen if they are not set correctly. If you want a layout component to stretch all the way from left to right, set android:layout_width to fill_parent; if not, set it to wrap_content. The same goes for top to bottom. If you want to cover the whole screen, set android:layout_height to fill_ parent; if not, set it to wrap_content.

Likewise, if you expect to share a particular direction with more than one component or layout, you will use wrap_content for that direction. Note how the two TableLayouts have wrap_content as their android:layout_height setting

Figure 3.4
Emulator image with table rows of different colors.

because they are expected to fit on top of each other. Experiment with these on your own. Typically, the outermost layout has both of these set to fill_parent.

I cannot imagine an Android application that didn't involve some amount of text, whether it's a default entry in a TextView or EditText control, labels for radio buttons, text in lists, and so on; text is certainly ubiquitous. Because of text's universality in applications, it is a good idea to spend a little time on it here. Java programmers are familiar with creating Font objects. Following is an example:

```
Font myfont=new Font("SansSerif", Font.BOLD, 32);
```

The example specifies a type name, a typestyle (bold), and a point size. These, along with color, are typical settings you would want to control for your application's text. Of course, you can use different styles for different text on the application.

For each layout or control, you can make the following specifications regarding text:

```
android:textColor
android:textAppearance
android:textSize
android:typeface
android:textStyle
```

You would enter these specifications, with allowable values of course, just as you would with the other attributes in the main.xml file. However, the more variations you want to use, the more tedious entering these attributes can become. There is another option. You can create some standard combinations, give them names, and refer to them as you need them.

Although we have discussed many of the XML files that Eclipse builds automatically, there is nothing to stop us from creating our own, assuming we format them in the correct XML format and put them in the right directories. Table 3.4 shows a brief list of common files, suggested filenames, their resource types, and the ideal place to put them in the project. Filenames must be lowercase and simple, containing numbers, letters, and underscores only.

Table 3.4   Resource File Types and Details

Resource Type	Directory Location	Suggested Filename	XML Tag, If Applicable
Strings	/res/values	strings.xml	<string>
Arrays of strings	/res/values	arrays.xml	<string-array>
Color values	/res/values	colors.xml	<color>
Bitmap graphics	/res/drawable	Any with .png, .jpg, or .gif extensions	n/a
Menu files	/res/menu	menu1.xml	<menu>
XML files (special purpose not described elsewhere)	/res/xml	special.xml	Defined by programmer
Raw files (for example, text files)	/res/raw	Any with .txt, .mp3, and so on extensions	n/a
Layout files	/res/layout (created by Eclipse)	start.xml, secondary.xml	n/a
Styles and themes	/res/values	textstyles.xml	<style>

Let's assume that we want to create a bolder type style we will call shout to emphasize particular text items. We want to use red for the text, make it a bigger size than the default, and use bold print to add even more emphasis. We see that files controlling text styles belong in the /res/values directory. In the Package Explorer window of Eclipse, right-click the /res/values folder and select New from the menu; then select File from the list. Name the file textstyles.xml or something similar of your own choosing, and enter the following:

```
<?xml version="1.0" encoding="utf-8"?>
<resources>
<style name="shout">
<item name="android:textColor">#ff0000</item>
<item name="android:textSize">20pt</item>
<item name="android:textStyle">bold</item>
</style>
</resources>
```

Notice that in the name-value pairs, the names are the attributes you would use in the main.xml file if you chose to create the special effects there. The same holds true for the values. Be careful to properly form the XML file. Now, whenever you want to use this configuration for emphasized text, simply add the following line to the item in the main.xml file (or any other layout file for that matter).

```
style="@style/shout"
```

Test your special effects by adding this line to the first TextView entry in the main.xml file. The first TextView entry in the main.xml file should look like this:

```
<TextView
   style="@style/shout"
   android:layout_width="wrap_content"
   android:layout_height="wrap_content"
   android:text="Column 1"
   android:layout_column="0"
   />
```

When you restart the application, the results should look like Figure 3.5 in the emulator.

Try adding some other specification combinations in your styles.xml file, apply them to other controls or layouts in your main.xml file as we did earlier, and examine the results. Remember that name-value pairs in the styles file should be appropriate for the control or layout you attempt to apply them to; for instance, type styles should be applied to items that have text as a feature.

You will see as we go on that different XML and other types of resource files are accessed differently as applications are created. Each of these will be addressed at the appropriate time.

Figure 3.5
Emulator image showing special effects on first TextView object.

COMPONENT IDS

When we looked at an example of the RelativeLayout, we gave one of the controls a name with an android:id attribute. Here is the line of code from the main.xml file:

```
android:id="@+id/centertext"
```

The @ sign in the ID is a signal to the XML parser how to deal with the ID string. The + indicates that this is an ID the user has created; it is not part of the Android framework namespace. You can find further clarification on creating IDs at http:// developer.android.com/guide/topics/ui/declaring-layout.html.

The android:id attribute was important to the RelativeLayout, but it is also important if the programmer wants to identify components from the XML layout file in the application's Java code. For example, suppose we write an application with a text field where the user would enter her name. The programmer would need a way to identify that particular text field to extract the entered name to do something with it. There must be a way to link a component from the static design of the screen during development (the XML file) to the application at run-time (the Java code). If we think in terms of the MVC paradigm, we must connect the view to the control. In the Java code, we declare and assign an instance of an object matching the class of the element in the XML. In the case we are describing, it would be an EditText control. The assignment step uses the ID from the XML file to make the connection. We will see examples of this as soon as we begin coding an application, but we bring it up here because we are in the middle of discussing layouts and the `main.xml` file.

It is a good idea for reasons that will become apparent soon to put an `android:id` attribute on your layouts. For example, you could identify the lowest level layout, the one represented with the first opening tag, as "base." When we added two `TableLayouts` to the underlying `LinearLayout`, the `LinearLayout` could be IDed as "base," the first `TableLayout` as `level2a` or `table_1`. Do whatever you think is appropriate.

A FEW SIMPLE CONTROLS

Soon we will be coding in Java; therefore, we should build some functional controls into a `main.xml` file so we can actually watch an application do something. So far, we have used `TextView` objects to display some simple text. Two more basic but useful controls, or *widgets* as they are called, are the `EditText` and the `Button`. Java programmers are already familiar with `Buttons`, and `EditText` controls are similar to `TextFields`. (The Android `TextView` is similar to the Java `Label` class.) Let's begin a simple application that will take the contents of a predefined `TextView` and use a button to cause the application to take that text, convert it to uppercase, and display it in an `EditText` field. A basic `main.xml` file could look like the following:

```
<?xml version="1.0" encoding="utf-8"?>
<LinearLayout xmlns:android="http://schemas.android.com/apk/res/android"
    android:orientation="vertical"
    android:layout_width="fill_parent"
    android:layout_height="fill_parent"
    android:id="@+id/base"
    >
<TextView
    android:layout_width="fill_parent"
    android:layout_height="wrap_content"
    android:text="My first android application"
    android:id="@+id/my_TextView"
    />
<Button
    android:layout_width="wrap_content"
    android:layout_height="wrap_content"
    android:text="Touch me"
    android:id="@+id/my_Button"
/>
```

```
<EditText
   android:layout_width="fill_parent"
   android:layout_height="wrap_content"
   android:id="@+id/my_EditText"
/>
</LinearLayout>
```

Take a moment to look at the R.java that is created based on the configuration of the main.xml. In particular, look at how the id attributes are interpreted in the R.java file:

```
/* AUTO-GENERATED FILE. DO NOT MODIFY.
 *
 * This class was automatically generated by the
 * aapt tool from the resource data it found. It
 * should not be modified by hand.
 */

package com.sheusi.DemoApp;

public final class R {
   public static final class attr {
   }
   public static final class drawable {
      public static final int icon=0x7f020000;
   }
   public static final class id {
      public static final int base=0x7f060000;
      public static final int my_Button=0x7f060002;
      public static final int my_EditText=0x7f060003;
      public static final int my_TextView=0x7f060001;
   }
   public static final class layout {
      public static final int main=0x7f030000;
   }
   public static final class string {
      public static final int app_name=0x7f040001;
      public static final int hello=0x7f040000;
   }
   public static final class style {
      public static final int shout=0x7f050000;
   }
}
```

We have seen before that Eclipse builds a basic framework for the main Java file. Again, it's found in the src subdirectory and has the name we filled into the Create

Activity field way back when we started the project. There is only enough code to put something into the emulator, so we know that the application was created, and not much more. This is where we need to turn now. Our first step is to decide what our application is designed to do. This is our model in the MVC paradigm. As stated, our application is meant to take the contents of a text field, convert them to uppercase, and place the results in another text field. Our view includes the original text in a text field, a button to start the conversion, and a text field to hold the results. Let's look at the Java code and peel it apart:

```
package com.sheusi.DemoApp;

import android.app.Activity;
import android.os.Bundle;
import android.view.*;
import android.widget.*;
import android.view.View.OnClickListener;
public class Demo extends Activity implements OnClickListener{
  /** Called when the activity is first created. */
  Button b=null;
  EditText et=null;
  TextView tv=null;
    @Override
    public void onCreate(Bundle savedInstanceState) {
      super.onCreate(savedInstanceState);
      setContentView(R.layout.main);
      b=(Button)findViewById(R.id.my_Button);
      et=(EditText)findViewById(R.id.my_EditText);
      tv=(TextView)findViewById(R.id.my_TextView);

      b.setOnClickListener(this);
    }
  public void onClick(View v){
    String temp=tv.getText().toString();
    temp=temp.toUpperCase();
    et.setText(temp);
  }
}
```

The first statement starts with the word `package`.

```
package com.sheusi.DemoApp;
```

You chose the package name when you created the project.

Next, notice the statements that begin with the word `import`. Java, like other object-oriented languages, uses groups of predefined classes called *packages*. Packages generally have multipart names separated by periods, such as android.view.View.Button. When packages are built, they have a tree-style organization, and the periods let the Java compiler navigate through the structure. The import statements are a convenience that relieves us from having to type the whole package name each time we use a class from the package. Here is an example. Without the import statement, if we wanted to declare and assign a couple of buttons, we would need these statements:

```
android.widget.Button b1;
android.widget.Button b2;
b1= new android.widget.Button("click me");
b2= new android.widget.Button("quit");
```

Using the import statement,

```
import android.widget.Button;
```

our declarations and assignments need only the class name:

```
Button b1;
Button b2;
b1= new Button("click me");
b2= new Button("quit");
```

You can imagine what a convenience this is in a long and complicated source code. If we want to indicate all classes in a given package, we can use an asterisk (*) as a wild card. For example:

```
import android.widget.*;
```

How do we know which packages to include? This is where it pays to have some Java programming experience. With some study and practice, you will begin to know what classes are necessary to achieve your programming goals; there are hundreds! A little research in textbooks and on the Internet will help with this. Whatever reference you use, the class documentation will always tell you the package name. You simply write an import statement for that particular package.

Not all packages, however, are included in the Java or Android SDKs. Specialized classes and packages sometimes have to be added to your SDK, and some even have to be purchased, but when this becomes necessary, the package vendor or supplier usually provides instructions. Back to the code!

The next line names the public class. Again, you provided the name for the public class when you created the project:

```
public class Demo extends Activity implements OnClickListener{
```

The way classes are structured in terms of syntax requires knowledge of Java or C++. The core of an Android application is built on the Activity class. When we create an application, we customize the Activity class, or *extend* it in Java-ese. Actually, Eclipse generated the beginning of this statement. We add the words implements OnClickListener as we customize the application. The class OnClickListener, as the name implies, lets our application "listen" or check for actions on the user interface, namely the Android device screens, hardware buttons, and so on. Only certain objects can send click messages, but the Android device knows what these are, and the Android application programming interface (API) tells the programmer what they are.

The next three lines declare the text areas and Button for the application's user interface. A TextView is similar to a Java Label class in that it contains text but cannot be edited by simply typing into it at run-time. For this, we use the EditText class.

The next section is where we define whatever we want to happen when the application starts, including laying out the screen, setting initial values to variables, and so on. In our application, we assign values to our control (widget) objects, and we connect the application's "listener" code to the Button:

```
public void onCreate(Bundle savedInstanceState) {
    super.onCreate(savedInstanceState);
    setContentView(R.layout.main);
    b=(Button)findViewById(R.id.my_Button);
    et=(EditText)findViewById(R.id.my_EditText);
    tv=(TextView)findViewById(R.id.my_TextView);
    b.setOnClickListener(this);
  }
```

As you examine this code, a light should go on in your head. Notice all the statements that include R.id.*** You will recognize these as the id attribute values we added to the sections of the main.xml file. We then looked at how they manifested themselves in the R.java file. These statements connect our screen objects to the Java code. Finally, the Button variable, b, connects the listener code.

This last section

```
public void onClick(View v){
   String temp=tv.getText().toString();
   temp=temp.toUpperCase();
   et.setText(temp);
  }
```

defines what we want to happen when we touch the button on the screen. In plain English, we create a text string and assign to it the contents of the TextView on the screen. The TextView got its original text from the android:text statement in the main.xml file. Then, through a built-in method of Java's String class, we convert all the letters to uppercase. Finally, we assign the converted text string to the text property of the EditText field.

Edit your .java file to match the previous code, run the application, and see what happens. The emulator should look like Figure 3.6 at start-up.

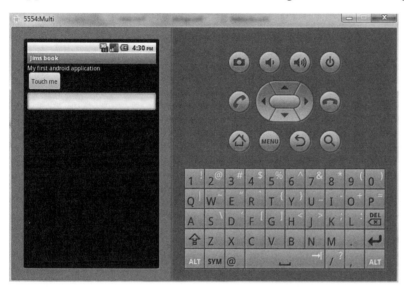

Figure 3.6
Emulator image of the application designed earlier.

To round out this simple application, let's add a second Button to close the application. Go back to the main.xml file and add another button directly below the EditText set of tags. Use the original button as your model. You can even copy and paste if you wish, but set the android:text attribute to Quit and the android:id to @+id/quit. Take care to align the opening and closing markers, < and />, correctly. Eclipse automatically makes corresponding changes to the R.java file, so there is no need to edit that manually. Finally, make the necessary changes to the Java file so that it matches the following:

```java
package com.sheusi.DemoApp;

import android.app.Activity;
import android.os.Bundle;
import android.view.*;
import android.widget.*;
import android.view.View.OnClickListener;
public class Demo extends Activity implements OnClickListener{
    /** Called when the activity is first created. */
    Button b=null;
```

```
EditText et=null;
TextView tv=null;
Button quitbutton=null;
@Override
public void onCreate(Bundle savedInstanceState) {
   super.onCreate(savedInstanceState);
   setContentView(R.layout.main);
   b=(Button)findViewById(R.id.my_Button);
   quitbutton=(Button)findViewById(R.id.quit);
   et=(EditText)findViewById(R.id.my_EditText);
   tv=(TextView)findViewById(R.id.my_TextView);
   b.setOnClickListener(this);
   quitbutton.setOnClickListener(this);
}
public void onClick(View v){
  if(v==b){
  String temp=tv.getText().toString();
  temp=temp.toUpperCase();
  et.setText(temp);
  }
  if(v==quitbutton){
    this.finish();
  }
 }
}
```

We have declared an additional Button object and assigned it using the same syntax as the original Button object. We have also assigned the same OnClickListener to the second Button. It may strike you that if we assign the same listener, the application would not know which Button was touched or clicked. We solve that problem with decision statements based on the parameter View v in the onClick( ) statement. Because the Button class is a child class of the View class in the Android SDK, the parameter can represent the buttons. The decision statements merely assess which Button was clicked or touched. The .finish( ) method is a method of the Activity class that ends the activity. Because our application extends the Activity class, we can use this method to end the application. The word this simply refers to the class using the .finish( ) method—in the previous case above, the Demo class.

Rerun the application and try the Quit button.

When working with EditText controls on the screen, you may want the application to respond to a particular keystroke rather than requiring the user to touch a button or take some other action. For instance, you may want to respond to keypad input as soon as the user touches the Enter key. We can do that by associating a

KeyListener with a given input field. We accomplish that by making some modifications to the previous example. Look at this revision of the previous code:

```
package com.sheusi.DemoApp;
import android.app.Activity;
import android.os.Bundle;
import android.view.*;
import android.widget.*;
import android.view.View.OnClickListener;
import android.view.View.OnKeyListener;
public class DemoAppActivity extends Activity implements OnClickListener,
OnKeyListener{
  /** Called when the activity is first created. */
  Button b=null;
  EditText et=null;
  TextView tv=null;
  Button quitbutton=null;
  @Override
  public void onCreate(Bundle savedInstanceState) {
    super.onCreate(savedInstanceState);
    setContentView(R.layout.main);
    b=(Button)findViewById(R.id.my_Button);
    quitbutton=(Button)findViewById(R.id.quit);
    et=(EditText)findViewById(R.id.my_EditText);
    tv=(TextView)findViewById(R.id.my_TextView);
    b.setOnClickListener(this);
    quitbutton.setOnClickListener(this);
    et.setOnKeyListener(this);
  }
  public void onClick(View v){
   if(v==b){
   String temp=tv.getText().toString();
   temp=temp.toUpperCase();
   et.setText(temp);
   }
   if(v==quitbutton){
     this.finish();
   }
  }
  public boolean onKey(View v, int keyCode, KeyEvent event){
   if(event.getAction()==KeyEvent.ACTION_DOWN){

     if(keyCode==KeyEvent.KEYCODE_ENTER){
       String temp=et.getText().toString();
       temp=temp.toUpperCase();
```

```
        et.setText(temp);
      }
    }
    return false;
  }
}
```

First, notice there is a new `import` statement to add the `OnKeyListener` interface to our namespace. If you are familiar with Java, you will know that implementation of interfaces requires that certain methods be defined in the code; in the case of the `OnKeyListener` interface, it is the `onKey( )` method. The method takes three arguments, or parameters, a `View` object, an integer representing the key you want to respond to, and finally a `KeyEvent` object. The `KeyEvent` object will represent one of two actions on a given key, when it is touched or pushed, and when it is released. These are represented by symbolic constants that can be found in the `KeyEvent`'s documentation, namely `ACTION_DOWN` and `ACTION_UP`. Traditionally, symbolic constants are represented in all uppercase letters. The `keyCode` integer variable also represents a set of symbolic constants defined in the `KeyEvent`'s documentation; there is a constant for each of the keys on the keypad.

Some of the common noncharacter keys on the Android devices and their corresponding symbolic constants are listed in Table 3.5.

Table 3.5   Keystrokes and Their Symbolic Constants

Device's Key	KeyEvent Symbolic Constant
Power button	KEYCODE_POWER
Back key	KEYCODE_BACK
Menu key	KEYCODE_MENU
Camera button	KEYCODE_CAMERA
Home key	KEYCODE_HOME
Search key	KEYCODE_SEARCH

For a complete list of keystrokes and their equivalents, view http://developer.android.com/reference/android/view/KeyEvent.html.

In our example, we want to respond to the user's touch on the Enter or Return key on the keypad; hence, the symbolic constant `KEYCODE_ENTER`. During run-time, the application assesses each keystroke entered into the `EditText` control we assigned the listener to. If the action matches ACTION_DOWN, the application goes on to check which key was pressed. If it was indeed the Enter key, we proceed with an action—in this case to convert all the characters typed in to uppercase—and then replace them in the EditText field. Make the necessary changes to the previous project or start a new one and try this technique.

CREATING AND CONFIGURING AN ANDROID EMULATOR

In Chapter 2, we discussed the different releases of the Android platform and the improvements and features added to the subsequent releases. Each of those versions had a version number starting at 1.0 and running to 3.2. In the same chapter, we discussed choosing an API for our project to correspond with the target platform when the project is started. Finally, we need to configure an emulator that will properly simulate the use of our application. As we progress through the exercises in the book, we will find it necessary to add features such as GPS and SD card for external storage.

We can add features to existing emulators and even create new emulators through Eclipse. Eclipse will maintain several emulators so the application designer can switch among several choices during development of a single application.

Under the Window menu in Eclipse, choose Android SDK and AVD Manager. AVD stands for Android Virtual Device, the emulator. Refer to Figure 3.7.

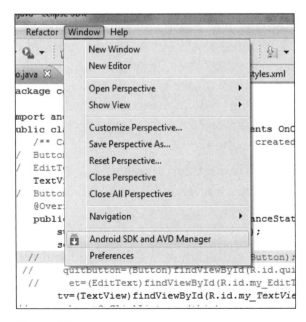

Figure 3.7
Window menu open showing Android SDK and AVD Manager choice.

Choosing that will give you the window in Figure 3.8.

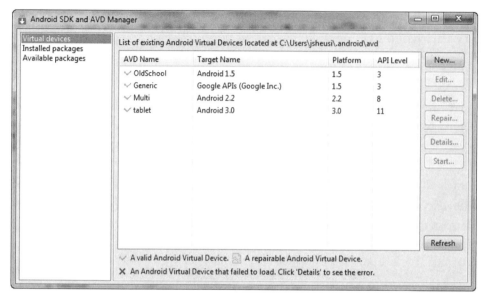

Figure 3.8
Emulator configuration panel.

Your screen may have only the "default" emulator in the list; that's okay. You will notice the New and Edit buttons on the right, which you will use to modify the chosen emulator or create new ones. We don't need to do either of these now, but you should know where to find these features for the future. Any time that you do choose to create a new emulator, remember the platforms we reviewed earlier and the features each offers. If you are writing an application that wants to take advantage of particular device features, be sure to build an emulator at that level. Otherwise, your application will not run in the emulator as you might expect.

To choose the emulator you want to use for your project development, you can click the down-facing arrow next to the green-circle icon and choose Run Configurations as indicated in Figure 3.9.

Alternatively, you can choose Project, Properties, Run/Debug Settings. Then choose your project and choose the Edit button on the right. Either way, you will end up with the window shown in Figure 3.10.

On this screen, you would select the Target tab and pick your emulator.

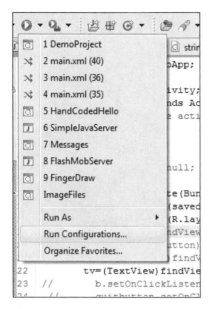

Figure 3.9
Run Configurations choice revealed in menu.

COMMUNICATING WITH THE EMULATOR

An application developer can communicate with a running emulator in two ways. One way is through a Telnet connection, which is a network-type connection that requires a Telnet/SSH client on the development machine. We will use this type of connection later in the book.

The second way to connect to a running emulator is through the Android Debug Bridge (ADB). The ADB is a stand-alone executable file that comes with the Android Development Kit (ADK). You can run it by starting a console session on your development machine. If you are using windows, you can click the Start button or Windows icon (Windows 7), and in the search box just type cmd. This starts a terminal screen. Navigate to the android-sdk directory, and in that directory you should find a subdirectory called platform-tools. Navigate into the platform-tools directory and type adb (enter) on the command line to run the program.

Note

An emulator has to be running if you want to connect; you cannot simply have an application project open in Eclipse.

The adb utility also allows the user to connect to his actual Android device if it is connected through a cable, but that is not our intent here.

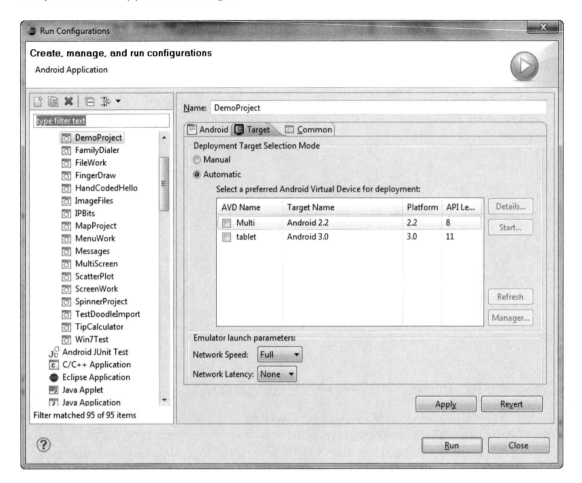

Figure 3.10
Run Configurations panel.

The adb command is used in conjunction with a keyword to cause a particular action. Some commands that you may find useful are detailed in Table 3.6.

If you are familiar with simple navigation commands used in Linux, such as ls, ls -l, and cd, feel free to try the adb shell command with a running emulator. If you are not familiar, here are some of the basics:

pwd [options] - "print working directory"—This gives you the complete path of the directory where you are currently located.

cd [options] [directoryname | ~ | ./ | ../ | -]—This changes your working directory.

ls [options] directoryname—Use this to list the files and subdirectories in the current (working) directory.

mkdir [options] directoryname—Use this to create a new directory.

Table 3.6 Commands and Their Emulator Responses

Command	Result
`adb install <application.apk>`	Installs a new application to the emulator or actual connected device.
`adb push <file on development machine> <location on emulator/ mobile device>`	Uploads a file to the emulator or connected device.
`adb pull <file on the emulator/ mobile device><location on development machine>`	Downloads a file from the emulator or connected device.
`adb shell`	Brings up a command line to the emulator or actual device that will respond to common Linux commands. (Remember, the core of the Android platform is Linux.) This is the easiest way to navigate the file system on the emulator or actual device.
`adb logcat`	Starts dumping debugging information to the screen. (Logcat is part of the debugging system in Eclipse as well, as we discussed in Chapter 2's section on debugging.

`rmdir [options] directoryname`—Use this to remove/delete the named directory.

`cp [options] source destination`—Use this to copy files and directories from source to destination.

`mv [options] source destination`—Use this to move files and directories from source to destination.

`rm [options] filenamelist`—Use this to remove/delete the named file(s).

FOLLOW-UP

1. Study and practice writing XML files.

2. Research and write a summary of the Model-View-Controller design paradigm.

3. Experiment with the XML settings for the `TextView`, `Button`, and `EditText` controls in the `main.xml` file.

4. Experiment with creation and configuration of different emulators for your projects.

5. Experiment with the Android Debug Bridge (adb) utility.

6. Become familiar with basic Linux navigational commands.

KEY CLASSES USED IN THIS CHAPTER

Button

Class	`Button`
Package	`android.widget`
Extends	`Android.widget.TextView`
Overview	Represents a push button on the screen. The user can click it or touch it to perform an action.

Methods used in this chapter:

`void setOnClickListener(View.OnClickListener ocl)`	Registers a callback to be invoked when this view or descendent class object is clicked. Inherited from the `View` class.

Other commonly used methods:

`void setOnTouchListener(View.OnTouchListener otl)`	Registers a callback to be invoked when a touch event is sent to this view or descendent class object. Inherited from the `View` class.
`void setOnLongClickListener (View.OnLongClickListener ocl)`	Registers a callback to be evoked when this view or descendent class object is clicked and held. Inherited from the `View` class.
`void setEnabled(boolean enabled)`	Sets the enabled state of this view or descendent class object. Inherited from the `TextView` class.
`void setHighlightedColor (int color)`	Sets the color used to display the section highlight. Inherited from the `TextView` class.
`void setText(CharSequence text)`	Sets the string value of the `TextView`. Inherited from the `TextView` class.
`void setTextColor(int color)`	Sets the text color for all the states (normal, selected, focused) to be this color. Inherited from the `TextView` class.
`void setTextSize(int unit, float size)`	Sets the default text size to a given unit and value. Inherited from the `TextView` class.

TextView

Class	`TextView`
Package	`android.widget`
Extends	`Android.view.View`
Overview	Displays text to the user, optionally allowing them to edit it. Although editing is possible, it is configured not to allow editing; it is similar to the `Label` class in the Java `awt` package in that respect.

Methods used in this chapter:

None

Other commonly used methods:

`setText(CharSequence text)`	Sets the string value of the `TextView`
`CharSequence getText( )`	Returns a `CharSequence`
`void setEnabled(boolean enabled)`	Sets the enabled state of this view or descendent class object
`void setHighlightedColor(int color)`	Sets the color used to display the section highlight
`void setTextColor(int color)`	Sets the text color for all the states (normal, selected, focused) to be this color
`void setTextSize(int unit, float size)`	Sets the default text size to a given unit and value
`void setAllCaps(boolean allCaps)`	Sets the properties of this field to transform input to ALL CAPS display
`void setLines(int lines)`	Makes the `TextView` exactly this many lines tall
`void setPadding(int left, int top, int right, int bottom)`	Sets the padding for this `TextView`

EditText

Class	`EditText`
Package	`android.widget`
Extends	`Android.view.View`
Overview	A `TextView`-type control configured to be editable

Methods used in this chapter:

`setText( )`   Inherited from `TextView`. Assigns text to the control.

Other commonly used methods:

`Editable getText( )`	Retrieves contents of the control. Contents can subsequently be assigned to a `String` through the use of the `toString( )` method.
`setTextColor(int color)`	Sets the text color for all the states (normal, selected, focused) to be this color. Inherited from `TextView`.
`void setTextSize(int unit, float size)`	Sets the default text size to a given unit and value. Inherited from `TextView`.
`void setAllCaps(boolean allCaps)`	Sets the properties of this field to transform input to ALL CAPS display. Inherited from `TextView`.
`void setLines(int lines)`	Makes the `TextView` exactly this many lines tall. Inherited from `TextView`.
`void setPadding(int left, int top, int right, int bottom)`	Sets the padding for this `TextView`. Inherited from `TextView`.

View.OnClickListener

Class	`View.OnClickListener` (an interface)
Package	`android.view.View`
Extends	n/a
Overview	Interface definition to be invoked when a view object is clicked.

Methods used in this chapter: (required)

`onClick( View v )`   Called when the view is clicked. v refers to the item that has been clicked.

Other commonly used methods:

n/a

READER'S NOTES

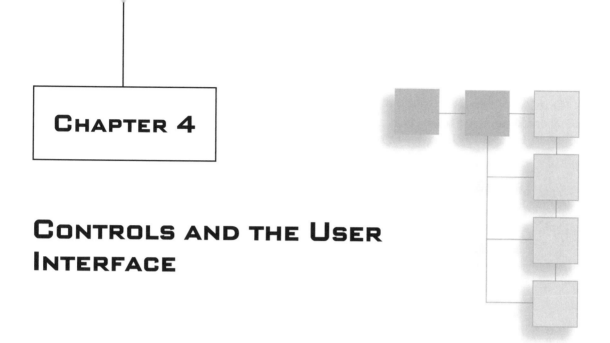

CHAPTER 4

CONTROLS AND THE USER INTERFACE

CHECK BOXES

In the previous chapter, we looked at two common and easy-to-implement user interfaces: the Button and the EditText. Both of these are standard in the Android software development kit (SDK) and can, for the most part, be configured in the main.xml file. This section examines a few more useful ways the user can interact with the application and how to handle the events they produce.

The controls, or *widgets* as they are sometimes called, are descendents of the Android widget class, just like all the layouts we looked at. A relatively easy widget to begin with here is the CheckBox. The CheckBox can be activated with a finger touch and can be polled in the application's code for a checked or unchecked state. To use this widget, let's create an application that allows construction of a shopping list so the user can check off items as they are picked up. For simplicity sake, let's make the list hold just five items. There will be no way to save or retrieve the items; they will only be on the application while it is running. Again, this is just an example of the CheckBox in action. We will use a TableLayout with five rows, each holding an EditText and a CheckBox. At the bottom, we will add a digital clock so the shopper can keep track of time, and a TextView that will display the word DONE! when all the CheckBoxes are checked.

Here is the main.xml file:

```
<?xml version="1.0" encoding="utf-8"?>
<TableLayout xmlns:android="http://schemas.android.com/apk/res/android"
  android:orientation="vertical"
```

```
      android:layout_width="fill_parent"
      android:layout_height="fill_parent"
   >
<TableRow
   android:layout_width="fill_parent"
   android:layout_height="wrap_content"
    >
    <EditText
    android:layout_width="wrap_content"
    android:layout_height="wrap_content"
    android:minWidth="250px"
    android:id="@+id/item1"
    android:paddingBottom="5px"
    />
    <CheckBox
    android:id="@+id/check1"
    />
    </TableRow>
    <TableRow
    android:layout_width="fill_parent"
    android:layout_height="wrap_content"
    >
    <EditText
    android:layout_width="wrap_content"
    android:layout_height="wrap_content"
    android:minWidth="250px"
    android:id="@+id/item2"
    android:paddingBottom="5px"
    />
    <CheckBox
    android:id="@+id/check2"
    />
    </TableRow>
    <TableRow
    android:layout_width="fill_parent"
    android:layout_height="wrap_content"
    >
    <EditText
    android:layout_width="wrap_content"
    android:layout_height="wrap_content"
    android:minWidth="250px"
    android:id="@+id/item3"
    android:paddingBottom="5px"
    />
```

```
<CheckBox
 android:id="@+id/check3"
 />
</TableRow>
<TableRow
android:layout_width="fill_parent"
android:layout_height="wrap_content"
 >
 <EditText
 android:layout_width="wrap_content"
 android:layout_height="wrap_content"
 android:minWidth="250px"
 android:id="@+id/item4"
 android:paddingBottom="5px"
 />
 <CheckBox
 android:id="@+id/check4"
 />
</TableRow>
<TableRow
android:layout_width="fill_parent"
android:layout_height="wrap_content"
 >
 <EditText
 android:layout_width="wrap_content"
 android:layout_height="wrap_content"
 android:minWidth="250px"
 android:id="@+id/item5"
 android:paddingBottom="5px"
 />
 <CheckBox
 android:id="@+id/check5"
 />
</TableRow>
<TableRow
 android:layout_width="fill_parent"
android:layout_height="wrap_content"
 >
<DigitalClock
android:textSize="20pt"
 android:layout_width="fill_parent"
android:layout_height="wrap_content"
/>
</TableRow>
```

```
<TableRow
android:layout_width="fill_parent"
android:layout_height="wrap_content"
>
<TextView
android:layout_width="wrap_content"
android:layout_height="wrap_content"
android:minWidth="250px"
android:id="@+id/done"
android:textSize="20pt"
android:paddingBottom="5px"
android:text=""
android:background="#ffffff"
 android:textColor="#ff0000"
/>
</TableRow>
</TableLayout>
```

We have added a couple of extra parameters to the XML file that we didn't mention previously, such as android:minWidth, but they should be fairly self-evident. As you might guess, the "px" on some of the values stands for pixels, and "pt" stands for points, each point being 1/72 of an inch. Note that the "px" unit is fixed; as the screen density of the device changes, the actual size in inches of an image changes. If you are developing for a broad range of devices, this may not be appropriate. An alternative is the "dp" unit. Dp stands for Density-independent Pixels, (sometimes referred to as "dip," and the compiler will accept both "dp" and "dip"), and it is based on a 160-pixel-per-inch screen. In practicality, the use of 160dp instead of 160px will ensure that the item displayed will be the same size no matter what device it is displayed on. The "sp" unit, which stands for Scale-independent Pixels, works the same way but is used for font size specifications.

Here is the code for the Java file:

```
package com.sheusi.ShoppingList;

import android.app.Activity;
import android.os.Bundle;
import android.widget.*;
import android.view.*;
import android.view.View.OnClickListener;
public class ShopList extends Activity implements OnClickListener{
   /** Called when the activity is first created. */
   EditText et1=null;
   CheckBox cb1=null;
```

```java
      EditText et2=null;
      CheckBox cb2=null;
      EditText et3=null;
      CheckBox cb3=null;
      EditText et4=null;
      CheckBox cb4=null;
      EditText et5=null;
      CheckBox cb5=null;
      TextView tv=null;
    @Override
    public void onCreate(Bundle savedInstanceState) {
        super.onCreate(savedInstanceState);
        setContentView(R.layout.main);
        et1=(EditText)findViewById(R.id.item1);
        cb1=(CheckBox)findViewById(R.id.check1);
        et2=(EditText)findViewById(R.id.item1);
        cb2=(CheckBox)findViewById(R.id.check2);
        et3=(EditText)findViewById(R.id.item1);
        cb3=(CheckBox)findViewById(R.id.check3);
        et4=(EditText)findViewById(R.id.item1);
        cb4=(CheckBox)findViewById(R.id.check4);
        et5=(EditText)findViewById(R.id.item1);
        cb5=(CheckBox)findViewById(R.id.check5);
        tv=(TextView)findViewById(R.id.done);
        cb1.setOnClickListener(this);
        cb2.setOnClickListener(this);
        cb3.setOnClickListener(this);
        cb4.setOnClickListener(this);
        cb5.setOnClickListener(this);
        cb1.setChecked(false);
        cb2.setChecked(false);
        cb3.setChecked(false);
        cb4.setChecked(false);
        cb5.setChecked(false);
    }
  public void onClick(View v){
    if(cb1.isChecked() & cb2.isChecked() & cb3.isChecked() & cb4.isChecked() &
cb5.isChecked())

      tv.setText("DONE!");
    else
      tv.setText("");
  }
}
```

Your running application should look like Figure 4.1.

Figure 4.1
Emulator image showing shopping list application.

Radio Buttons

Java programmers are familiar with check boxes and how combining them into a `CheckBox` group turns them into radio buttons. What makes radio buttons special is that they are mutually exclusive; that is if one is selected, all the others are automatically deselected. They are called radio buttons because they work like the station selectors on a car radio. An easy demonstration for radio buttons is a tip calculator. We will supply an `EditText` box in which the user can supply the dinner bill amount and select one of three radio buttons to determine a tip for 10, 15, or 20 percent. The tip is calculated upon selection of one of the buttons. The following code is the `main.xml` file for the tip calculator:

```
<?xml version="1.0" encoding="utf-8"?>
<LinearLayout xmlns:android="http://schemas.android.com/apk/res/android"
    android:orientation="vertical"
    android:layout_width="fill_parent"
    android:layout_height="fill_parent"
    >
<TableLayout
android:layout_width="fill_parent"
    android:layout_height="wrap_content"
>
```

```
<TableRow
  android:layout_width="fill_parent"
  android:layout_height="wrap_content"
  >
  <TextView
   android:layout_width="wrap_content"
  android:layout_height="wrap_content"
    android:textSize="9pt"
  android:text="Enter Bill Amount: $"

  />

  <EditText
  android:layout_width="wrap_content"
  android:layout_height="wrap_content"
    android:textSize="9pt"
  android:id="@+id/bill_amount"
  android:minWidth="100px"
  />

</TableRow>
</TableLayout>
<RadioGroup
  android:layout_width="wrap_content"
  android:layout_height="wrap_content"
  android:id="@+id/tip_choices"
  >

<RadioButton
  android:id="@+id/ten"
   android:layout_width="wrap_content"
  android:layout_height="wrap_content"
  android:text="10%"
  android:textSize="20pt"
  />
  <RadioButton
  android:id="@+id/fifteen"
   android:layout_width="wrap_content"
  android:layout_height="wrap_content"
  android:text="15%"
  android:textSize="20pt"
  />
  <RadioButton
  android:id="@+id/twenty"
   android:layout_width="wrap_content"
  android:layout_height="wrap_content"
```

```
    android:text="20%"
    android:textSize="20pt"
    />
  </RadioGroup>
<TableLayout
 android:layout_width="fill_parent"
  android:layout_height="wrap_content" >
<TableRow
  android:layout_width="fill_parent"
  android:layout_height="wrap_content"
  >
  <TextView
   android:layout_width="wrap_content"
  android:layout_height="wrap_content"
    android:textSize="9pt"
  android:text="The tip should be: "

  />

  <TextView
  android:layout_width="wrap_content"
  android:layout_height="wrap_content"
   android:textSize="9pt"
    android:minWidth="100px"
  android:id="@+id/tip_amount"
   android:background="#ffffff"
  android:textColor="#000000"
   />
  </TableRow>
</TableLayout>

</LinearLayout>
```

The `main.xml` files are getting longer, but they aren't getting more complicated. There are just more elements with essentially the same attributes that we have been using all along. The important addition here is the use of the `RadioButtons` and the `RadioGroup`. Notice how all the `RadioButtons` are set inside the `RadioGroup` tags. Also notice that we gave the `RadioGroup` an ID value. This is important because in the code the `RadioGroup` will be an object we have to modify. Study the Java source code for the tip calculator:

```
package com.sheusi.tips;

import android.app.Activity;
import android.os.Bundle;
import android.widget.*;
import android.view.*;
```

```
import android.widget.RadioGroup.*;
import java.text.DecimalFormat;

public class Tips extends Activity implements RadioGroup.OnCheckedChangeListener{
  /** Called when the activity is first created. */
  EditText ba=null;
  TextView ta=null;
  RadioButton t10=null;
  RadioButton t15=null;
  RadioButton t20=null;
  RadioGroup rg=null;
  DecimalFormat df=new DecimalFormat("$#####.00");
  @Override
  public void onCreate(Bundle savedInstanceState) {
    super.onCreate(savedInstanceState);
    setContentView(R.layout.main);
    ba=(EditText)findViewById(R.id.bill_amount);
    ta=(TextView)findViewById(R.id.tip_amount);
    t10=(RadioButton)findViewById(R.id.ten);
    t15=(RadioButton)findViewById(R.id.fifteen);
    rg=(RadioGroup)findViewById(R.id.tip_choices);
    rg.setOnCheckedChangeListener(this);
  }
  public void onCheckedChanged(RadioGroup rg,int i){
   if(i==t10.getId())
     ta.setText(df.format(Double.parseDouble(ba.getText().toString())*.10));
   if(i==t15.getId())
     ta.setText(df.format(Double.parseDouble(ba.getText().toString())*.15));
   if(i==t20.getId())
     ta.setText(df.format(Double.parseDouble(ba.getText().toString())*.20));
  }
}
```

It's interesting that, by simple line count, the main.xml exceeds the Java code. This goes to show how much work the main.xml file actually does. The first thing you might notice about the Java code is that we introduced a new listener, the OnCheckedChange-Listener. What is worth noting about this listener is that it is connected to the RadioGroup and not the individual RadioButtons. The onCheckedChanged( ) method of the listener takes two arguments: a RadioGroup and an integer value. We could share the method among several RadioGroups, so we need to know which one we are dealing with when an event occurs. The integer parameter identifies the RadioButton that was selected.

What are the integer values? Well, we really don't need to know them while we are coding because we can use the .getId( ) method of each button to retrieve the actual value, but if you are really curious look at the R.java file. You will notice there is a hexadecimal value associated with each object listed. (It starts with "0x" to indicate it is a hexadecimal value.) If you take any of these numbers and convert it to decimal, you will have the integer value returned by the corresponding object's .getId( ) method. Technically, the computer doesn't care if it's hex, decimal, or binary, but if you write code to print the value to a TextView for curiosity sake, the value will print as decimal by default. Once again, we see how the project files are tied to each other.

The if( ) statements take the bill amount that exists as text, convert it to a double data type, multiply by the appropriate factor, format the product according to the specification in the DecimalFormat object, and place it in the TextView at the bottom of the screen. The running application should look like Figure 4.2.

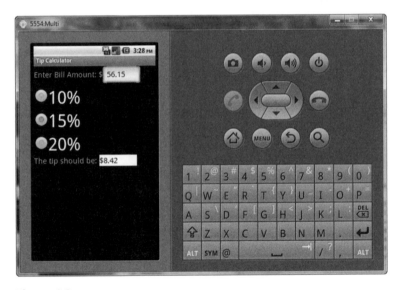

Figure 4.2
Emulator image showing Tip Calculator application.

THE SPINNER

You will notice in the RadioButton that the series of only three buttons takes up almost half the screen space. The programmer may need to contend with many items that must be displayed on the screen and many choices for a given item. A Spinner widget is ideal in this situation. The Spinner is similar to the java.awt.Choice class or the Visual Basic .NET ComboBox. The Spinner not only conserves screen space, it restricts the user to a list of valid, correctly spelled entries.

Because the entries are likely to be known at design time (for example, a list of states, a list of zip codes, and so on), they can be included in the XML files before Java code is written. The example we will look at displays the New England state names, allows the user to pick a state, and then displays the chosen entry in a `TextView` at the bottom of the list for confirmation's sake. Notice how little screen space the example actually occupies. The first item is the `strings.xml` file. This demonstrates how to enter an array of strings. We assume you understand the principle of an array in any programming language at this point. The `string.xml` file is found in the `values` directory under the `res` directory and is created by Eclipse when the project is created.

```xml
<?xml version="1.0" encoding="utf-8"?>
<resources>
   <string name="hello">Hello World, MySpinner!</string>
   <string name="app_name">Spinner Example</string>
   <string-array name="NewEnglandStates">
      <item>Maine</item>
      <item>New Hampshire</item>
      <item>Vermont</item>
      <item>Massachusetts</item>
      <item>Rhode Island</item>
      <item>Connecticut</item>
      </string-array>
   <string name="spinner_prompt">Pick A State</string>
</resources>
```

Next, let's look at the `main.xml` file where we make an entry for the `Spinner` widget.

```xml
<?xml version="1.0" encoding="utf-8"?>
<LinearLayout xmlns:android="http://schemas.android.com/apk/res/android"
   android:orientation="vertical"
   android:layout_width="fill_parent"
   android:layout_height="fill_parent"
   >
   <TextView
   android:layout_width="fill_parent"
   android:layout_height="wrap_content"
   android:text="A Spinner Example"
   />
   <Spinner
   android:id="@+id/NEStates"
    android:layout_width="fill_parent"
   android:layout_height="wrap_content"
   android:entries="@array/NewEnglandStates"
   android:prompt="@string/spinner_prompt"
```

```
></Spinner>
<TextView
android:id="@+id/tv1"
android:layout_width="fill_parent"
android:layout_height="wrap_content"
/>
</LinearLayout>
```

In the Spinner element, the android:prompt places a string at the top of the list when it is opened. It is optional, and without it the first choice in the list simply appears at the top of the list. The TextView entry at the bottom of the LinearLayout demonstrates that the Spinner works and is unnecessary to a functional application. However, the programmer should be aware that the first entry in the Spinner's list (the array defined in the strings.xml file) will be the default entry when the application is started, and any variable that uses the results of the user's choice for its value will have the first choice as its value when the application starts.

Finally, let's look at the Java code for the application.

```
package com.sheusi.SpinnerExample;
import android.app.Activity;
import android.os.Bundle;
import android.widget.*;
import android.view.*;
public class MySpinner extends Activity implements AdapterView.OnItemSelectedListener{
    /** Called when the activity is first created. */
    Spinner statespinner=null;
    TextView tv1=null;
   @Override
    public void onCreate(Bundle savedInstanceState) {
       super.onCreate(savedInstanceState);
       setContentView(R.layout.main);
       statespinner=(Spinner)findViewById(R.id.NEStates);
       tv1=(TextView)findViewById(R.id.tv1);
       statespinner.setOnItemSelectedListener(this);
    }
    public void onItemSelected(AdapterView<?> parent, View view, int pos, long id) {

       tv1.setText(((TextView)view).getText());
      }
    public void onNothingSelected(AdapterView<?> parent) {
     // do nothing
    }
}
```

Notice the introduction of a new Listener interface required to support the Spinner: the AdapterView.OnItemSelectedListener. Use of this interface requires definition of two methods: onItemSelected( ) and onNothingSelected( ). As a Java programmer, you should know that Java allows multiple adapters to be used as long as the required methods for each adapter are defined in the class implementing the adapters. You can also create inline classes to implement the adapters, which is common in examples you might find on the Internet. Other than that, the code should look familiar and be pretty straightforward by now.

The programmer may have occasion to create the array of choices dynamically in code, such as assigning a list of cities to a Spinner object based on the state chosen by another Spinner object, or entered in an EditText; or even the results of a database query. The modification of the original Java code to achieve this is shown here. The Spinner here is loaded from an array of states entered by assignment statements for convenience and clarity.

```java
package com.sheusi.SpinnerExample;
import android.app.Activity;
import android.os.Bundle;
import android.widget.*;
import android.view.*;
public class MySpinner extends Activity implements AdapterView.OnItemSelectedListener{
   /** Called when the activity is first created. */
   Spinner statespinner=null;
   TextView tv1=null;
  @Override
   public void onCreate(Bundle savedInstanceState) {
      super.onCreate(savedInstanceState);
      setContentView(R.layout.main);
      statespinner=(Spinner)findViewById(R.id.NEStates);

      // Begin dynamically loaded Spinner object
      String[] southernstates=new String[5];
      southernstates[0]="Florida";
      southernstates[1]="Louisiana";
      southernstates[2]="Texas";
      southernstates[3]="California";
      southernstates[4]="Arizona";
      ArrayAdapter<String> adapter = new ArrayAdapter<String>( this,
         android.R.layout.simple_spinner_item,southernstates);
   adapter.setDropDownViewResource(
     android.R.layout.simple_spinner_dropdown_item);
   statespinner.setAdapter(adapter);
```

```
        // End dynamically loaded Spinner object

        tv1=(TextView)findViewById(R.id.tv1);
        statespinner.setOnItemSelectedListener(this);


    }
    public void onItemSelected(AdapterView<?> parent,
View view, int pos, long id) {
        tv1.setText(((TextView)view).getText());
    }
    public void onNothingSelected(AdapterView<?> parent) {

    }
}
```

The lines that follow create an instance of an ArrayAdapter for strings and load it with the contents of the Southern States array as indicated by the third parameter. The second parameter, android.R.layout.simple_spinner_item, is part of the Android SDK, so leave it as it is.

```
ArrayAdapter<String> adapter = new ArrayAdapter<String>( this,
        android.R.layout.simple_spinner_item,southernstates);
```

The following runs the setDropDownViewResource( ) method for our adapter instance. As above, the parameter android.R.layout.simple_spinner_drop down_item, one of several constants of the R.layout class, is part of the SDK, so leave that as is.

```
adapter.setDropDownViewResource(
        android.R.layout.simple_spinner_dropdown_item);
```

Finally, the next line simply connects our newly created Adapter instance to the Spinner:

```
statespinner.setAdapter(adapter);
```

Recall that the android:entries parameter in the main.xml file assigned the list of values to the Spinner. The Java code replaces these with the new array. If you intend to assign the values in your Java code, you could eliminate this parameter in the main.xml file.

Your running application should look like Figure 4.3.

DATEPICKER

Two more attractive and useful widgets in the Android SDK are the DatePicker and the TimePicker. They, like the Spinner, are ideal because the programmer doesn't have to worry about the application user choosing invalid date values, such

Figure 4.3
Emulator image showing an open Spinner object.

as the 33rd of the month, spelling the month incorrectly due to the tiny keyboard on a mobile device, or using an improper date format. The `DatePicker` and the `TimePicker` have their own listeners that we can implement by putting the appropriate methods in our main class, just as we did with the `Spinner`. What is different about these classes is that, to be useful, we need to look at two other Java classes: the `Calendar` class and the `Date` class. One or both of these classes typically store the date chosen by the user. Although the results of the widgets' fields are technically treated as integers, as we will see in the methods, the whole point of these widgets is to store and perform calculations with dates and times, not primitive integer values. Therefore, we must look at these Java classes. A little research on these classes will reveal what they can and cannot do and how they are typically used. There is some interchangeability between them, and each can be instantiated as an object using the other to supply its initial values.

Most documentation you might find on the `DatePicker` (which we concentrate on in this section) will show how to construct a `Date` object using the values from the `DatePicker`. However, if you look at documentation of Java's `Date` classes, you will see that the constructor often used by examples is actually deprecated, or obsolete. What's more, there are actually two `Date` classes: the `java.util.Date` and the `java.sql.Date`. This requires the programmer to take extra care when using a `Date` class. Some Java documentation recommends replacing the use of the `Date` class(es) with an instance of the `Calendar` class, which is what we will do in our example.

Our application will be a simple implementation of the DatePicker and a TextView field below the DatePicker to display the chosen date each time we change the Date Picker. You will notice in this application, just as we pointed out in the Spinner application, how much room on the screen is actually consumed by the DatePicker. A little later we will learn how to solve this problem by placing the DatePicker on a pop-up so it will appear over the rest of the screen until we dismiss it.

First, look at our main.xml file:

```xml
<?xml version="1.0" encoding="utf-8"?>
<LinearLayout xmlns:android="http://schemas.android.com/apk/res/android"
   android:orientation="vertical"
   android:layout_width="fill_parent"
   android:layout_height="fill_parent"
   >
   <DatePicker
      android:layout_width="fill_parent"
   android:layout_height="wrap_content"
   android:id="@+id/mydatepicker"/>
   <TextView
   android:layout_width="fill_parent"
   android:layout_height="wrap_content"
   android:textSize="12pt"
   android:background="#ffffff"
   android:textColor="#000000"
   android:id="@+id/myChosenDate"
   />
</LinearLayout>
```

There is nothing too special here, except we need to be sure to put android:id attributes in our elements. Look at the Java code here.

```java
package com.sheusi.DatePickerDemo;

import android.app.Activity;
import android.os.Bundle;
import android.widget.*;
import java.util.*;

public class DatePickerDemo extends Activity implements DatePicker.OnDateChangedListener{
   /** Called when the activity is first created. */
   DatePicker dp=null;
   Calendar cal=null;
   TextView mcdate=null;
   @Override
```

```
public void onCreate(Bundle savedInstanceState) {
    super.onCreate(savedInstanceState);
    setContentView(R.layout.main);
    dp=(DatePicker)findViewById(R.id.mydatepicker);
    mcdate=(TextView)findViewById(R.id.myChosenDate);
    cal=Calendar.getInstance();
    dp.init(dp.getYear(),dp.getMonth(),dp.getDayOfMonth(),this);
}
public void onDateChanged(DatePicker dpview,int year, int monthOfYear,
int dayOfMonth){
    cal.set(year,monthOfYear, dayOfMonth);
    java.util.Date d=cal.getTime();
    mcdate.setText(String.valueOf(d.getMonth()+1)+"/"+String.valueOf(d.getDate())+"/
"+String.valueOf(d.getYear()+1900));

}
}
```

As you have seen before, we implement a listener class and add the necessary method(s) to our code. Here we implement the `DatePicker.OnDateChangedListener` and add the necessary method, `onDateChanged( )`. You can see that we declared a `Calendar` variable at the top of the code.

In the `onCreate( )` method, we assign the `Calendar` variable with the factory method, `Calendar.getInstance( )`. This places the system's date's values into the instance variable. Likewise, when we assign the `DatePicker` object variable, "dp," it will be initialized with the system date. The `.init( )` method takes four parameters. The first three should be self-evident, and the fourth is set to the listener class instance to be associated with this particular `DatePicker`. In our case we use the word "this" because the listener is implemented in the surrounding class.

In the `onDateChanged( )` method, we first assign new date, month, and year values to our already-existing `Calendar` class variable. As we mentioned before, there are some things a `Date` object does better than a `Calendar` object, and vice versa. One of the things the `Date` class does better is allow access to its fields for printing. Therefore, we declare a local `Date` object and assign it with the values from the `Calendar` object. This is done in this line:

```
java.util.Date d=cal.getTime();
```

Finally, we fill our text field with values from the `Date` object formatted to look like the common form mm/dd/yyyy. There are many ways to do this; this is just one way.

You will see when you run the application that the date in the TextView field changes every time we change the DatePicker. As stated before concerning the Spinner, it is not necessary to display the results each time you change the date, but the programmer should retain the DatePicker's values to be used where necessary.

You may notice some arithmetic statements where the date display is assigned to the TextView object. First, we add one to the month because the months are stored as zero-based values in the DatePicker and subsequently in the Date object; in other words, January is month zero, not one. Again, when we display the year, we must add 1900 for essentially the same reason.

The TimePicker implementation is similar to the DatePicker's, so we will not give an example here. The programmer should just note that the listener is the TimePicker.OnTimeChangedListener, and the method that must be implemented is the onTimeChanged( ) method.

Your running application should look like Figure 4.4.

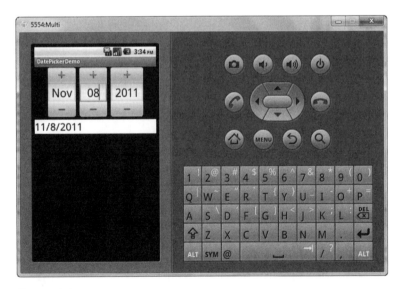

Figure 4.4
Emulator image showing a DatePicker object.

Follow-Up

1. Experiment with the following listener classes and methods that can be associated with the View class and its subclasses.

Listener Class	Method	Description
`View.OnClickListener`	`onClick( )`	This method is called when the user touches the item or focuses on the item with navigation keys or a trackball and then presses the Enter key or presses the trackball.
`View.OnLongClickListener`	`onLongClick( )`	Called when the user touches and stays on an item or holds down the Enter key or the trackball.
`View.OnFocusChange Listener`	`onFocusChange( )`	Called when the user navigates to or away from the item using navigation keys or the trackball.
`View.OnKeyListener`	`onKey( )`	Called when the user is focused on the item and presses or releases a key on the device. Typically, the developer wants to detect a specific key.
`View.OnTouchListener`	`onTouch( )`	Called when the user performs an action qualified as a touch event, such as a press, release, or movement within the bounds of the item associated with the listener.

2. Experiment with the `TimePicker` class by substituting it for the `DatePicker` in the last exercise.

3. Experiment with `onKey( )` listeners by responding to specific characters entered in `EditText` objects.

KEY CLASSES USED IN THIS CHAPTER

CheckBox

Class	`CheckBox`
Package	`android.widget`
Extends	`android.widget.CompoundButton`
Overview	The `CheckBox` is similar to a `Button` but has only two states: checked and unchecked.

Methods used in this chapter:

`void setChecked(boolean chked)`	Inherited from `CompoundButton`. This method changes the state of the `CheckBox`.
`boolean isChecked()`	Inherited from `CompoundButton`. This method returns the state of the `CheckBox`.
`void setOnClickListener(View.OnClickListener listener)`	Inherited from `View`. Registers a listener and process to be invoked when the control is clicked.

Other commonly used methods:

`void setOnCheckChangedListener (CompoundButton.OnCheckChangedListener listener)`	Registers a listener and process to be invoked when the control is changed. Inherited from `CompoundButton`.
`boolean performClick()`	Calls the view's `onClickListener`, if it is defined. Inherited from `CompoundButton`.
`void toggle()`	Changes the state of the check box to its inverse. Inherited from `CompoundButton`.

RadioButton

Class	`RadioButton`
Package	`android.widget`
Extends	`android.widget.CompoundButton`
Overview	The radio button is a two-state widget similar to the `CheckBox`; however, once it is checked, the user cannot uncheck it.

Methods used in this chapter:

`void setOnCheckChangedListener (CompoundButton.OnCheck-ChangedListener occl)`	Inherited from `CompoundButton`

Other commonly used methods:

`toggle( )`	Forces the state to be changed from the current state to the opposite state.
`boolean isChecked( )`	This method returns the state of the `CheckBox`. Inherited from `CompoundButton`.
`boolean performClick()`	Calls the view's `onClickListener`, if it is defined. Inherited from `CompoundButton`.

RadioGroup

Class	`RadioGroup`
Package	`android.widget`
Extends	`android.widget.LinearLayout`
Overview	This class creates a multiple exclusion group of radio buttons. In other words, if one radio button is checked, all others will become unchecked. Only one radio button in a group can be checked at a time. Initially, all buttons are unchecked. `RadioButtons` are added to a `RadioGroup` in a layout XML file similar to the way `TableRows` are added to a `TableLayout`.

Methods used in this chapter:

`setOnCheckChangedListener` `(CompoundButton.OnCheck-` `ChangedListener occl)`	Inherited from `CompoundButton`. Assigns a listener to the `RadioGroup`.

Other commonly used methods:

`void clearCheck()`	Clears all the `RadioButtons` in the group
`void check( int ID )`	Checks the `RadioButton` indicated by the ID
`void addView(View child, int index, ViewGroup.LayoutParams params)`	Adds a child view with the specified layout parameters
`int getCheckedRadioButtonId()`	Returns the identifier of the currently selected radio button in this group
`void clearCheck()`	Clears the current selection

Spinner

Class	`Spinner`
Package	`android.widget`
Extends	`android.widget.AbsSpinner`
Overview	A view that displays one child at a time and lets the user pick among them

Methods used in this chapter:

`setOnItemSelectedListener (AdapterView.OnItemSelected Listener listener)`	Assigns a listener to the `Spinner`. Inherited from `AdapterView`.
`setAdapter(SpinnerAdapter adapter)`	Associates an adapter to the `Spinner`. The adapter is the source of the items in the `Spinner`.

Other commonly used methods:

`setPrompt(CharSequence prompt)`	Sets the prompt to display when the `Spinner` is shown.
`int getCount()`	Returns the number of items in the `Spinner`. Inherited from `AbsSpinner`.
`CharSequence getPrompt()`	Retrieves the prompt from the `Spinner`.
`void setPromptId(int id)`	Sets the prompt to display when the dialog is shown.
`void setGravity()`	Describes how the selected item view is positioned.
`Object getSelectedItem()`	Returns selected item. Inherited from `AdapterView`.
`long getSelectedItemId()`	Returns selected item `id`. Inherited from `AdapterView`.

ArrayAdapter

Class	`ArrayAdapter`
Package	`android.widget`
Extends	`android.widget.BaseAdapter`
Overview	A `BaseAdapter` that is backed by an array of arbitrary objects. If the `ArrayAdapter` is used for anything other than a `TextView`, care must be taken to choose the correct constructor.

Methods used in this chapter:

`void setDropDownViewResource (int resource)`	Sets the layout resource to create the drop-down views

Other commonly used methods:

`void add(Object object)`	Adds an object at the end of the array
`void remove(Object object)`	Removes the specified object from the array
`void insert(Object object, int index)`	Inserts the specified object at the specified index position
`Object getItem(int position)`	Returns the object at the specified position
`int getPosition(Object item)`	Returns the position of the specified item in the array

DatePicker

Class	`DatePicker`
Package	`android.widget`
Extends	`android.widget.FrameLayout`
Overview	This class is a widget for selecting a date. The date is set by a series of `Spinners`. The date can be selected by a year, month, and day `Spinners` or a `CalendarView` object.

Methods used in this chapter:

`init(int year, int monthOfYear, int dayOfMonth, DatePicker.OnDateChanged Listener onDateChanged Listener)`	This method sets the initial date for the `DatePicker` object and assigns `OnDateChangedListener`.

Other commonly used methods:

`CalendarView getCalendarView( )`	Returns a `CalendarView`
`int getDayOfMonth( )`	Returns the day of the month set on this object
`int getMonth( )`	Returns the month set on this object
`int getYear( )`	Returns the year set on this object
`boolean getSpinnersShown()`	Gets whether the `Spinners` are shown
`boolean isEnabled()`	Gets whether the `DatePicker` is enabled
`void setEnabled(boolean enabled)`	Sets the enabled state of this view
`void updateDate(int year, int month, int dayOfMonth)`	Updates the current date

DatePicker.OnDateChangedListener

Class	`DatePicker.OnDateChangedListener` (interface)
Package	`android.widget`
Extends	n/a
Overview	Signals that the user has changed the date on the `DatePicker` associated with this listener

Methods used in this chapter: (required)

```
public abstract void onDateChanged(DatePicker view, int year, int
monthOfYear, int dayOfMonth)
```

Other commonly used methods:

n/a

READER'S NOTES

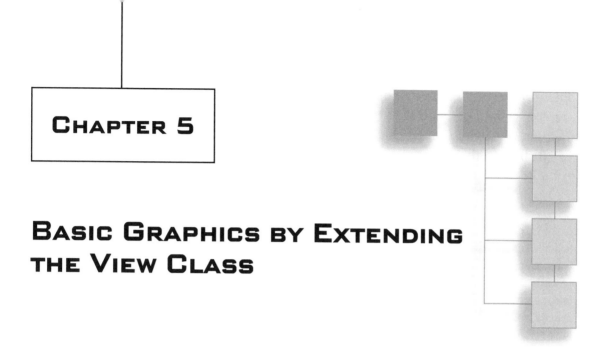

CHAPTER 5

BASIC GRAPHICS BY EXTENDING THE VIEW CLASS

COMBINING GRAPHICS WITH A TOUCH LISTENER

Up to this point we have been using widgets included in the Android software development kit (SDK). Sometimes you will want to build custom widgets that will actually extend a built-in base class. After all, this is one of the advantages of using an object-oriented programming language. The following two examples will extend the View class to become something uniquely suited to our purpose.

The first example extends the View class and attaches a touch listener to become a "doodle pad." First, take a look at the main.xml for the project:

```xml
<?xml version="1.0" encoding="utf-8"?>
<LinearLayout xmlns:android="http://schemas.android.com/apk/res/android"
   android:orientation="vertical"
   android:layout_width="fill_parent"
   android:layout_height="fill_parent"
   android:id="@+id/base"
   >
<TextView
   android:layout_width="fill_parent"
   android:layout_height="wrap_content"
   android:text="My Doodle Pad"
   android:textSize="15pt"
   />
</LinearLayout>
```

You will notice that it is simple, containing only a `LinearLayout` in the background, and a single embedded `TextView`. What you should also notice is something it doesn't have: any kind of an element to represent a doodle pad on the screen. In this exercise, we will design that in the Java code and attach it dynamically to the screen. In Chapter 3, "Application Design," we mentioned that it is desirable to add an `android:id` attribute to the `LinearLayout`; now we will see why. We need to use the identifier in the Java code to attach our custom class object. Examine the following source code:

```java
package com.sheusi.FingerDraw;

import android.app.Activity;
import android.os.Bundle;
import android.widget.*;
import android.content.Context;
import android.view.View.OnTouchListener;
import android.graphics.*;
import android.view.MotionEvent;
import android.view.View;
import java.util.ArrayList;

public class DoodlePad extends Activity {
  /** Called when the activity is first created. */
  LinearLayout ll=null;
  DoodleView dv=null;
 @Override
  public void onCreate(Bundle savedInstanceState) {
    super.onCreate(savedInstanceState);
    setContentView(R.layout.main);
    ll=(LinearLayout)findViewById(R.id.base);
    dv=new DoodleView(this);
    ll.addView(dv,1);
  }
}
class DoodleView extends TextView implements OnTouchListener{
ArrayList<dot> sketch =new ArrayList<dot>();
Paint myPaint=new Paint();

public DoodleView(Context myContext){
  super(myContext);
  this.setBackgroundColor(Color.WHITE);
  this.setHeight(120);
  this.setFocusable(true);
  this.setFocusableInTouchMode(true);
  this.setOnTouchListener(this);
  myPaint.setColor(Color.BLACK);
```

```
      myPaint.setStyle(Paint.Style.FILL_AND_STROKE);
  }
  public void onDraw(Canvas c){
    for(dot d:sketch)
    c.drawCircle(d.x,d.y,2,myPaint);

  }
  public boolean onTouch(View v, MotionEvent me){
    if(me.getAction()==MotionEvent.ACTION_DOWN){}
    if(me.getAction()==MotionEvent.ACTION_MOVE){
      sketch.add(new dot(me.getX(),me.getY()));

    }
    if(me.getAction()==MotionEvent.ACTION_UP){}
    invalidate();
    return true;
  }
  class dot{
    private float x;
    private float y;
    //constructor
    public dot(float x, float y){
      this.x=x;
      this.y=y;
    }
  }
}
}
```

Notice that we create a LinearLayout object variable and assign it using findViewById(R.id.base). This allows us to manipulate the object that appeared first in the main.xml file. You will notice that the source code actually has two classes: the "main" class that extends the Activity class, and another class that extends the TextView class. This additional class defines our doodle pad.

The doodle pad works by saving a series of dots and repainting the screen every time a dot is added. The "dot" class stores the x,y coordinates any time the user's finger is moved across the screen. Because MotionEvent.ACTION_UP and MotionEvent.ACTION_DOWN are empty methods, nothing will happen when the user touches the screen or the pad. The invalidate( ) method causes the redraw. The onDraw( ) method instructs the device to redraw all the dots that are in the ArrayList of dots called "sketch."

Although the code in the class is interesting enough, the lesson here is in adding a widget subclass to the screen in the Java code instead of the main.xml file. The following line does that:

```
ll.addView(dv,1);
```

The name of the `LinearLayout`'s variable is `11` (el-el), and the `addView( )` method adds the widget represented by `dv` to position one in the list. The widget at position zero is the `TextView` specified in the `main.xml` file. There is a second version of the `addView( )` method that only takes the widget variable as the argument with no index value. If you use that version (for example, `.addView(dv)`), your custom widget appears below any previously added method calls on the screen.

Your application in the emulator should look like Figure 5.1.

Figure 5.1
Emulator image of the DoodlePad application.

Our `DoodleView` class is an extension of the `TextView` class that is part of the Android Development Kit (ADK). It would be convenient to be able to use that class or any other custom subclass in future applications without having to rewrite the code. We can do this by creating a `.jar` (Java Archive) file in its own package and store it on our development machine until we need it. At that point, we can just add it to a future project as is and make it an element in our `main.xml` file. Following is a description of the necessary steps.

Create a new Android project with a unique project name, package name, and so on. This time, however, when you complete the project setup screen, remove the check from the Create Activity check box. (Refer to section 1 of the tutorial, if necessary.) Go back to the project from which you want to "borrow" the custom class (such as the `DoodlePad` project), copy *only* the source code for the custom subclass and the necessary import statements, and paste them into the new project. For an example, look at the following source code:

```java
package com.sheusi.Doodle;

import android.widget.*;
import android.content.Context;
import android.view.View.OnTouchListener;
import android.graphics.*;
import android.view.MotionEvent;
import android.view.View;
import java.util.ArrayList;
import android.util.AttributeSet;

class DoodleOnly extends TextView implements OnTouchListener{
ArrayList<dot> sketch =new ArrayList<dot>();
Paint myPaint=new Paint();

public DoodleOnly(Context myContext){
  super(myContext);
  this.setBackgroundColor(Color.WHITE);
  this.setHeight(120);
  this.setFocusable(true);
  this.setFocusableInTouchMode(true);
  this.setOnTouchListener(this);
  myPaint.setColor(Color.BLACK);
  myPaint.setStyle(Paint.Style.FILL_AND_STROKE);
}
public DoodleOnly(Context myContext, AttributeSet attrs){
  super(myContext, attrs);
  this.setBackgroundColor(Color.WHITE);
  this.setHeight(120);
  this.setFocusable(true);
  this.setFocusableInTouchMode(true);
  this.setOnTouchListener(this);
  myPaint.setColor(Color.BLACK);
  myPaint.setStyle(Paint.Style.FILL_AND_STROKE);
}
public DoodleOnly(Context myContext, AttributeSet attrs, int defStyle){
  super(myContext, attrs, defStyle);
  this.setBackgroundColor(Color.WHITE);
  this.setHeight(120);
  this.setFocusable(true);
  this.setFocusableInTouchMode(true);
```

```
      this.setOnTouchListener(this);
      myPaint.setColor(Color.BLACK);
      myPaint.setStyle(Paint.Style.FILL_AND_STROKE);
    }
    public void onDraw(Canvas c){
      for(dot d:sketch)
      c.drawCircle(d.x,d.y,2,myPaint);

    }
    public boolean onTouch(View v, MotionEvent me){
      if(me.getAction()==MotionEvent.ACTION_DOWN){}
      if(me.getAction()==MotionEvent.ACTION_MOVE){
        sketch.add(new dot(me.getX(),me.getY()));

      }
      if(me.getAction()==MotionEvent.ACTION_UP){}
      invalidate();
      return true;
    }
    class dot{
      private float x;
      private float y;
      //constructor
      public dot(float x, float y){
        this.x=x;
        this.y=y;
      }
    }
  }
}
```

Of course, if you choose, you can type in code by hand. If you do this be careful, because there will be no way to test the code in an emulator because there is no associated activity. You are at the mercy of the Eclipse debugger.

Remember, there is no Activity class, only the subclass we created from the TextView class. It is also important to note that I have extended *all* the constructors for the TextView class in my DoodleOnly class. This is essential, or you will encounter an *inflation* error at run-time, meaning that your subclass was unusable. Also note that because there is no Activity class or subclass, this project will not run in an emulator, so you shouldn't bother to try. Instead, we need to archive it. In the Package Explorer, right-click on the source code filename and select Export, Jar File from the menu. Then click the Next button. You will see a screen like the one shown in Figure 5.2. In it, be sure to deselect every item in the project except the src folder and the .classpath and .project names on the right.

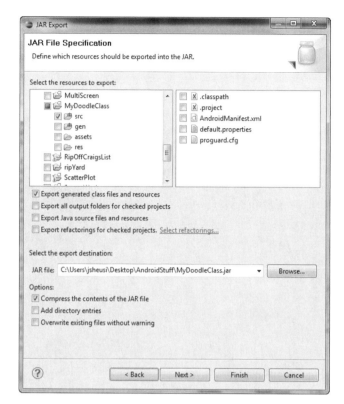

Figure 5.2
Eclipse JAR Export panel.

Expand the directory tree on the left side as shown, so you can deselect everything necessary.

Under Select the Export Destination, select the location where you want to store the .jar file.

Now click the Next button twice, and you will reach the screen shown in Figure 5.3.

Be sure to check the Save the Manifest in the Workspace box and choose the src directory of your project to store the manifest in. Don't confuse this with the AndroidManifest file we have used in the past; the two are different. You can leave the Main Class field blank. Now click the Finish button. Note where you saved this .jar file for future use.

Now let's assume you are in a new project and you want to use your custom subclass. In the current project, choose Properties from the Eclipse Project menu. Then select Java Build Path on the left and choose Add External JARs. Select your .jar file from wherever you stored it.

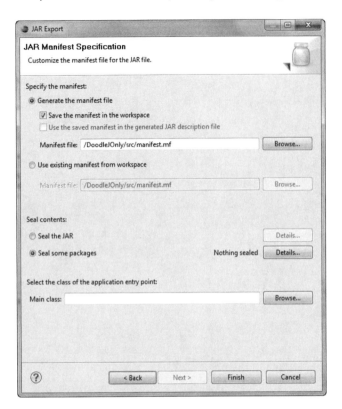

Figure 5.3
Manifest section of JAR export process.

You can now use your custom class by name in your main.xml or any other screen setup .xml you may have. Just be sure to use the complete package name, not just the class name by itself. Refer to the sample main.xml file that follows:

```
<?xml version="1.0" encoding="utf-8"?>
<LinearLayout xmlns:android="http://schemas.android.com/apk/res/android"
   android:orientation="vertical"
   android:layout_width="fill_parent"
   android:layout_height="fill_parent"
   >
<TextView
   android:layout_width="fill_parent"
   android:layout_height="wrap_content"
   android:text="@string/hello"
   />
   <com.sheusi.Doodle.DoodleOnly
    android:layout_width="fill_parent"
```

```
    android:layout_height="wrap_content"
    android.id="@+id/doodlepad"
    />
</LinearLayout>
```

You will now have a fully functional doodle text field in your new application. If you choose to create an instance of the class in the Java code, just be sure to either use the full package name for the class in your variable declarations or put the package in an import statement as you would any other package.

Some Practical Uses for Graphics

This next exercise is another application of the technique that allowed us to create a doodle pad by adding an onDraw( ) method to a class that is a child class of TextView. Rather than simply drawing a stick man or circles on the screen, we will produce a graphic representation of the Poisson distribution for an average the user provides. Depending on where you are in your academic career and what you are studying, there is a chance that you may never run into the Poisson distribution principle and formula. This is perfectly fine; most of the work is taken care of for us by existing classes and methods. However, graphing in an application is a worthwhile effort because it forces the programmer to deal with the screen dimensions of the device, specifically the TextView hosting the Canvas, the x,y coordinates of the Canvas, and mixing text and graphics on the Canvas.

Our exercise will apply the Poisson formula to a number the user enters and produce a series of values that represent the percentage probability that any number (starting with zero) will occur in place of the average. We will count up from zero, and for each value we will apply the formula and obtain the corresponding probability, save each probability, and accumulate a running total of the probabilities. When we cover 99 percent of the probabilities, we will stop calculating and place a dot on the screen in a spot corresponding to the counting value and the corresponding probability. We will treat the Canvas as a graph with the X-axis representing the count value and the Y-axis as the corresponding probability.

Note

Stopping at 99 percent is arbitrary, but the alternative is to continue calculating and producing ever-smaller probabilities for the higher numbers until the values are meaningless.

Let us look at an example. Suppose the number of phone calls an operator gets is 10 per hour. What is the likelihood that in some given hour he will only receive 8? Or the likelihood he will receive 12? Here is what we do to find answers. Using L to represent the average of 10 (normally we use the Greek symbol lambda) and x to represent the experimental value, we apply the formula:

$P(x) = (L^x * e^ - L) / x!$ e represents the constant, 2.71828

$P(8) = (10^8 * 2.71828 ^ -10) / 8!$

$P(8) = .1125$ or 11.25%

Likewise, P(12) is .0947 or 9.47%

That's enough of the Poisson distribution for now. You can study more about it in a statistics or modeling book or on the Internet, such as at http://en.wikipedia.org/wiki/ Poisson_distribution. At any rate, the Poisson distribution gives us a challenging graphic subject, so let's get to work. The easiest part of this application is the screen design. We just need an EditText to receive the user input, a Button to start the calculations, and a few appropriate labels in the XML file. Here is the main.xml file we will use:

```xml
<?xml version="1.0" encoding="utf-8"?>
<LinearLayout xmlns:android="http://schemas.android.com/apk/res/android"
    android:orientation="vertical"
    android:layout_width="fill_parent"
    android:layout_height="fill_parent"
    android:id="@+id/base"
    android:background="#ffffff"
    >
<TextView
    android:layout_width="fill_parent"
    android:layout_height="wrap_content"
    android:text="POISSON DISTRIBUTION GRAPHER"
    android:textColor="#000000"
    />
<TableLayout
android:layout_width="fill_parent"
 android:layout_height="wrap_content" >
 >
    <TableRow >
<TextView
    android:layout_width="fill_parent"
    android:layout_height="wrap_content"
    android:text="Lambda (average)"
    android:layout_column="1"
    android:layout_weight=".5"
    android:textColor="#000000"
    />
```

```
<TextView
android:layout_width="fill_parent"
android:layout_height="wrap_content"
android:text="     "
android:layout_column="2"
android:layout_weight=".5"
/>

</TableRow>
  <TableRow >
<EditText
android:layout_width="fill_parent"
android:layout_height="wrap_content"
android:text=""
android:id="@+id/et1"
android:layout_column="1"
android:layout_weight=".5"
/>
<Button
android:layout_width="fill_parent"
android:layout_height="wrap_content"
android:text="Touch to graph"
android:id="@+id/b1"
/>
</TableRow>
</TableLayout>
</LinearLayout>
```

We added white to the LinearLayout, purely for aesthetics. We will add a TextView at run-time that also will be white. If we place white-on-white at run-time, the transition on the screen will be transparent. We also assign black to the text in the labels for clarity. No changes are necessary in the manifest file, so we don't have to touch that.

The Java code is where the real work is. Before we get started on our own, we'll see if there is a predesigned class that we can incorporate in our application to save some steps. In the previous exercise, we learned how to save a reusable doodle pad by creating a .jar file so we could add it to subsequent projects. Allowing for possible licensing issues, occasionally we can find .jar files from other programmers. Of course, it is up to the developer to determine if someone else's code is trustworthy. It so happens that a quick Google search yielded at least one package containing a Poisson distribution calculator available as an open-source downloadable .jar. The JAR download can be found at www.java2s.com/Code/Jar/c/Downloadcommonsmath11jar.htm. Documentation can be found at http://commons.apache.org/math/apidocs/org/apache/commons/math/distribution/PoissonDistributionImpl.html.

The `PoissonDistributionImpl` class is derived from the `PoissonDistribution` interface. We are interested in the `probability( )` method that takes one argument, an integer, representing the average value that the distribution is built around. We can download the `org.apache.commons.math.distribution` package as a `.jar` file. Using the downloaded package and the physical `.jar` file involves two steps. The first and easiest is including an `import` statement in our code to add the namespace to the Java code. You will see that in the code listing later. The second and more involved step is to tell Eclipse where the package actually is on your development machine so the code can be added to your project. We will address that first.

Once you have found the `.jar` file to download, make a note of where your computer is storing it. Although there is no strict requirement for a location, it is a good idea to move it to a "permanent" location and out of folders such as Downloads or the desktop; in other words don't leave it in a location where it could be accidently lost when you periodically "clean house" on your computer. And don't store it on a flash drive or CD, which may not be available in the future. Once you've stored the `.jar` file and you have started a project in Eclipse for this exercise, choose Properties under the Project menu, and you will see a screen like Figure 5.4.

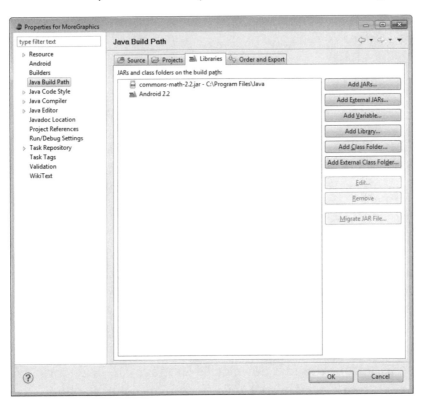

Figure 5.4
Eclipse panel used to add components to a project.

Choose Java Build Path on the right side, and then click the Add External JARs button on the right. You will be asked to select the path and name for the `.jar` file you want to add to the project. In this case it will probably be the `commons-math-2.2.jar` file you see listed in the illustration. Once it appears in the window, click the OK button and move on.

Next is a listing of the Java code:

```java
package com.sheusi.MoreGraphics;

import android.app.Activity;
import android.os.Bundle;
import android.view.*;
import android.widget.*;
import android.content.Context;
import android.graphics.Color;
import android.graphics.Canvas;
import android.graphics.Paint;
import java.util.ArrayList;
import org.apache.commons.math.distribution.*;
import android.util.Log;

public class MoreGraphicsActivity extends Activity {
    /** Called when the activity is first created. */
    EditText avg=null;
    LinearLayout base=null;
    PoissonView poisson=null;
    Button grapher=null;
    ArrayList<Double> series=null;
    int graphsize;
    @Override
    public void onCreate(Bundle savedInstanceState) {
        super.onCreate(savedInstanceState);
        setContentView(R.layout.main);
        avg=(EditText)findViewById(R.id.et1);
        grapher=(Button)findViewById(R.id.b1);
        base=(LinearLayout)findViewById(R.id.base);

        series=new ArrayList<Double>();
        grapher.setOnClickListener(new View.OnClickListener(){
        public void onClick(View v){

        int lam=Integer.parseInt(avg.getText().toString());
        PoissonDistributionImpl pdi=new PoissonDistributionImpl(lam);
        double accum=0;
        double prob=0;
        int x=0;
```

```
      do{
       prob=pdi.probability(x);
       series.add(new Double(prob));
       x=x+1;
       accum=accum+prob;
      }while(accum<.99);
      // after .99, the accum value will increase by ever-tinier amounts without
end
       poisson=new PoissonView(getApplicationContext(),series);

       base.addView(poisson);
      }
      });
    }

  private class PoissonView extends TextView{
    Canvas myCanvas=null;
    Paint myPaint=null;
    int screenheight=0;
    int screenwidth=0;
    public PoissonView(Context c,ArrayList<Double> series){
    super(c);
    myPaint=new Paint();
    myPaint.setStyle(Paint.Style.FILL);
    myPaint.setColor(Color.BLACK);
    Display display =
    ((WindowManager) c.getSystemService(Context.WINDOW_SERVICE))
  .getDefaultDisplay();
    screenwidth=display.getWidth();
    screenheight=display.getWidth();
    // make a square graph area as large as the screen width
    this.setHeight(screenheight);
    //this.setHeight(300);
    this.setWidth(screenwidth);
    this.setBackgroundColor(Color.WHITE);

    }
  @Override
  protected void onDraw(Canvas myCanvas){
    super.onDraw(myCanvas);

    //below draws the y-axis scale for percentages values of probabilities
    for(int ct=9;ct>=0;--ct){
      myCanvas.drawText("."+String.valueOf(ct*5),3,screenheight-
  ((screenheight/10)*ct),myPaint);
    }
```

```
double[] points= new double[series.size()];
for(int ct=0;ct<series.size();++ct){
  points[ct]=series.get(ct).doubleValue();
}
int xjump=(int)(screenwidth/series.size());
myCanvas.drawText("First point is p(0)", 5.0f, 10.0f, myPaint);
//draw a border line on the bottom of the graph
myCanvas.drawLine(0f,screenheight-1.0f, screenwidth,screenheight-1.0f, myPaint);
myPaint.setColor(Color.BLUE);
//below, the constant 46 represents the number of positions on the scale 0-45
for(int ct=0;ct<series.size();++ct){
  myCanvas.drawCircle((float)(xjump*ct),(float)(screenheight-
((int)(points[ct]*100*(screenheight/46)))),(float) 4.0, myPaint);
}

}
}//ends inner class PoissonView
@Override
public void onPause(){
  super.onPause();
  this.finish();
}
}
```

If we start with the import statements, you will see that the import for the Poisson distribution class appears second to last. Below that is the package containing the Log class, which is not really necessary unless you intend to make entries to the Log section in the debugger. In the onClick( ) method we get some important work done. First we get the average value to base the distribution on from an EditText field on the screen. Next, we continually apply the correct method from the PoissonDistributionImpl class object to get the probabilities for all the values around the average starting with zero and finishing when we have accounted for 99 percent of probabilities. These are stored in a Java ArrayList and later converted to an array. All of this is well enough, but we are primarily interested in rendering the graphics. As you have seen before, the unit of graphics we use is the pixel. The way we lay out the graph is based on how many pixels are available on the given device. Because the application could be used on any number of devices, we cannot hard-code values, but we must calculate everything at run-time based on the host device. We can determine the screen dimensions for any device that might host the application using the Android Display class. Look at the lines here:

```
Display display =
  ((WindowManager) c.getSystemService(Context.WINDOW_SERVICE)).getDefaultDisplay();
  screenwidth=display.getWidth();
  screenheight=display.getWidth();
```

We create an instance of the `Display` class called display (with a lowercase "d") to determine the screen dimensions of the device. Then we make sure the graph area is square to reduce distortion by setting both the height and width to the same number. We store these as separate variables for clarity. From here on, any plotting we do is based on a product or quotient of the height or width and the number of pieces we want to divide it into. For instance, the spacing left to right of the points on the graph is a result of the screen width divided by the number of points we need to graph. Likewise, the position of the points is a result of the screen height divided by the number of positions on our scale, namely 50. The scale itself on the left side is accomplished using a loop repeating a similar calculation.

Each "point" on the graph is actually a circle that is four pixels wide, which is what the 4.0 represents in the call to `.drawCircle( )`.

Maybe you have noticed that while plotting the scale and points we subtract the positions from the screen height. For example, look at the lines that follow:

```
myCanvas.drawCircle((float)(xjump*ct),(float)(screenheight-
((int)(points[ct]*100*(screenheight/46)))),(float) 4.0, myPaint);
```

Unlike graphs you may have done by hand on graph paper where the (0,0) position is in the lower-left corner of the graph (or at least the lower-left corner of the positive-x, positive-y quadrant), the (0,0) position is in the upper-left corner of the canvas. The y-value decreases from the bottom of the canvas to the top. To compensate, we subtract the position from the screen height. Java programmers are used to this from graphics on `Frames` or `Panels`.

Finally, the running application using an average of four (4) should look like Figure 5.5.

You can compare your results to the Poisson distribution examples shown on web pages such as www.wikipedia.org/wiki/Poisson_distribution or any other Poisson distribution graphing tool. With some practice, you could graph histograms using the `drawLine( )` method, scatterplots, or other similar diagrams.

SAVING YOUR MASTERPIECE

Whether you are simply doodling on the doodle pad or have coded and implemented a serious graphic application, you may want to save the image on the `View` portion of your screen. This isn't difficult; in fact, it requires only a few extra lines of code. First, you will need to add the Java IO package to your import statements to provide the name space for the classes necessary for saving a file. Also, if you want to log the

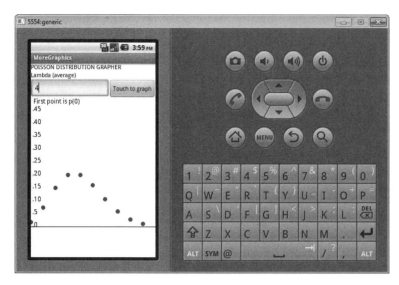

Figure 5.5
Emulator image showing Poisson distribution curve.

results of the file-save attempt (or just its failure), you should add the Android Log class to the import statements:

```
import java.io.*;
import android.util.Log;
```

To save the image, add the setDrawingCacheEnabled(true) method to the extended View class that will contain your drawing.

Next, add a Context class variable to hold a reference to the application's context. Declare it in your global variables, and then assign it in the onCreate( ) method. The application will need a button or some other way to trigger the save process for your drawing. The application programmer can create a button in the main.xml file or add one in the Java code. For the OnClickListener class associated with the button, the onClick( ) method will have the following code:

```
public void onClick(View v){
    try{
     File f=new File(myContext.getFilesDir()+"/sketch.jpg");
     FileOutputStream fos=newFileOutputStream(f);
     dv.getDrawingCache().compress(Bitmap.CompressFormat.JPEG,100,fos);
    }catch(IOException ioe){
    Log.i("file info","Couldn't save the file");
    }
    }
```

The first line creates a hard-coded filename for the saved file, which will be saved in JPEG format. The application programmer could allow the user to choose a name, but for convenience sake, it is hard-coded here. The `.getFilesDir( )` is a path that defaults to the standard directory associated with any given application and belongs to the `Context` class. Literally, the path is `/data/data/` `<application's complete package name>/files`. You can find more on the file storage process on the following web page: http://developer.android.com/guide/topics/data/data-storage.html.

In the previous code, the `getDrawingCache( )` method returns an instance of the `Bitmap` class, and the `Bitmap` class's `compress( )` method has parameters used to choose the format, in this case JPEG, the quality (100), and finally the file output stream. The variable name, `dv`, refers to an instance of the "DoodleView" class from which this code snippet was taken. The entire Java code, revised from the example found earlier in the chapter to implement the saving of the image, is shown here:

```java
package com.sheusi.FingerDraw;

import android.app.Activity;
import android.os.Bundle;
import android.widget.*;
import android.content.Context;
import android.view.View.OnTouchListener;
import android.graphics.*;
import android.view.MotionEvent;
import android.view.View;
import java.util.ArrayList;
import java.io.*;
import android.util.Log;

public class DoodlePad extends Activity {
  /** Called when the activity is first created. */
  LinearLayout ll=null;
  DoodleView dv=null;
  Button save=null;
  Context myContext=null;
  @Override
  public void onCreate(Bundle savedInstanceState) {
    super.onCreate(savedInstanceState);
    setContentView(R.layout.main);
    myContext=this.getApplicationContext();
    ll=(LinearLayout)findViewById(R.id.base);
```

```
        save=(Button)findViewById(R.id.savebutton);
        dv=new DoodleView(this);
        ll.addView(dv,1);
        save.setOnClickListener(new View.OnClickListener(){
          public void onClick(View v){
            try{
              File f=new File(myContext.getFilesDir()+"/sketch.jpg");
              FileOutputStream fos=new FileOutputStream(f);
              dv.getDrawingCache().compress(Bitmap.CompressFormat.JPEG,100,fos);
            }catch(IOException ioe){
              Log.i("file info","Couldn't save the file");
            }
          }
        });
    }
}
class DoodleView extends TextView implements OnTouchListener{
ArrayList<dot> sketch =new ArrayList<dot>();
Paint myPaint=new Paint();

public DoodleView(Context myContext){
  super(myContext);
  setDrawingCacheEnabled(true); //added code
  this.setBackgroundColor(Color.WHITE);
  this.setHeight(120);
  this.setFocusable(true);
  this.setFocusableInTouchMode(true);
  this.setOnTouchListener(this);
  myPaint.setColor(Color.BLACK);
  myPaint.setStyle(Paint.Style.FILL_AND_STROKE);
}
public void onDraw(Canvas c){
  for(dot d:sketch)
  c.drawCircle(d.x,d.y,2,myPaint);

}
public boolean onTouch(View v, MotionEvent me){
  if(me.getAction()==MotionEvent.ACTION_DOWN){}
  if(me.getAction()==MotionEvent.ACTION_MOVE){
    sketch.add(new dot(me.getX(),me.getY()));

  }
  if(me.getAction()==MotionEvent.ACTION_UP){}
  invalidate();
  return true;
}
```

```
class dot{
  private float x;
  private float y;
  //constructor
  public dot(float x, float y){
    this.x=x;
    this.y=y;
  }
}
}
```

You can verify that the image was in fact saved at the location stated by using the adb utility to explore the running emulator's directories.

FOLLOW-UP

1. Complete the following chart of some other commonly used Canvas class methods.

Method Name	Purpose
drawRGB(int r, int g, int b)	
drawLine(float startX, float startY, float stopX, float stopY, Paint paint)	
drawPoint(float x, float y,Paint paint)	
drawRect(float left, float top, float right, float bottom, Paint paint)	
drawText(String text, float x, float y, Paint paint)	

2. Practice using the various drawing methods of the Canvas class.

3. Using the basic techniques used in the Poisson distribution program, try displaying a straight line using the formula $y = ax + b$.

KEY CLASSES USED IN THIS CHAPTER

Canvas

Class	`Canvas`
Package	`android.graphics`
Extends	`java.lang.Object`
Overview	Holds the "draw" calls that write to a `Bitmap`

Methods used in this chapter:

`void drawCircle(float cx, float cy, float radius, Paint paint)`	Draws a circle at the specified x,y coordinates with the specified radius and other features specified by the `Paint` object variable, such as the color

Other commonly used methods:

`void drawLine(float startX, float startY, float stopX, float stopY, Paint paint)`	Draws a line from start x,y coordinates to stop x,y coordinates using features specified in the `Paint` object variable, such as the color
`void drawRect(float left, float top, float right, float bottom, Paint paint)`	Draws a rectangle from top, left to bottom, right using features specified in the `Paint` object variable, such as the color
`void drawText(String text, float x, float y, Paint paint)`	Draws text starting at the x,y coordinates using features specified in the Paint object variable such as the color
`void drawCircle(float cx, float cy, float radius, Paint paint)`	Draw the specified circle using the specified paint
`void drawColor(int color)`	File the entire canvas bitmap (restricted to the current clip) with the specified color
`void drawPicture(Picture picture)`	Save the canvas state, draw the picture, and then restore the canvas state

`void drawPoint(float x, float y, Paint paint)`	Draws a single point at the coordinates indicated
`int getHeight()`	Returns the height of the current drawing layer
`int getWidth()`	Returns the width of the current drawing layer
`int save()`	Saves the current matrix and clip into a private stack
`void rotate(float degrees)`	Preconcat the current matrix with the specified rotation
`void scale(float x, float y)`	Preconcat the current matrix with the specified scale

Bitmap

Class	`Bitmap`
Package	`android.graphics`
Extends	`java.lang.Object`
Overview	Holds the "draw" calls that write to a `Bitmap`

Methods used in this chapter:

`boolean compress(Bitmap.CommpressFormat format, int quality, OutputStream stream)`	Writes a compressed version of the `Bitmap` to the output stream

Other commonly used methods:

`void copyPixelsFromBuffer (Buffer src)`	Copy the pixels from the buffer, beginning at the current position, overwriting the `Bitmap`'s pixels
`static Bitmap createBitmap (Bitmap source)`	Returns an immutable `Bitmap` from the source `Bitmap`
`final int getByteCount()`	Returns the number of bytes used to store this `Bitmap`'s pixels
`int getDensity()`	Returns the density for this `Bitmap`
`final int getHeight()`	Returns the height of this `Bitmap`
`final int getWidth()`	Returns the width of this `Bitmap`
`void writeParcel(Parcel p, int flags)`	Writes this `Bitmap` and its pixels to the specified parcel

Paint

Class	`Paint`
Package	`android.graphics`
Extends	`java.lang.Object`
Overview	Holds the "draw" calls that write to a `Bitmap`

Methods used in this chapter:

`setColor(int color)`	Sets the `Paint`'s color.
`setStyle(Paint.Style style)`	Sets the `Paint`'s style. `Paint.Style` sets how the line is filled, stroked, or both. Three choices are available: FILL, FILL_AND_STROKE, and STROKE.

Other commonly used methods:

`setTextSize(float size)`	Sets the `Paint`'s text size
`int getColor( )`	Returns the `Paint`'s current color setting
`float measureText(String text)`	Returns the width of the text
`void setStrokeWidth(float width)`	Sets the width for stroking
`void setStyle(Paint.Style style)`	Set the `Paint`'s style, used for controlling how primitives' geometries are interpreted
`Shader setShader(Shader shader)`	Sets or clears the shader object
`Typeface setTypeface (Typeface typeface)`	Sets or clears the typeface object
`void setFlags(int flags)`	Sets the `Paint`'s flags

MotionEvent

Class	`MotionEvent`
Package	`android.view`
Extends	`Android.view.InputEvent`
Overview	Used to report movement

Methods used in this chapter:

n/a

Symbolic constants used:

`ACTION_DOWN`	Signals the start of a gesture. Contains the starting location.
`ACTION_MOVE`	Signals a change has happened since `ACTION_DOWN`.
`ACTION_UP`	Signals a gesture has finished. Contains the release location.

Other commonly used methods:

`final long getDownTime(float size)`	Returns the time (in ms) when the user originally pressed Down
`final int getRawX( )`	Returns the original raw X coordinate of the event
`final int getAction()`	Returns the kind of action being performed
`final int getButtonState()`	Gets the state of all buttons that are pressed, such as a mouse or stylus button
`final int getDeviceId()`	Gets the identification for the device that this event came from
`final long getEventTime()`	Gets the time in milliseconds when this specific event was generated
`final int getSource()`	Gets the source of the event

READER'S NOTES

CHAPTER 6

FIND A LOCATION WITH GOOGLE MAPS

No one would be content with her Android programming knowledge unless she were able to put a map on the screen. There are a couple of ways to do this. The first is by invoking a build-in Intent on the Android device, similar to switching to the browser or using the phone dialer. In the next chapter we will present at length some of the built-in actions that are represented by symbolic constants that are part of the Intent class. Some of the built-in actions that use the same name, such as ACTION_VIEW, respond with different services depending on the uniform resource identifier (URI) that is submitted to it. For example, ACTION_VIEW, when supplied with http:// and a web address, returns a web page. When supplied with the prefix geo: and geocodes, it returns a Google Map for the location. For now, let us look at a Google Map example.

Examine the next code, which could be assigned to any button's OnClickListener. The latitude and longitude values are hard-coded, but they could just as easily be variables. The prefix geo: signals that the activity should return a Google map page:

```
public void onClick(View v){

    String geoURI=String.format("geo:%f,%f?z=15",41.841892,-71.413631);
    Uri geo=Uri.parse(geoURI);
    Intent mapIt=new Intent(Intent.ACTION_VIEW);
    mapIt.setData(Uri.parse(geoURI));
    startActivity(mapIt);
    }
});
```

The z=15 in the geoURI string assignment is a zoom factor. A slight variation in the string can use an address instead of geocodes. Although this is a quick way to flash a map on the screen, there isn't much control. For instance, there is no pin or other icon to mark the exact spot. Also, realize we have actually started another activity and abandoned our screen and whatever user interface it had. We can go back to our application with the Back button on the device, but then we lose sight of the map. We cannot have it both ways.

The second way to use mapping is much more controllable, but much more complicated step in application-programming skills development. This is because it involves an external library to be obtained from Google, more new classes and methods, and modifications to the Android Manifest file. However, with a little patience it is certainly within reach.

The first step is to be sure we have the necessary application programming interfaces (APIs) to use Google Maps. You should note that the Android APIs do not include these; you must download them from Google. However, Eclipse will handle this for you. Under the Window menu in Eclipse, choose Android SDK and AVD Manager, which opens a window. (If you are using a version of Eclipse that separates the SDK and AVD Managers, choose the SDK Manager.) When it does, choose Installed Packages on the left. You should see the screen shown in Figure 6.1.

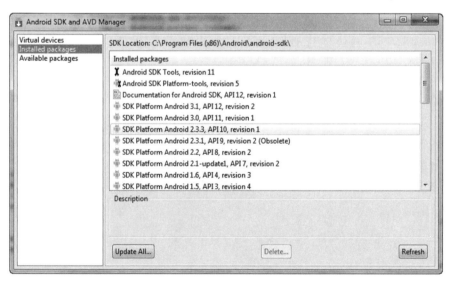

Figure 6.1
Eclipse SDK and AVD Manager panel.

Scroll down the list on the right side, and be sure you have a list of Google APIs. If they aren't present, choose Available Packages on the left side and wait for a list of additional packages to generate. Choose the Google packages and install them. This may take a few minutes. (An Internet connection must be present.) After you've downloaded the packages (if necessary), you need to include them in the build of your application. To do this, choose Properties under the Project menu on Eclipse. You will be presented with the screen shown in Figure 6.2. Choose Android on the left; then check Google APIs on the right side under Project Build Target. You will want to choose the Google APIs that go with the same platform as the Android target you were using.

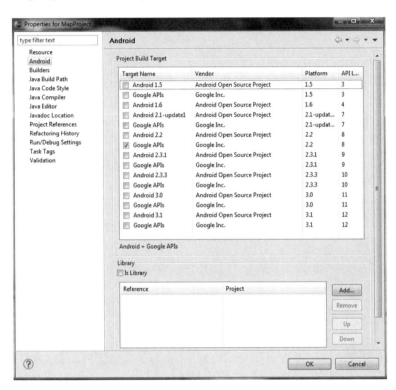

Figure 6.2
Eclipse Project Properties panel.

The next step is to be sure that our emulator is able to display maps. You will follow a similar procedure. In Eclipse under the Window menu, choose Android SDK and AVD Manager. You should see the window shown in Figure 6.3.

Choose the emulator you have been working with (you may have only one in your list), and click the Edit button on the right. Now you should see the screen shown in Figure 6.4. Notice the pick-list next to the word Target. In this pick-list, choose the same Google API that you chose for the project. Next, check the hardware settings for the emulator. If you don't see GPS support in the Property List, click the New button on the right, and add it. Finally, click the Edit AVD button to go back to Eclipse.

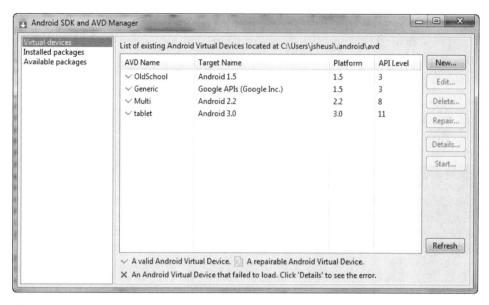

Figure 6.3
Eclipse SDK and AVD Manager panel showing the Virtual device list.

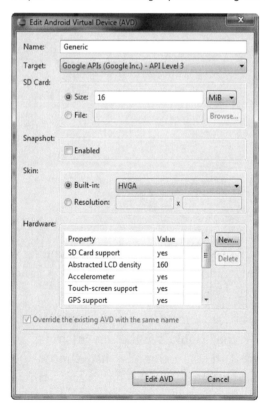

Figure 6.4
Eclipse AVD Edit panel.

Next, you need to create a Google Maps API key. There are actually two keys available: the production key that you must obtain from Google, and the "debug" key that you can obtain from your own system. The former is to be used for a production application that you intend to distribute or use on an actual mobile device. You'll learn how to obtain that later in the tutorial. For now, we just need the latter. You obtain the debug key from your downloaded Android software development kit (SDK) by performing the following steps:

1. Find the `debug.keystore` file in your system. You can either search for the file by name using your operating system's file-search utility, or from Eclipse you can choose Preferences from the Window menu and you will see the panel shown in Figure 6.5.

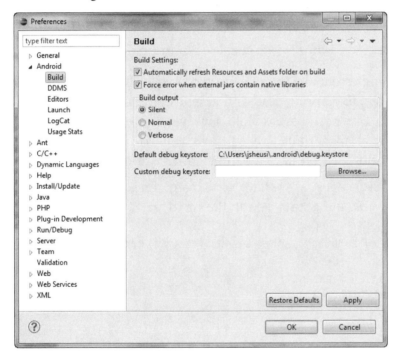

Figure 6.5
Eclipse Project Preferences panel.

If you pick the Build choice under the Android heading on the left, you will see the location of the `debug.keystore` file on your system; in this case, it's `c:\Users\jsheusi\.android\debug.keystore`.

2. Next, open a console screen. (In Windows, use the Start button or the Windows icon in Windows 7; then type `cmd` in the text field.) In the console screen, navigate to the location you found for the `debug.keystore` file. If you are unfamiliar with console commands, please consult the guide on the following

web page: www.microsoft.com/resources/documentation/windows/xp/all/
proddocs/en-us/ntcmds.mspx, specifically the chdir or cd command.

3. When you have reached the location of the debug.keystore file, type the
   following command:

```
keytool -v -list -keystore debug.keystore (enter)
```

If you are prompted for a password, just press Enter. You will see many
fingerprints using different mathematical formulas; Google requires the MD5
fingerprint. You should see a set of 16 hex values separated by colons next to
"MD5:" under the heading "Certificate Fingerprints." Write it in the space below
for safe-keeping. Be careful that you write the password correctly. It might also
be a good idea to save a screen shot with the "fingerprint" on it or copy and
paste it to a Word document and store it in a safe place on your computer.

4. Using your browser, go to http://code.google.com/android/maps-api-signup.html.

On that page you will find essentially the same instructions as listed here. You will also
find a place to enter your fingerprint, read and accept the terms and conditions, and
continue as instructed. The next page should give you a debug key and show an
example of how to use it in a MapView entry in your main.xml file. Write the
debug key on the line below so you have a permanent record of it.

Now it's time to start a project just as we have done many times before. Our project will
simply contain a TextView and a MapView in the main.xml. It should look like this.

```xml
<?xml version="1.0" encoding="utf-8"?>
<LinearLayout xmlns:android="http://schemas.android.com/apk/res/android"
   android:orientation="vertical"
   android:layout_width="fill_parent"
   android:layout_height="fill_parent"
   >
<TextView
   android:id="@+id/myTextView"
   android:layout_width="fill_parent"
   android:layout_height="wrap_content"
   android:text="Where Am I?"
   />
   <com.google.android.maps.MapView
           android:layout_width="fill_parent"
           android:layout_height="wrap_content"
           android:id="@+id/myMapView"
           android:apiKey="0GblCZOB21y******N8v3fNHtZD1CYaq96AeUWA"
           />

</LinearLayout>
```

Please note that I replaced six of my key characters with asterisks so you would not be tempted to simply use my key. You can copy this element directly from the example that Google presented to you when you obtained your key. Just change the `layout_height` parameter to `wrap_content` if you intend to share the screen between the `TextView` and the `MapView`. You should also add an `id` tag as I did in the code.

This is a good time to address another component of the project we haven't paid much attention to until now: the `AndroidMainifest.xml` file. You can find it in the Package Explorer tab on the left side of the Eclipse screen. Eclipse builds most of the manifest file, but you must make at least two additional entries to use the `MapView`. First, before the closing `/application` tag, make the following entry:

```
<uses-library android:name="com.google.android.maps" />
```

And before the closing `/manifest` tag, add the following entries:

```
<uses-permission android:name="android.permission.INTERNET" />
<uses-permission android:name="android.permission.ACCESS_FINE_LOCATION" />
```

The entire `AndroidManifest.xml` file should look like this:

```
<?xml version="1.0" encoding="utf-8"?>
<manifest xmlns:android="http://schemas.android.com/apk/res/android"
    package="com.sheusi.WhereAmI"
    android:versionCode="1"
    android:versionName="1.0">
  <uses-sdk android:minSdkVersion="3" />

  <application android:icon="@drawable/icon" android:label="@string/app_name">
    <activity android:name=".WhereAmI"
            android:label="@string/app_name">
      <intent-filter>
        <action android:name="android.intent.action.MAIN" />
        <category android:name="android.intent.category.LAUNCHER" />
      </intent-filter>
    </activity>
    <uses-library android:name="com.google.android.maps" />
  </application>
  <uses-permission android:name="android.permission.INTERNET" />
  <uses-permission android:name="android.permission.ACCESS_FINE_LOCATION" />
 <uses-permission android:name="android.permission.ACCESS_COARSE_LOCATION" />
</manifest>
```

Notice the `uses-library` and the `uses-permission` tags. The first tells Eclipse to use the Google Maps objects in the build, and the permissions allow the device user to be warned if she does indeed want these services to be active on the device while the application is running. When a user downloads an application from the Android Market, there will be warnings that such services will be used.

The first step in this project will be to display the current latitude and longitude values for the device. These will be displayed in the TextView we included in the main.xml file. The emulator itself does not have real GPS capabilities, so we will have to communicate with the emulator to install some coordinates. We do this using a terminal program such as *PuTTY*, which is an open-source download from the Internet (search Google for PuTTY download sites), or a terminal emulator included with your operating system. Before we get into that, let's look at the main Java file for the application:

```java
package com.sheusi.WhereAmI;

import android.content.Context;
import android.os.Bundle;
import android.location.*;
import android.widget.*;
import android.util.Log;
import java.io.IOException;
import com.google.android.maps.*;
public class WhereAmI extends MapActivity {
    /** Called when the activity is first created. */
    Location myLocation=null;
    LocationListener myLocListener=null;
    LocationManager myLocMgr=null;
    Criteria myCriteria=null;
    TextView latlon=null;
    @Override
    public void onCreate(Bundle savedInstanceState) {
        super.onCreate(savedInstanceState);
        this.setContentView(R.layout.main);
      try{
        myLocMgr=(LocationManager)this.getSystemService(Context.LOCATION_SERVICE);
        myLocListener=new MyLocationListener();
        myCriteria=new Criteria();
        latlon=(TextView)findViewById(R.id.myTextView);
        myLocMgr.requestLocationUpdates(LocationManager.GPS_PROVIDER,0, 0,
myLocListener);
        myCriteria.setAccuracy(Criteria.ACCURACY_FINE);
        String GPSName =myLocMgr.getBestProvider(myCriteria,true);

        myLocation=myLocMgr.getLastKnownLocation(GPSName);
        String here;
        here= String.valueOf(myLocation.getLatitude())+",
```

```
"+String.valueOf(myLocation.getLongitude());
   latlon.setText(here);
   }catch(IOException e){
   Log.i("Mapping Info","IO error occured");
   }
   }
  public boolean isRouteDisplayed(){
   return true;
  }
}
class MyLocationListener implements LocationListener{
  public void onLocationChanged(Location l){}
  public void onProviderDisabled(String provider){}
  public void onProviderEnabled(String provider){}
  public void onStatusChanged(String provider, int status, Bundle extras){}

}
```

First notice the import statements at the top of the file, especially the
com.google.android.maps.* import statement. We added this library to the
manifest file. If you did not include the Google APIs in your project as instructed
earlier, this line and others will cause errors. This package is found in the Google
APIs, not the standard Android APIs. Next, notice that your class extends the
MapActivity class, not the Activity class as our applications did earlier.

If you look at previous applications we developed, you will notice that we generally
implemented some Listener interface and added the necessary methods to our
application. This application needs a LocationListener. However, instead of
implementing the LocationListener in the main class, I added a separate class
definition called MyLocationListener and implemented the LocationListener. I
also defined the four necessary methods required by the LocationListener interface;
I left them empty for the time being. I declared a LocationListener variable,
myLocListener, and assigned an instance of MyLocationListener to it in the
code. Finally, in the code I declared a String variable named here and assigned it
the latitude and longitude values obtained by the GPS service. Then I filled in the
TextView with the string.

For the application to show actual latitude and longitude values on the emulator, we
need to communicate them. The top of the emulator shows the emulator's name,
assigned by you when you configured it, preceded by the number 5554. This number
is a port number that you will use to communicate with the emulator. There is a brief
set of commands you can use to interact with the emulator; one of them is the geo
command. Open a terminal emulator such as PuTTY, set it on Telnet (not SSH), set

the IP address to 127.0.0.1 (or localhost), and set the port number to 5554. The emulator needs to be running before you can do this. You can start the emulator without running any of your applications by choosing Android SDK and AVD Manager under Eclipse's Window menu. Choose the correct emulator, if there is more than one in the list, click the Start button on the right. Once the emulator is running, start your terminal emulator as described, and connect to the Android emulator.

The emulator will take geocode values as decimals, not degrees and minutes, and the longitude value will come first. For example, for a latitude of 41.6539999 and a longitude of −71.2620000, enter the following command:

```
geo fix -71.2620000 41.6539999 (enter)
```

The terminal emulator should respond with OK. Note that each time you close and reopen the Android emulator, you have to reset the values, so it's a good idea to minimize the emulator when you are working on your code and then restore it when you are ready to rerun an application. If you have your manifest.xml file, your main.xml file, and your source code file completed, start your application.

When the application runs, it should look like Figure 6.6. Notice the latitude and longitude values at the top. Yours may not match, but there should be two values separated by a comma and a space.

Figure 6.6
Emulator showing the Google Map application.

The next step is to alter the code to mark our location on the map based on the geocodes we have entered. Study the following revised source code. Notice the comments preceded by double slashes (//):

```java
package com.sheusi.WhereAmI;

import android.content.Context;
import android.os.Bundle;
import android.location.*;
import android.widget.*;
import android.widget.RadioGroup.LayoutParams;
import android.util.Log;
import com.google.android.maps.*;
public class WhereAmI extends MapActivity {
  /** Called when the activity is first created. */
  Location myLocation=null;
  LocationListener myLocListener=null;
  LocationManager myLocMgr=null;
  Criteria myCriteria=null;
  TextView latlon=null;
  // new variables for mapping location
  MapView myMapView=null;
  MapView.LayoutParams myLayoutParams=null;
  MapController myMapController=null;
  ImageView myMarker=null;
  GeoPoint mySpot=null;
  // end new variables
  @Override
  public void onCreate(Bundle savedInstanceState) {
    super.onCreate(savedInstanceState);
    this.setContentView(R.layout.main);
   try{
    myLocMgr=(LocationManager)this.getSystemService(Context.LOCATION_SERVICE);
    myLocListener=new MyLocationListener();
    myCriteria=new Criteria();
    latlon=(TextView)findViewById(R.id.myTextView);
    myLocMgr.requestLocationUpdates(LocationManager.GPS_PROVIDER,0, 0,
myLocListener);
    myCriteria.setAccuracy(Criteria.ACCURACY_FINE);
    String GPSName =myLocMgr.getBestProvider(myCriteria,true);
    myLocation=myLocMgr.getLastKnownLocation(GPSName);
    String here;
    here= String.valueOf(myLocation.getLatitude())+",
```

```
"+String.valueOf(myLocation.getLongitude());
    latlon.setText(here);
    // new mapping assignments
    myMapView=(MapView)findViewById(R.id.myMapView);
    myMapController=myMapView.getController();
    mySpot=new
GeoPoint((int)(myLocation.getLatitude()*1e6),(int)
(myLocation.getLongitude()*1e6));
    myLayoutParams= new MapView.LayoutParams(LayoutParams.WRAP_CONTENT,
        LayoutParams.WRAP_CONTENT,mySpot,MapView.LayoutParams.BOTTOM);
    myMarker=new ImageView(this);
    // end new assignments
    // new method calls
    myMapController.setZoom(17);
    myMapView.setBuiltInZoomControls(true);
    myMapController.animateTo(mySpot);
    myMarker.setImageResource(R.drawable.icon);
    myMapView.addView(myMarker,myLayoutParams);
    // end new method calls
  }catch(Exception e){
  Log.i("Mapping Info","IO error occurred");
  }
  }
  public boolean isRouteDisplayed(){
   return true;
  }
}
class MyLocationListener implements LocationListener{
  public void onLocationChanged(Location l){}
  public void onProviderDisabled(String provider){}
  public void onProviderEnabled(String provider){}
  public void onStatusChanged(String provider, int status, Bundle extras){}

}
```

Most of the new variables in the declarations section have to do with the MapView class. One of the variables is an ImageView instance; this will be the marker for the location based on the geocodes entered into the emulator or the actual geocodes determined by the location of a real Android device. Normally this would be a push-pin graphic, but for the sake of convenience I will just use the Android logo that is always included with the SDK and is built into each application started in Eclipse automatically. It is called icon.png and is found in the drawable folder under the res folder in the project.

The next commented section contains the assignments for the declared variables. One of them assigns a `GeoPoint` and uses the coordinates we previously entered as the arguments. Look at the following lines of code:

```
mySpot=new
GeoPoint((int)(myLocation.getLatitude()*1e6),(int)
(myLocation.getLongitude()*1e6));
```

The `GeoPoint` object takes two integers in the constructor. Note that we entered our coordinates into the emulator as floating point numbers (−71.234567). These floating point numbers must be multiplied by a power of ten (*1e6) to convert them to the appropriate integer values; then they are type-cast to ints.

Finally, we call several methods belonging to the mapping objects to render the map and the location marker on the screen. The value in the `setZoom( )` method is one you will have to play with to suit yourself. However, the `setBuiltInZoomControls ( )` method, if set to `true`, will put zoom toggles on the map so the user can zoom in and out at will. Also note that I put the marker in the middle of Mount Hope Bay. That's probably not a very good place to find an Android device!

The running application in the emulator should look like Figure 6.7.

Figure 6.7
Revised Google Maps application showing location.

If you intend to publish an application using Google Maps, you need a production key from Google that is not based on the `debug.keystore`. To obtain this, use the generated MD5 fingerprint you will produce in Chapter 11, "Publishing Your Application."

Follow-Up

1. Visit http://developer.android.com/guide/appendix/g-app-intents.html and complete the following table.

Target Application	Intent URI	Intent Action	Result
Browser			
Dialer			
Google Maps			
Google Streetview			

2. Create an application using the first example of an onClick( ) method associated with a button. Try to make the application accept an address from the user. Using the information from the chart, try to display a map using the address the user entered.

KEY CLASSES USED IN THIS CHAPTER

Location

Class	`Location`
Package	`android.location`
Extends	`java.lang.object`
Overview	A representation of a location sensed at a particular time. It consists of a latitude, a longitude, and a timestamp, and optionally information on altitude, speed, and bearing.

Methods used in this chapter:

`double getLatitude( )`	Returns the latitude of this fix
`double getLongitude( )`	Returns the longitude of this fix

Other commonly used methods:

`float getAccuracy( )`	Returns the accuracy of this fix in meters
`String getProvider( )`	Returns the name of the provider that provided this fix
`long getTime( )`	Returns the UTC time for this fix in milliseconds since Jan 1, 1970
`float distanceTo(Location dest)`	Returns the approximate distance in meters between the `Location` parameter supplied and the current location
`float getSpeed()`	Returns the speed of the device over ground in meters per second
`boolean hasAltitude()`	Returns `true` if this fix contains altitude information; `false` otherwise
`boolean hasSpeed()`	Returns `true` if this fix contains speed information; `false` otherwise
`void reset()`	Clears the contents of this location

`void setAccuracty(float accuracy)`	Sets the accuracy of this fix
`void setAltitude(float altitude)`	Sets the altitude of this fix
`void setBearing(float bearing)`	Sets the bearing of this fix
`void setLatitude(double latitude)`	Sets the latitude of this fix
`void setLongitude(double longitude)`	Sets the longitude of this fix
`void setTime(long time)`	Sets the UTC time of this fix, in milliseconds since Jan 1, 1970

LocationManager

Class	`LocationManager`
Package	`android.location`
Extends	`java.lang.object`
Overview	A class that provides access to the device's location services. It can also fire an `Intent` as the device enters proximity to a given location.

Methods used in this chapter:

`void requestLocationUpdates (String provider, long minTime, float minDistance, LocationListener listener)`	Registers the current activity to be periodically notified by the provider

Other commonly used methods:

`boolean isProviderInabled( )`	Returns the status of a given provider
`List<String> getAllProviders( )`	Returns a list of all location providers
`List<String> getProviders (boolean enabledOnly)`	Returns a list of enabled location providers
`String getBestProvider (Criteria criteria, boolean enabledOnly)`	Returns the name of the provider that best meets the given criteria
`Location getLastKnownLocation (String provider)`	Returns a `Location` object indicating the data from the last known location fix obtained from the given provider
`void requestSingleUpdate (String provider, Pending Intent intent)`	Requests a single location update from the named provider

LocationListener

Class	`LocationListener (interface)`
Package	`android.location`
Extends	n/a
Overview	A class that provides access to the device's location services. It can also fire an `Intent` as the device enters proximity to a given location.

Methods used in this chapter: (required)

`void onLocationChanged (Location location)`	Called when the location changes
`void onProviderDisabled (String provider)`	Called when the user disables the provider
`void onProviderEnabled(String provider)`	Called when the user enables the provider
`void onStatusChanged(String provider, int status, Bundle extras)`	Called when the provider's status changes

Other commonly used methods:

n/a

Criteria

Class	`Criteria`
Package	`android.location`
Extends	`java.lang.object`
Overview	A class indicating the criteria by which the system selects the location provider. It could be based on a multitude of variables including accuracy, provision of speed data, and cost. Several symbolic constants represent the various parameters and values, including `ACCURACY_HIGH`.

Methods used in this chapter:

`void setAccuracy(int accuracy)`	Names accuracy as a criteria

Other commonly used methods:

`void setCostAllowed(boolean costAllowed)`	Names cost as a criterion. Determines whether or not the provider is allowed to incur a cost.
`void setSpeedRequired(boolean speedRequired)`	Indicates whether or not the provider must provide speed information.
`void setBearingRequired (boolean bearingRequired)`	Indicates whether or not the provider must provide bearing information.
`int getHorizontalAccuracy()`	Returns a constant indicating the desired horizontal accuracy (latitude and longitude).
`int getVerticalAccuracy()`	Returns a constant indicating the desired vertical accuracy (altitude).
`boolean isAltitudeRequired()`	Returns whether the provider must provide altitude information.

`boolean isBearingRequired()`	Returns whether the provider must provide bearing information.
`boolean isCostRequired()`	Returns whether the provider is allowed to incur monetary cost.
`boolean isSpeedRequired()`	Return whether the provider must provide speed information.
`void setHorizontalAccuracy (int accuracy)`	Indicates the desired horizontal accuracy (latitude and longitude).
`void setVerticalAccuracy (int accuracy)`	Indicates the desired vertical accuracy (altitude).

GeoPoint

Class	`GeoPoint`
Package	`com.google.android.maps`
Extends	`java.lang.object`
Overview	Class representing a latitude and longitude pair, held as integer numbers of microdegrees. A microdegree is $1/1{,}000{,}000$ ($10\,\wedge{-}6$) of a degree.

Methods used in this chapter:

n/a

Other commonly used methods:

`int getLatitudeE6( )`	Returns the latitude of this point in microdegrees
`int getLongitudeE6( )`	Returns the longitude of this point in microdegrees
`boolean equals(java.lang. Object object)`	Determines equality between the GeoPoint object and the parameter object
`int hashCode()`	Returns the hash code of the GeoPoint
`java.lang.String toString()`	Returns a string description of the GeoPoint

READER'S NOTES

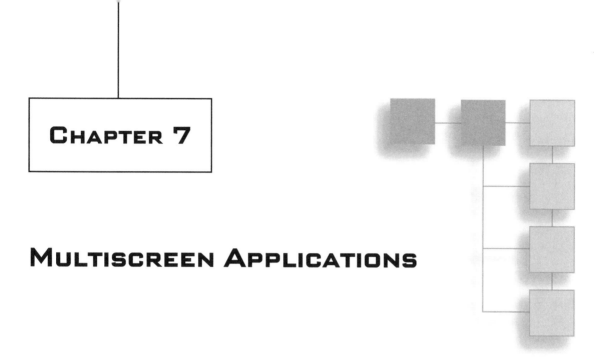

CHAPTER 7

MULTISCREEN APPLICATIONS

STRETCHING THE SCREEN

There will be times when no matter how hard you try to plan your screen correctly, there will not be enough room for all the controls you need to use. In this case, you will need to plan for multiple screens on the same application. There are several approaches you can use. The first and easiest is simply to design beyond the normal boundaries of the device. This is done with two classes we haven't looked at yet: the ScrollView and the HorizontalScrollView. These two classes are typically used in an XML file for a screen layout, such as the main.xml file, and become the outermost elements. They work by allowing the user to use his finger to roll the screen up and down or left to right to gain access to controls beyond the physical screen. In the examples that follow we will simply load the screen with TextViews that far outnumber what would fit on a normal screen. The application serves no useful purpose; it just demonstrates the principle discussed here. First, let's look at the main.xml file:

```xml
<?xml version="1.0" encoding="utf-8"?>
<ScrollView xmlns:android="http://schemas.android.com/apk/res/android"

    android:layout_width="fill_parent"
    android:layout_height="fill_parent"
    >

<LinearLayout
    android:orientation="vertical"
```

```
    android:layout_width="fill_parent"
    android:layout_height="fill_parent"
    android:id="@+id/L1"
    >

<TextView
    android:layout_width="fill_parent"
    android:layout_height="wrap_content"
    android:text="@string/hello"
    />

</LinearLayout>

</ScrollView>
```

The most important thing to note is that the `ScrollView` encapsulates the outer-most layout—in this case, the `LinearLayout`. In fact, you are restricted to placing only one object inside the `ScrollView` or `HorizontalScrollView`; not adhering to this rule will cause your application to crash with a run-time exception. That being said, you can still pack your single inner object with objects of its own as you see here. It's just that between the `ScrollView`'s pair of tags, there can be only one pair of tags at the next level in. A minor but necessary point is the following line:

```
xmlns:android="http://schemas.android.com/apk/res/android"
```

It must be associated with the outermost tag pair in the XML file. Notice that I moved it from the `LinearLayout` tag to the `ScrollView` tag. This is an XML rule, and it has nothing to do with the Android objects used here. The `ScrollView` extends the screen vertically, so make sure the orientation for your `LinearLayout` is vertical. Otherwise, you are defeating the purpose of the scroll effect. Now let's look at the Java source code:

```
package com.sheusi.ScrollViews;

import android.app.Activity;
import android.os.Bundle;
import android.widget.*;
import android.content.Context;
import android.graphics.Color;

public class ScrollViewsActivity extends Activity {
    /** Called when the activity is first created. */
TextView[] tvarray=new TextView[30];
LinearLayout myLayout=null;
Context myContext=null;
```

```
@Override
public void onCreate(Bundle savedInstanceState) {
  super.onCreate(savedInstanceState);
  setContentView(R.layout.main);
  myContext=this.getApplicationContext();
  myLayout=(LinearLayout)findViewById(R.id.L1);
  for(int ct=0;ct<=29;++ct){
    int colormult;
    tvarray[ct]=new TextView(myContext);
    tvarray[ct].setText(" TextView number "+String.valueOf(ct));
    colormult=ct*8;
    tvarray[ct].setBackgroundColor(Color.rgb(colormult,colormult,
    colormult));
    tvarray[ct].setTextSize(30);
    myLayout.addView(tvarray[ct]);
    }
  }
}
```

Again, realize that this is a junk application, only to demonstrate scrolling screens. This code will create 30 TextViews of various shades of gray on the screen, and the user will have to scroll the screen to see all of them. What you might also notice here is the use of one of the principles we saw in Chapter 2, "Starting an Android Application Project": that of dynamically adding controls to the screen in the Java code. To make the code more efficient, I declare an array of TextViews and then, using a loop in the main code, I instantiate each of them, give them an individual shade of gray, and add text to number the control in the array. The coloring is just for effect. Remember that a 30-element array has index values 0 through 29; if you try to use index value 30, you will get a run-time exception, and the application will crash.

Note

Notice that the TextViews are added to the LinearLayout, not the ScrollView. The rule must be followed in XML and in Java code.

Figure 7.1 shows the application scrolled halfway through the TextViews.

As you might assume, the HorizontalScrollView is used and behaves in the same way, only left to right on the screen. You can modify the previous XML and Java code to see how it works. First, in your main.xml file, change the ScrollView tags to HorizontalScrollView. Be sure to change both the opening and closing tags. Next, change the orientation for the LinearLayout element to horizontal. In

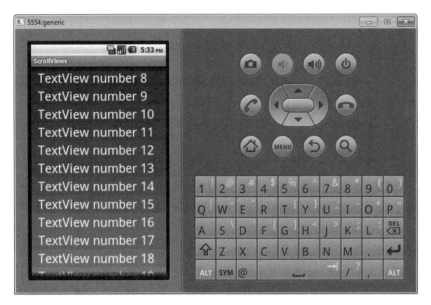

Figure 7.1
Emulator showing an application using a ScrollView object. When the user actually scrolls the screen (you can do it on the emulator with a mouse drag), you will see a scrollbar on the right side. The scrollbar disappears as you release the screen, or the mouse in the case of the emulator.

the Java code, we will change the size of the TextView from 30 to 8 and make changes to the loop according to the following code snippet:

```
for(int ct=0;ct<=7;++ct){
  int colormult;
  tvarray[ct]=new TextView(myContext);
  tvarray[ct].setText(" TextView number "+String.valueOf(ct));
  colormult=ct*30;
  tvarray[ct].setBackgroundColor(Color.rgb(colormult, colormult, colormult));
  tvarray[ct].setTextSize(30);
  myLayout.addView(tvarray[ct]);
  }
```

We will reduce the loop size to reflect the size of the array and increase the grayscale multiplier to 30.

Note

Color values cannot exceed 255 for any of the red, green, and blue settings, so the variable colormult must stay below 255.

The running application should now look like Figure 7.2.

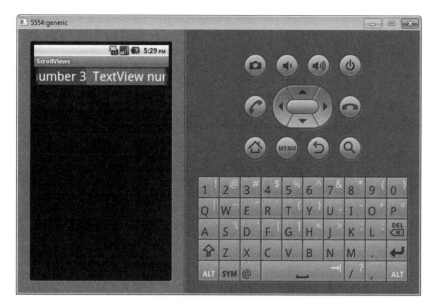

Figure 7.2
Emulator showing an application using a HorizontalScrollView object.

The other ways to expand your usable screen space are a little more difficult and need a lot more planning. For instance, instead of making one screen hold more information, we can use multiple screens if it is more appropriate. The next we will look at is using separate instances of the Activity class to produce a multi-screen application. Each screen is treated as a separate activity, so it is written into its own Java class file and has its own XML file for the screen layout. The manifest file also has an entry for each activity class used in the application.

Activities start other activities by using an instance of Android's Intent class. An Intent is created by taking the Activity class as an argument to its *constructor*. Data can be passed back and forth among activities using a method built into the Intent class called putExtra( ). Standard services that the device provides, such as dialing the phone, are also built into the Intent class as integer values for the Intent's action field represented by symbolic constants. A *symbolic constant* is an English word or phrase that represents a numeric value, used to make source code more readable. A programmer can declare her own symbolic constants in applications, but the ones used here build into the Intent class.

The following are some of the actions built into the Intent class:

```
ACTION_DIAL
ACTION_CALL
ACTION_SENTTO
ACTION_ANSWER
```

```
ACTION_INSERT
ACTION_DELETE
ACTION_MAIN
ACTION_EDIT
ACTION_VIEW
```

For instance, to dial a phone number from within an application, you could use the following:

```
Uri theNumber = Uri.parse(tel:8005551212);
Intent dialMe= new Intent(Intent.ACTION_DIAL,theNumber);
startActivity(dialMe);
```

Another possibility is to use an `onClick( )` or `onTouch( )` method belonging to a screen component to view a web page using the built-in action `ACTION_VIEW`. The target URL of the browser can be delivered along with the call based on some condition of the original screen. The code could look like this:

```
public void onClick(View v){
  String myUrl=someEditText.getText( ).toString( );
  Intent myIntent=new Intent(Intent.ACTION_VIEW);
  myIntent.setData(Uri.parse(myUrl));
  startActivity(myIntent);
}
```

Of course, the appropriate `import` statements to include the necessary classes are required, and the necessary permissions such as access to the Internet must be entered into the manifest file.

To demonstrate a multiscreen application, we will make two screens, each containing a `Button` object that will be used to switch back and forth between screens, and a `TextView` to let us know which screen we are viewing at any given time. The first step will be to create two XML files for the screen design: the `main.xml` file Eclipse creates for the primary screen, and an additional file called `second.xml`. To create an additional screen XML file, right-click on the `layout` folder under the `res` folder in the Package Explorer in Eclipse, and choose New, File from the menu. Be sure to add `.xml` to the filename; the `.xml` file extension is required. You can leave the file blank for the time being.

The `main.xml` file, automatically created by Eclipse, should be edited to look like this:

```
<?xml version="1.0" encoding="utf-8"?>
<LinearLayout xmlns:android="http://schemas.android.com/apk/res/android"
  android:orientation="vertical"
  android:layout_width="fill_parent"
```

```
  android:layout_height="fill_parent"
  >
<TextView
  android:layout_width="fill_parent"
  android:layout_height="wrap_content"
  android:textSize="20px"
  android:text="Primary Screen"
  />
<Button
  android:id="@+id/SwitchToSecond"
  android:layout_width="fill_parent"
  android:layout_height="wrap_content"
  android:textSize="20px"
  android:text="Switch to Second Screen"
  />

</LinearLayout>
```

For convenience sake, you can copy the entire contents of the main.xml file and paste it on your new, blank second.xml file. Make some edits to the second.xml file so that it looks like the following:

```
<?xml version="1.0" encoding="utf-8"?>
<LinearLayout xmlns:android="http://schemas.android.com/apk/res/android"
  android:orientation="vertical"
  android:layout_width="fill_parent"
  android:layout_height="fill_parent"
  >
<TextView
  android:textSize="20px"
  android:layout_width="fill_parent"
  android:layout_height="wrap_content"
  android:text="Secondary Screen"
  />
  <Button
  android:id="@+id/SwitchToMain"
  android:layout_width="fill_parent"
  android:layout_height="wrap_content"
  android:textSize="20px"
  android:text="Back to Main Screen"
  />
</LinearLayout>
```

Be particularly careful to change the id attribute in the Button tag so that you won't be confused when writing the Java code later. The XML files all tend to look the same, so it is a good idea to create id attributes that indicate which screen they belong to. The next step is to add the following lines to the manifest file to provide for the additional Activity class we will create for the second screen:

```
<activity android:name=".SecondScreen">
    </activity>
```

Be careful to place this *inside* the application tags, but *outside* any other activity tag pair, as shown in the following snippet:

```
<application android:icon="@drawable/icon" android:label="@string/app_name">
  <activity android:name=".MultiScreen"
    android:label="@string/app_name">
    <intent-filter>
      <action android:name="android.intent.action.MAIN" />
        <category android:name="android.intent.category.LAUNCHER" />
    </intent-filter>
  </activity>
  <activity android:name=".SecondScreen">
  </activity>
</application>
```

Finally, we can work on our Java code. First, let's create a second Java class file called SecondScreen (remember: it is important that this class filename matches the activity name we just put in the manifest file) by right-clicking the package name under the src directory in the Package Explorer, as we did when we created the second XML file in the res\layout directory. This time choose New-Class. It will automatically have the .java extension added, so simply enter SecondScreen for the filename.

Note

The file that Eclipse creates will be a bare-bones class file, so make any necessary additions so that it extends Android's Activity class and has the required methods.

Initially, the file should look like the following:

```
package com.sheusi.MultiScreen;

import android.app.Activity;
import android.os.Bundle;

public class SecondScreen extends Activity{
  @Override
  public void onCreate(Bundle savedInstanceState) {
```

```
    super.onCreate(savedInstanceState);
    setContentView(R.layout.second);
  }
}
```

Now let's turn our attention back to the main Java class, the `MultiScreen.java` file. We have added some additional import statements, a `Button` declaration and assignment, and most importantly, the `onClick( )` listener that switches to the second screen. The listener is done as an "in-line" class declaration, which essentially creates a new `OnClickListener` class and defines its `onClick( )` method all in one statement:

```
screen2Button.setOnClickListener(new View.OnClickListener(){
  public void onClick(View v){
    Intent myIntent=new Intent(v.getContext(),SecondScreen.class);
    startActivity(myIntent);
  }
});
```

This is a common convenience in Java code as long as the `onClick( )` method we define never has to be used by any other control. In other words, no other `Button` object will need to share it. The complete `MultiScreen.java` file should look like this:

```
package com.sheusi.MultiScreen;

import android.app.Activity;
import android.os.Bundle;
import android.widget.*;
import android.view.*;
import android.content.Intent;

public class MultiScreen extends Activity {
  /** Called when the activity is first created. */
  Button screen2Button=null;
  @Override
  public void onCreate(Bundle savedInstanceState) {
    super.onCreate(savedInstanceState);
    setContentView(R.layout.main);
    screen2Button=(Button)findViewById(R.id.SwitchToSecond);
    screen2Button.setOnClickListener(new View.OnClickListener(){
    public void onClick(View v){
      Intent myIntent=new Intent(v.getContext(),SecondScreen.class);
      startActivity(myIntent);
    }
```

```
    });
    }
}
```

If you run the application, you will see that clicking the button gets us to the second screen; we just cannot get back yet. To do this, we have to add more code to the `SecondScreen.java` file. We need to add the import statements that we added to the other Java file, the `Button` declaration and assignment, and finally the in-line `View.OnClickListener` class definition. You will see that the simple method call, `finish( )`, will get us back to the main screen. The `SecondScreen.java` file should now look like this:

```java
package com.sheusi.MultiScreen;

import android.app.Activity;
import android.os.Bundle;
import android.widget.*;
import android.view.*;

public class SecondScreen extends Activity{
  Button returnButton=null;
  @Override
  public void onCreate(Bundle savedInstanceState) {
    super.onCreate(savedInstanceState);
    setContentView(R.layout.second);
    returnButton=(Button)findViewById(R.id.SwitchToMain);
    returnButton.setOnClickListener(new View.OnClickListener(){
  public void onClick(View v){
    finish();
      }
    });
   }
}
```

You should be able to switch back and forth between screens. Again, this is an over-simplified example, but it lays a foundation for multiscreen applications.

Applications with multiple activities can pass data back and forth in an Android class called the `Bundle`. The `Bundle` is a collection of key-value pairs associated with the `Intent` class; it is loaded and unloaded using the `Intent`'s `putExtra()` and `getExtras()` methods. Remember that an application's main `Activity` can branch off into more than one secondary `Activity`, and they can either return to the main `Activity` or branch somewhere else; either pass data back or not; and so on. For the application programmer, this, of course, means more code, but it also means another level of design consideration because he must determine which data items are going where and whether they need to come back. To do this, we have to carefully plot data paths, name the bundles, and name the key-value pairs. It is a good idea to sketch this out before sitting down to code.

The example presented next is based on the previous two-screen example, but it is done as a different project. You are certainly welcome to modify the code you wrote for the previous example for convenience. It will include an EditText field on the opening screen, which will allow the user to enter any text. When the user touches the button to go on to the secondary activity (screen), the text entered on the first screen will appear in the EditText field on the second screen. The user can edit the text on the second screen, and the new text will be returned to the first screen when the button labeled Return is pressed. Following is a breakdown of the objects and labels used in the demonstration application:

Screen 1 (Activity 1)

Key/value pair -> payload/contents of the EditText field

Bundle name when received at Screen 2 -> incoming

Screen 2 (Activity 2)

Key/value pair -> returnpayload/contents of the EditText field

Bundle name when received back at Screen 1 -> response

First let's take a look at the two XML files for the main and secondary screens.

main.xml

```xml
<?xml version="1.0" encoding="utf-8"?>
<LinearLayout xmlns:android="http://schemas.android.com/apk/res/android"
    android:orientation="vertical"
    android:layout_width="fill_parent"
    android:layout_height="fill_parent"
    >
    <TextView
    android:layout_width="fill_parent"
    android:layout_height="wrap_content"
    android:textSize="20px"
    android:text="Primary Screen"
    />
    <Button
    android:layout_width="fill_parent"
    android:layout_height="wrap_content"
    android:text="Switch to Second Screen"
```

```
android:textSize="20px"
android:id="@+id/SwitchToSecond"
/>
<EditText
android:layout_width="fill_parent"
android:layout_height="wrap_content"
android:text=""
android:textSize="20px"
android:id="@+id/payloadValue"
/>
</LinearLayout>
```

second.xml

```
<?xml version="1.0" encoding="utf-8"?>
<LinearLayout xmlns:android="http://schemas.android.com/apk/res/android"
  android:orientation="vertical"
  android:layout_width="fill_parent"
  android:layout_height="fill_parent"
  >
  <TextView
  android:layout_width="fill_parent"
  android:layout_height="wrap_content"
  android:textSize="20px"
  android:text="Secondary Screen"
  />
  <Button
   android:layout_width="fill_parent"
  android:layout_height="wrap_content"
  android:text="Back to Main Screen"
  android:textSize="20px"
  android:id="@+id/SwitchToMain"
  />
  <EditText
  android:layout_width="fill_parent"
  android:layout_height="wrap_content"
  android:text=""
  android:textSize="20px"
  android:id="@+id/payloadValue"
    />
</LinearLayout>
```

As you can see, the two files are nearly identical except for the text that appears on the buttons and some of the android:id fields. As in the previous example and with any multiactivity application, you need to make an entry in the manifest file for each `Activity` class file. Here is the manifest used for this project:

```xml
<?xml version="1.0" encoding="utf-8"?>
<manifest xmlns:android="http://schemas.android.com/apk/res/android"
   package="com.sheusi.ActivitiesNBundles"
   android:versionCode="1"
   android:versionName="1.0">
   <uses-sdk android:minSdkVersion="8" />
   <application android:icon="@drawable/icon"
     android:label="@string/app_name">
     <activity android:name=".ActivitiesNBundlesActivity"
android:label="@string/app_name">
       <intent-filter>
         <action android:name="android.intent.action.MAIN" />
         <category android:name="android.intent.category.LAUNCHER" />
       </intent-filter>
     </activity>
     <activity android:name=".SecondActivity">
     </activity>
   </application>
</manifest>
```

Now let's take a look at the Java code for the first screen: `ActivitiesNBundles Activity.java`.

```java
package com.sheusi.ActivitiesNBundles;
import android.app.Activity;
import android.os.Bundle;
import android.widget.*;
import android.view.*;
import android.content.Intent;
public class ActivitiesNBundlesActivity extends Activity {
   /** Called when the activity is first created. */
   Button screen2Button=null;
   EditText et=null;
   private final int SECOND_ACTIVITY=2;
   @Override
   public void onCreate(Bundle savedInstanceState) {
     super.onCreate(savedInstanceState);
     setContentView(R.layout.main);
     screen2Button=(Button)findViewById(R.id.SwitchToSecond);
     et=(EditText)findViewById(R.id.payloadValue);
     screen2Button.setOnClickListener(new View.OnClickListener(){
```

```
      public void onClick(View v){
      Intent myIntent=new Intent(v.getContext(),SecondActivity.class);
      myIntent.putExtra("payload",et.getText().toString());
      //key-value pair
      startActivityForResult(myIntent,SECOND_ACTIVITY);
        }
     });
   }
  @Override
   //This method is necessary if you expect data to be returned
   //when the second activity ends
   public void onActivityResult(int requestID, int resultID, Intent i){
   super.onActivityResult(requestID, resultID, i);

   Bundle response=i.getExtras();
   Et.setText(response.getString("returnpayload"));
   }
}
```

There is a lot to pay attention to here. First, be sure to import the appropriate packages. Next, notice that we use a symbolic constant to represent the second screen. Remember that data in bundles is associated with specific Intent objects, so we want to associate the right Intent with the right target Activity. In other words, we want to deliver the right package(s) to the right address. You will see where this symbolic constant is used near the end of the code.

As in the previous example, clicking the button creates a new Intent object. What is different this time is that we add a piece of data in a name-value pair to the Intent using the putExtra( ) method. Finally, because we expect to get something back, we use the startActivityForResult( ) method instead of startActivity( ); and we override the onActivityResult( ) method to pull off the data and do what we want with it. Here is the Java code for the second screen:

```
package com.sheusi.ActivitiesNBundles;
import android.app.Activity;
import android.os.Bundle;
import android.widget.*;
import android.view.*;
import android.content.Intent;
public class SecondActivity extends Activity {
   /** Called when the activity is first created. */
   Button returnButton=null;
   EditText et2s=null;
```

```
@Override
public void onCreate(Bundle savedInstanceState) {
  super.onCreate(savedInstanceState);
  setContentView(R.layout.second);
  returnButton=(Button)findViewById(R.id.SwitchToMain);
  et2s=(EditText)findViewById(R.id.payloadValue);
  Bundle incoming=this.getIntent().getExtras();
  et2s.setText(incoming.getString("payload"));
  returnButton.setOnClickListener(new View.OnClickListener(){
    public void onClick(View v){
    Intent goBack=new Intent();
    goBack.putExtra("returnpayload",et2s.getText().toString());
    setResult(RESULT_OK, goBack);
    finish();
    }
  });
  }
}
```

The big difference here is that you can see the declaration of the Bundle object and its assignment using the Intent's getExtras( ) method. Remember that more than one key-value pair can be inserted into a bundle, so we use the key name to identify the data item we want to use at a given time. Notice that it is used as the parameter in the getString( ) method of the bundle's instance when it is inserted into the EditText field. Finally, the same process is used again to send the edited text value back to the main screen when the button is clicked. A new Intent object is instantiated, and a key-value pair is created. This time the key is named returnpayload and it is attached to the Intent; then the second screen is finished. The parameter, RESULT_OK, is a value for a field of the Activity class, which signals that the Activity was completed correctly.

POP-UP DIALOG BOXES AND TOASTS

It is common to give the user some notification during the operation of an application, such as an instructional message or a confirmation, or to request some bit of information. However, we may not want to waste precious screen space for something that may have a temporary and fleeting use. For this, pop-up messages or requests and Toasts are ideal. Toasts are a feature unique to the Android application; they appear as quick bursts of text that quickly fade away without user intervention. They can be done in one or two lines of code. Toasts are useful to inform the application user that something has occurred that might not be readily obvious to the user, such as a record change, an Internet connection made, and so on. Pop-ups are a little more involved but can request information from the user. To give some examples, we will construct an application that has three buttons. The first button will simply fire a toast message; the second two buttons will fire some pop-ups. Start a project, and set the `main.xml` to look like the following:

```xml
<?xml version="1.0" encoding="utf-8"?>
<LinearLayout xmlns:android="http://schemas.android.com/apk/res/android"
   android:orientation="vertical"
   android:layout_width="fill_parent"
   android:layout_height="fill_parent"
   >
<TextView
   android:layout_width="fill_parent"
   android:layout_height="wrap_content"
   android:text="@string/hello"
   />
<TableLayout
   android:layout_width="fill_parent"
   android:layout_height="wrap_content"
>
<TableRow
   android:layout_width="wrap_content"
   android:layout_height="wrap_content" >
<Button
   android:layout_width="wrap_content"
   android:layout_height="wrap_content"
   android:layout_weight=".5"
   android:text="Toast"
   android:id="@+id/toastbutton"/>
<Button
   android:layout_width="wrap_content"
   android:layout_height="wrap_content"
   android:layout_weight=".5"
   android:text="Request"
   android:id="@+id/requestpopup"/>
<Button
   android:layout_width="wrap_content"
   android:layout_height="wrap_content"
   android:layout_weight=".5"
   android:text="Date Picker"
   android:id="@+id/datepopup"/>

</TableRow>
</TableLayout>
</LinearLayout>
```

Remember: each button needs to have an ID element so that we can access it in the Java code.

The Toast class is a member of the Widget class, like Buttons and TextViews, so the android.widget package needs to be in the import statement. Its constructor takes the application's context as an argument. You will see the assignment for the Toast object in the onClick( ) method for the first button. Write your Java file to look like this:

```java
package com.sheusi.Messages;

import android.app.Activity;
import android.os.Bundle;
import android.widget.*;
import android.view.*;
import android.content.Context;

public class Messages extends Activity {
  /** Called when the activity is first created. */
  Button toastButton=null;
  Button popupRequest=null;
  Button popupCal=null;
  Context myContext=null;
  @Override
  public void onCreate(Bundle savedInstanceState) {
    super.onCreate(savedInstanceState);
    setContentView(R.layout.main);
    myContext=this.getApplicationContext();
    toastButton=(Button)findViewById(R.id.toastbutton);
    toastButton.setOnClickListener(new View.OnClickListener(){
      public void onClick(View v){
      Toast myToast=new Toast(myContext);
      myToast.makeText(myContext,"This is my toast message",Toast.LENGTH_LONG). show();
      }
    });
  }
}
```

The Toast class has methods that allow you to set the location of the message on the screen. You can also change the length of time the message shows by setting the duration constant to Toast.LENGTH_SHORT. Furthermore, you can use a static method call to display a Toast with one statement, as shown in this line:

```java
Toast.makeToast(myContext,"This is my message,Toast.LENGTH_LONG).show();
```

The next example will be a pop-up message that requests a response from the user. The class that causes a pop-up message is the AlertDialog, and it is an Android class. It requires another class called the AlertDialog.Builder. The latter is configured with all the components required by the programmer, such as the question to be asked of the user, the text on the buttons it will contain, and the code that the choices trigger. In the example, I have added a TextView object to the screen to display which choice the user made. To do the same, modify your main.xml to look like this. Notice the new TextView object at the bottom.

```xml
<?xml version="1.0" encoding="utf-8"?>
<LinearLayout xmlns:android="http://schemas.android.com/apk/res/android"
    android:orientation="vertical"
    android:layout_width="fill_parent"
    android:layout_height="fill_parent"
    >
<TextView
    android:layout_width="fill_parent"
    android:layout_height="wrap_content"
    android:text="@string/hello"
    />
<TableLayout
    android:layout_width="fill_parent"
    android:layout_height="wrap_content"
>
<TableRow
    android:layout_width="wrap_content"
    android:layout_height="wrap_content" >
<Button
    android:layout_width="wrap_content"
    android:layout_height="wrap_content"
    android:layout_weight=".5"
    android:text="Toast"
    android:id="@+id/toastbutton"/>
<Button
    android:layout_width="wrap_content"
    android:layout_height="wrap_content"
    android:layout_weight=".5"
    android:text="Request"
    android:id="@+id/requestpopup"/>
<Button
    android:layout_width="wrap_content"
    android:layout_height="wrap_content"
    android:layout_weight=".5"
```

```
     android:text="Date Picker"
     android:id="@+id/datepopup"/>
</TableRow>
</TableLayout>
<TextView
  android:id="@+id/responses"
  android:layout_width="fill_parent"
  android:layout_height="wrap_content"
  android:text=""
  android:background="#808080"
  android:textColor="#000000"
  />
</LinearLayout>
```

There are quite a few lines of code used to implement an `AlertDialog`, so study the following Java code carefully:

```java
package com.sheusi.Messages;

import android.app.Activity;
import android.os.Bundle;
import android.widget.*;
import android.view.*;
import android.content.Context;
import android.app.*;
import android.content.DialogInterface;

public class Messages extends Activity {
  /** Called when the activity is first created. */
  Button toastButton=null;
  Button popupRequest=null;
  Button popupCal=null;
  Context myContext=null;
  AlertDialog.Builder adb=null;
  AlertDialog ad=null;
  TextView responses=null;
  @Override
  public void onCreate(Bundle savedInstanceState) {
     super.onCreate(savedInstanceState);
     setContentView(R.layout.main);
     myContext=this.getApplicationContext();
     responses=(TextView)findViewById(R.id.responses);
     toastButton=(Button)findViewById(R.id.toastbutton);
     toastButton.setOnClickListener(new View.OnClickListener(){
       public void onClick(View v){
```

```
       //Toast myToast=new Toast(myContext);
       Toast.makeText(myContext,"This is my toast message",Toast.LENGTH_LONG).show();
         }
     });
    adb=new AlertDialog.Builder(this);
    adb.setCancelable(false);
    adb.setMessage("Respond Yes or No");
    adb.setPositiveButton("Yes", new DialogInterface.OnClickListener(){
      public void onClick(DialogInterface di, int id){
responses.setText("You answered YES to the popup");
      }
    });
    adb.setNegativeButton("No", new DialogInterface.OnClickListener(){
      public void onClick(DialogInterface di, int id){
      responses.setText("You answered NO to the popup");
      }
    });
    ad=adb.create();
    ad.setTitle("Yes or no?");
    popupRequest=(Button)findViewById(R.id.requestpopup);
    popupRequest.setOnClickListener(new View.OnClickListener(){
      public void onClick(View v){
        ad.show();
    }
    });
  }
}
```

First, notice the two additional import statements. These packages include classes we will need.

Next, notice the declarations for the AlertDialog, the AlertDialog.Builder, and the additional TextView object variables. In the onCreate( ) method, the additional class variables are assigned, and several methods are called for the AlertDialog.Builder. Notice that the OnClickListener objects for the Yes and No buttons on the AlertDialog are written as in-line classes as we have done before for some on-screen Button objects. Their onClick( ) methods are defined in-line as well. You will insert all the code needed to run when a Yes or No choice is made in these in-line definitions. Finally, the AlertDialog.Builder method, create( ), is used to assign the AlertDialog variable, ad. All that is left is for the in-line onClick( ) method for the pop-up button on the main screen to call the .show( ) method for the AlertDialog. That's not too complicated if you are careful with the syntax.

Figure 7.3 shows what the running application should look like.

Figure 7.3
Emulator showing application with an AlertDialog object.

There are a few useful subclasses to the AlertDialog class: the DatePicker Dialog, the TimePickerDialog, and the ProgressDialog. Because we discussed the DatePicker earlier and understand how it is used, we will create a DatePicker Dialog and assign it to the third button on the main screen. We will use our additional TextView to display the date the user chose in the DatePickerDialog.

Because you can customize the basic AlertDialog with other widgets besides the basic yes and no buttons, the AlertDialog.Builder class assembles it. The Date PickerDialog, on the other hand, is predesigned. We are only allowed to customize what happens when the user chooses a new date (or chooses to keep the original date) and confirms the choice. The DatePickerDialog can be returned by the protected method, onCreateDialog( ), which belongs to the Activity class, or it can be created with its constructor. If the programmer uses the Activity class's onCreateDialog( ) to create the dialog, features of the activity will be associated with the dialog. For instance, when the dialog is open and the user clicks the menu button, the options menu choices written into the activity will be revealed. If the programmer decides to use the constructor, the DatePickerDialog will not be attached to the activity.

In our example, the onCreateDialog( ) method is inserted and annotated on top of the onCreate( ) method.

The DatePickerDialog takes five arguments in its constructor: the Context referred to by the keyword; this, an OnDateSetListener; and three integer values to set the initial day, month, and year. In this example, I defined the OnDateSet Listener in-line just as I did the listeners for the Button objects. It can also be defined as an inner class and added to the constructor through the use of a variable.

Other things to note are the use of the Calendar class, which is in the java.util package. It is used to set the original date on the DatePickerDialog to the current system date. The day of the month, the month, and the year are handled by global integer variables. Note that months are zero-based; that is, January is month zero, so we add one to the value of the month when we display it in our TextView. Here is the revised code:

```
package com.sheusi.Messages;
import android.app.Activity;
import android.os.Bundle;
import android.widget.*;
import android.view.*;
import android.content.Context;
import android.app.*;
import android.content.DialogInterface;
import java.util.Calendar;
public class Messages extends Activity {
  /** Called when the activity is first created. */
  Button toastButton=null;
  Button popupRequest=null;
  Button popupCal=null;
  Context myContext=null;
  AlertDialog.Builder adb=null;
  AlertDialog ad=null;
  TextView responses=null;
  int myYear;
  int myMonth;
  int myDay;
  Calendar myCal=null;
  //overridden method definition to implement a DatePickerDialog
  @Override
  protected Dialog onCreateDialog(int id){
    return new DatePickerDialog(this,
      new DatePickerDialog.OnDateSetListener(){
        public void onDateSet(DatePicker dp,int year, int monthOfYear,
      int dayOfMonth){
          myYear=year;
          myMonth=monthOfYear;
```

```
            myDay=dayOfMonth;
            responses.setText("Your chosen date was "+
String.valueOf(myMonth+1)+"/"+
String.valueOf(myDay)+"/"+
String.valueOf(myYear));
        }
      },
      myYear,
      myMonth,
      myDay);
  }
  @Override
  public void onCreate(Bundle savedInstanceState) {
    super.onCreate(savedInstanceState);
    setContentView(R.layout.main);
    myContext=this.getApplicationContext();
    responses=(TextView)findViewById(R.id.responses);
    toastButton=(Button)findViewById(R.id.toastbutton);
    //Begin code for DatePickerDialog
    myCal=Calendar.getInstance();
    myYear=myCal.get(Calendar.YEAR);
    myMonth=myCal.get(Calendar.MONTH);
    myDay=myCal.get(Calendar.DAY_OF_MONTH);
    popupCal=(Button)findViewById(R.id.datepopup);
    popupCal.setOnClickListener(new View.OnClickListener(){
      public void onClick(View v){
      showDialog(0);
      }
    });
  //end code for DatePickerDialog
    toastButton.setOnClickListener(new View.OnClickListener(){
      public void onClick(View v){
      Toast.makeText(myContext,"This is my toast message",Toast.LENGTH_LONG).show();
      }
    });


    adb=new AlertDialog.Builder(this);
    adb.setCancelable(false);
    adb.setMessage("Respond Yes or No");
    adb.setPositiveButton("Yes", new DialogInterface.OnClickListener(){
      public void onClick(DialogInterface di, int id){
```

```
//decision=true;
    responses.setText("You answered YES to the popup");
    }
  });
  adb.setNegativeButton("No", new DialogInterface.OnClickListener(){
    public void onClick(DialogInterface di, int id){
  //decision=false;
    responses.setText("You answered NO to the popup");
    }
  });
  ad=adb.create();
  ad.setTitle("Yes or no?");
  popupRequest=(Button)findViewById(R.id.requestpopup);
  popupRequest.setOnClickListener(new View.OnClickListener(){
    public void onClick(View v){
      ad.show();
    }
  });
  }
}
```

When the application runs, it should look like Figure 7.4.

Figure 7.4
Emulator showing application with a DatePickerDialog object.

MENUS ON THE ANDROID DEVICE

If an application's design has too many buttons on the screen and appears too cluttered, or the designer simply needs to free some space, she might consider using Android's menu facility. There are two types of menus: the option menu and the context menu. An *option menu* is a global menu, functionally similar to a menu bar at the top of an application. The second, the *context menu*, is functionally similar to a right-click on a computer application. An option menu is activated by the hardware button on the Android device. (Actually, it's not so much a hardware button, but a hardware touch-pad location.)

This example illustrates use of the option menu. We start by designing the menu as an XML file. The example has three choices. The first two are "dummies"; in other words, they will do nothing in our example. They are included for illustration purposes here but could do anything a button could do at the application level. The third choice simply closes the application.

Following is the XML file we will eventually call `mymenu.xml`:

```xml
<?xml version="1.0" encoding="utf-8"?>
<menu xmlns:android="http://schemas.android.com/apk/res/android">
<item android:id="@+id/dummy"
   android:icon="@drawable/icon"
   android:title="Do Something"/>
<item android:id="@+id/anotherdummy"
   android:icon="@drawable/icon"
   android:title="Do Something Else"/>
<item android:id="@+id/close"
   android:icon="@drawable/icon"
   android:title="close"/>
</menu>
```

Notice that the `mymenu.xml` file is similar to the `main.xml` file, but the outermost tags are menu tags instead of layout tags. Where does this file go? In the Project Explorer, right-click on the `res` folder and create a new folder called `menu`. Next, right-click on the `menu` folder you just created, choose New from the menu, and create a new file. Call the file `mymenu.xml`. Finally, type in the XML code shown previously and save it.

All the item tags have `id` attributes in them. They will be used to identify the menu choices in your Java code. Remember that in the `R.java` file, anything with an `id` attribute will be identified and associated with an integer value. We have seen this many times. Following is the Java file for the application:

```java
package com.sheusi.MenuStuff;

import android.app.Activity;
import android.os.Bundle;
```

```
import android.view.Menu;
import android.view.MenuInflater;
import android.view.MenuItem;
public class MenuWerx extends Activity {
  /** Called when the activity is first created. */

 @Override
 public boolean onCreateOptionsMenu(Menu menu){
   MenuInflater inflater=getMenuInflater();
   inflater.inflate(R.menu.mymenu,menu);
   return super.onCreateOptionsMenu(menu);
 }
 @Override
 public boolean onOptionsItemSelected(MenuItem mi){
   if(mi.getItemId()==R.id.dummy){
     //do nothing
     return true;
   }
   if(mi.getItemId()==R.id.anotherdummy){
     //again, do nothing
     return true;
   }
   if(mi.getItemId()==R.id.close){
     this.finish();
     return true;
   }
   return true;
 }
 @Override
 public void onCreate(Bundle savedInstanceState) {
   super.onCreate(savedInstanceState);
   setContentView(R.layout.main);
 }
}
```

There is something new here. We override the onCreateOptionsMenu( ) and the onOptionsItemSelected( ) methods that are part of the Activity class. There are also a few menu-related include statements added to the application.

Next, we flesh out the onOptionsItemSelected( ) method using the references from the R.java file to identify the user's menu choice. Java programmers may encounter a similar code block when they use the same ActionListener implementation and onClick( ) method to be shared by several buttons. The principle is the same. Here, depending on which menu choice is tapped, a different action will take place in the application. Figure 7.5 shows how the application should look on the screen. All of the images on the menu choices are the same Android icon, which is included by Eclipse in every new project. The icon to be used needs to be specified in the menu's XML file. Different icons can be used for each menu choice, or no icons at all. Just be sure to include the icons according to Android graphics guidelines described and illustrated elsewhere in this book.

Figure 7.5
Emulator showing application using an options menu.

Note

When you're using the options menu technique, remember that the hardware menu may not be intuitive to the user. The application designer should determine some way to indicate use of the menu feature to the user, such as displaying an image of the menus open on the application's page of the Android Market.

Follow-Up

1. Review the Intent class at http://developer.android.com/reference/android/content/Intent.html and complete the following chart.

Standard Activity Actions	Descriptions

2. Review the `TimePickerDialog` class at http://developer.android.com/reference/android/app/TimePickerDialog.html and replace the `DatePickerDialog` in this chapter with a `TimePickerDialog`.

KEY CLASSES USED IN THIS CHAPTER

Intent

Class	Intent
Package	android.content
Extends	java.lang.Object
Overview	An Intent is an abstract description of an operation to be performed. It generally starts an activity; thus, it connects multiple activities in an application.

Methods used in this chapter:

Intent setData(Uri data)	Set the data this Intent will operate on
Intent putExtra(String name, String value)	Adds extended data to the Intent
Bundle getExtras( )	Retrieves a map of extended data from the Intent

Other commonly used methods:

float getFloatExtra(String name, float defaultValue)	Retrieves extended data from the Intent
int getIntExtra(String name, int defaultValue)	Retrieves extended data from the Intent
double getDoubleExtra(String name, double defaultValue)	Retrieves extended data from the Intent
String getPackage( )	Retrieves the application package name that this Intent is limited to
Intent putExtra(String name, double value)	Adds extended data to the Intent

`Intent putExtra(String name, int value)`	Adds extended data to the Intent
`Intent putExtra(String name, float value)`	Adds extended data to the Intent
`Intent putExtra(String name, char value)`	Adds extended data to the Intent
`Intent putExtras(Bundle extras)`	Adds a set of extended data to the Intent
`Intent replaceExtras(Bundle extras)`	Replaces the extras in the Intent with the given bundle of extras
`void removeExtra(String name)`	Removes the extended data from the Intent

Bundle

Class	`Bundle`
Package	`android.os`
Extends	`java.lang.Object`
Overview	A mapping of `String` values to various `Parcelable` data types.

Methods used in this chapter:

`String getString(String key)`	Returns the string value associated with a given key, or a `null` if a `null` is associated with this key or no mapping to a `String` data type is associated with this key.

Other commonly used methods:

`boolean isEmpty( )`	Returns `true` if `Bundle` is empty, `false` if otherwise
`boolean getBoolean(String key)`	Returns the `boolean` value associated with the given key, or `false` if no mapping of the desired type exists for the key
`byte getByte(String key)`	Returns the `byte` value associated with the key or zero (0) if no mapping of the desired type exists for the key
`float getFloat(String key)`	Returns the `float` value associated with the key or zero (0) if no mapping of the desired type exists for the key
`double getDouble(String key)`	Returns the `double` value associated with the key or zero (0) if no mapping of the desired type exists for the key
`int getInt(String key)`	Returns the `int` value associated with the key or zero (0) if no mapping of the desired type exists for the key

`void putBoolean(String key, boolean value)`	Inserts a `boolean` value into this `Bundle`'s mapping, replacing the current value for the key if there is one
`void putDouble(String key, double value)`	Inserts a `double` value into this `Bundle`'s mapping, replacing the current value for the key if there is one
`void putChar(String key, char value)`	Inserts a `char` value into this `Bundle`'s mapping, replacing the current value for the key if there is one
`void putFloat(String key, float value)`	Inserts a `float` value into this `Bundle`'s mapping, replacing the current value for the key if there is one
`void putInt(String key, int value)`	Inserts an `int` value into this `Bundle`'s mapping, replacing the current value for the key if there is one

Toast

Class	`Toast`
Package	`android.widget`
Extends	`java.lang.Object`
Overview	Produces a quick, floating message to the user. `Toast` never receives focus. A `Toast` is typically used as a confirmation to the user that some event has occurred that would not otherwise be apparent, such as the successful saving of a file.

Methods used in this chapter:

`Toast MakeText(Context context, CharSequence text, int duration)`	Make a standard `Toast` that just contains a text view. The duration uses two symbolic constants: `LENGTH_LONG` and `LENGTH_SHORT`.
`void show( )`	Shows the message for the specified duration.

Other commonly used methods:

`void setText(CharSequence text)`	Updates the text in the `Toast`
`void setGravity(int gravity, int xOffset, int yOffset)`	Sets the location on the screen for the `Toast`
`void setDuration(int duration)`	Sets how long the `Toast` will show using the symbolic constants `LENGTH_LONG` and `LENGTH_SHORT`
`int getXOffset( )`	Returns the X offset in pixels to apply to the gravity's location
`int getYOffset( )`	Returns the Y offset in pixels to apply to the gravity's location
`float getHorizontalMargin( )`	Returns the horizontal margin
`float getVerticalMargin( )`	Returns the vertical margin

AlertDialog

Class	`AlertDialog`
Package	`android.app`
Extends	`android.app.Dialog`
Overview	A subclass of `Dialog` that can contain one, two, or three buttons. A string can be displayed using the `setMessage( )` method.

Methods used in this chapter:

`void setTitle(CharSequence title)`	Sets the title for this `AlertDialog`

Other commonly used methods:

`void setMessage(CharSequence message)`	Sets the message for this `AlertDialog`
`void setIcon(Drawable icon)`	Sets the icon to appear on this `AlertDialog`
`void setView(View view)`	Sets the `View` (or child of the `View` class) to be displayed on this `AlertDialog`
`Button getButton(int whichButton)`	Gets one of the `Button` objects used in the dialog, using `whichButton` as an index value
`ListView getListView( )`	Gets the `ListView` object used in the dialog

AlertDialog.Builder

Class	`AlertDialog.Builder`
Package	`android.app`
Extends	`java.lang.Object`
Overview	Class for creating `AlertDialogs`

Methods used in this chapter:

`AlertDialog create( )`	Creates an `AlertDialog` with the arguments supplied to this `Builder`

Other commonly used methods:

`void setTitle(CharSequence title)`	Sets the title for the `AlertDialog(s)` to be produced
`void setMessage(CharSequence message)`	Sets message for the `AlertDialog(s)` to be produced
`void setIcon(Drawable icon)`	Sets the icon for the `AlertDialog(s)` to be produced
`void setView(View view)`	Sets the `View` (or child of the `View` class) for the `AlertDialog(s)` to be produced
`void show( )`	Builds, then shows an `AlertDialog`

DatePickerDialog

Class	`DatePickerDialog`
Package	`android.app`
Extends	`android.app.AlertDialog`
Overview	A simple dialog containing only a `DatePicker`

Methods used in this chapter:

n/a

Other commonly used methods:

`DatePicker getDatePicker()`	Retrieves the `DatePicker` object contained in this dialog
`void onClick(DialogInterface dialog, int which)`	Method is evoked when a button in the dialog is clicked
`void onDateChanged(DatePicker view, int year, int month, int day)`	Method is called when the date on the `DatePicker` is changed
`void onRestoreInstanceState (Bundle savedInstanceState)`	Restores the state of the dialog from a previously saved bundle
`Bundle onSaveInstanceState()`	Saves the state of the dialog into a bundle
`void updateDate(int year, int month, int day)`	Sets the current date

DatePickerDialog.OnDateSetListener

Class	`DatePickerDialog.OnDateSetListener` (interface)
Package	`android.app`
Extends	`java.lang.Object`
Overview	The callback used to indicate the user is done filling in the date

Methods used in this chapter:

`abstract void onDateSet` `(Datepicker view, int year,` `int month, int day)`	Method to respond to date set on this `DatePicker`

Other commonly used methods:

n/a

Menu

Class	`Menu (interface)`
Package	`android.menu`
Extends	n/a
Overview	An interface for managing items on a menu. Note: If six or more menu choices are necessary, they can be reached by the More item on the icon menu. However, they will not show icons, and item check marks are discouraged.

Methods used in this chapter:

n/a

Other commonly used methods:

`abstract MenuItem add (CharSequence title)`	Adds a new menu item to the menu
`abstract SubMenu addSubMenu (int groupid, int itemid, int order, CharSequence title)`	Adds a new submenu to the menu
`abstract void close( )`	Closes the menu
`abstract void clear( )`	Removes all existing items from the menu, leaving it empty as if it had just been created
`abstract MenuItem getItem(int index)`	Gets the menu item at the given index.
`abstract MenuItem findItem(int id)`	Gets the menu item with a particular identifier
`abstract int size( )`	Returns the number of items in the menu

MenuInflater

Class	`MenuInflater`
Package	`android.menu`
Extends	`java.lang.Object`
Overview	This class is used to convert XML files into menus.

Methods used in this chapter:

`void inflate(int menuRes, Menu menu)`	Inflate a menu hierarchy from the specified XML resource. The `menuRes` value refers to the integer value found in the `R.java` file associated with the `menu.xml file`.

Other commonly used methods:

n/a

MenuItem

Class	`MenuItem (interface)`
Package	`android.view`
Extends	n/a
Overview	Interface for direct access to a previously created menu item

Methods used in this chapter:

`abstract int getItemId( )`	Returns the identifier for this menu item.

Other commonly used methods:

`abstract intent getIntent( )`	Returns the `Intent` associated with this menu item
`abstract int getOrder( )`	Returns the category and order within the category for this menu item
`abstract CharSequence getTitle( )`	Returns the current title of this menu item
`abstract SubMenu getSubMenu( )`	Returns the `SubMenu` for this menu item, if it has one
`abstract MenuItem setIcon (Drawable icon)`	Change the icon associated with this item
`abstract MenuItem setIntent (Intent intent)`	Change the `Intent` associated with this item
`abstract MenuItem setNumeric Shortcut(char numericChar)`	Change the numeric shortcut associated with this item

READER'S NOTES

CHAPTER 8

WORKING WITH IMAGES

DISPLAYING IMAGES

Displaying images on the Android device is fairly simple. Android supports the four common image formats: PNG, JPG, BMP, and GIF. Images that you want to bundle with your application are stored in the res directory. Starting with software development kit (SDK) 1.6, users can have some control over the resolution of their images by storing three versions of the same image. The correct version will be displayed depending on the device the end user employs. You will notice that in the Package Explorer in Eclipse, the res directory has three subdirectories: drawable-ldpi (low resolution), drawable-mdpi (medium resolution), and drawable-hdpi (high resolution). You will also see that the Package Explorer already has three versions of the default Android launch icon, icon.png. If resolution doesn't concern you, you can place a single image in any of the subdirectories, or better yet you can create a subdirectory under the res directory called simply drawable. Note that all image filenames should be lowercase and contain only letters, numbers, and underscores.

The device will adjust the size of the image and maintain the aspect ratio when the image is displayed. Images are displayed in an ImageView object. Like a TextView object, an ImageView object can be added to the screen in the XML file that is used to lay out the screen, such as main.xml, or it can be declared and assigned in the Java code. A particular image can be assigned to an ImageView either in the XML file or in the Java code, the latter allowing the application to change the image while it is running. Images can also be downloaded and displayed, but that procedure is not covered here.

Our example actually displays two images in two ImagesViews to show both techniques. First, look at the main.xml file. Notice that the width and height specifications are set to wrap_content. This provides better centering of the images.

```xml
<?xml version="1.0" encoding="utf-8"?>
<LinearLayout xmlns:android="http://schemas.android.com/apk/res/android"
    android:orientation="vertical"
    android:layout_width="fill_parent"
    android:layout_height="fill_parent"

    >
<TextView
    android:layout_width="wrap_content"
    android:layout_height="wrap_content"
    android:text="@string/hello"
    />
    <ImageView
    android:id="@+id/myimage"
    android:layout_width="wrap_content"
    android:layout_height="wrap_content"
    android:src="@drawable/harbor"/>
    <ImageView
    android:id="@+id/myimage2"
    android:layout_width="fill_parent"
    android:layout_height="wrap_content"/>
    </LinearLayout>
```

Also note that the second ImageView doesn't need to have an android:id value assigned, because it will be done in the Java code. You might also note that a new attribute, android:src, is used in the first ImageView and that the value starts with @drawable. Remember that images are stored in directories starting with the name drawable.

The Java code for the application is listed here:

```java
package com.sheusi.images;

import android.app.Activity;
import android.os.Bundle;
import android.widget.ImageView;

public class ImageDisplay extends Activity {
   /** Called when the activity is first created. */
   ImageView myImageView=null;
   ImageView myImageView2=null;
   @Override
```

```
  public void onCreate(Bundle savedInstanceState) {
    super.onCreate(savedInstanceState);
    setContentView(R.layout.main);
    myImageView=(ImageView)findViewById(R.id.myimage);
    myImageView2=(ImageView)findViewById(R.id.myimage2);
    myImageView2.setImageResource(R.drawable.lighthouse);
  }
}
```

Note that in the last line of the code the image to be displayed in the second
ImageView is assigned at run-time. This provides an interesting possibility. Take a
look at the auto-generated file, R.java. You can find it in the gen folder under the
package name in the Package Explorer. Notice that all the images are assigned a hex
integer to represent them.

```
public static final class drawable {
  public static final int harbor=0x7f020000;
  public static final int icon=0x7f020001;
  public static final int lighthouse=0x7f020002;
}
```

In your code, you could create an array of integers to represent a series of images.
Simply assign each image to the array as follows:

```
int[] album=new int[2];
    album[0]=R.drawable.harbor;
    album[1]=R.drawable.lighthouse;
```

To display any given image, use a line such as

```
myImageView2.setImageResource(album[0]);
```

and change the image by changing the index value on the array. This could be done
with forward and back Button objects, which change an index variable in their listeners. Study this variation of the Java code:

```
package com.sheusi.images;

import android.app.Activity;
import android.os.Bundle;
import android.widget.ImageView;
import android.widget.Button;
import android.view.View;

public class ImageDisplay extends Activity {
  /** Called when the activity is first created. */
```

```
ImageView myImageView2=null;
Button forward=null;
Button back=null;
int pic;
int[] album=new int[2];
@Override
public void onCreate(Bundle savedInstanceState) {
  super.onCreate(savedInstanceState);
  setContentView(R.layout.main);
  forward=(Button)findViewById(R.id.forward);
  back=(Button)findViewById(R.id.back);
  album[0]=R.drawable.harbor;
  album[1]=R.drawable.lighthouse;
  myImageView2=(ImageView)findViewById(R.id.myimage2);
  myImageView2.setImageResource(album[0]); //start app with first picture
  forward.setOnClickListener(new View.OnClickListener(){
    public void onClick(View v){
      if(pic<album.length-1)
      pic++;
      myImageView2.setImageResource(album[pic]);
    }
  });
  back.setOnClickListener(new View.OnClickListener(){
   public void onClick(View v){
     if(pic>0)
       pic--;
       myImageView2.setImageResource(album[pic]);
   }
  });
 }
}
```

I eliminated the first ImageView in the main.xml file and in the Java code, because only one ImageView is now able to display all images. I also added Forward and Back buttons to the screen.

When this version is run, it should look like Figure 8.1.

In the previous chapter we looked at how to use some built-in Android activities such as ACTION_DIAL and ACTION_VIEW to build multiscreen applications. We even saw how we can create multiscreen applications using multiple Activity classes and XML files of our own. We then looked at how to pass data back and forth through the use of the Bundle class.

Figure 8.1
Emulator showing ImageDisplay application.

USING IMAGES STORED ON THE ANDROID DEVICE

In the `ImageDisplay` application we just completed, we learned how to display images shipped with the application on the screen. Let us now combine all these techniques and learn how to pull images from the photo gallery on the mobile phone into our own applications. To select the photo from the gallery, we use the built-in activity `ACTION_PICK`, but let's take things slow and do some prep work first.

Android devices can store data items internally or externally (using an SD card). There are two constructs we will look at for retrieving data from these sources. The Android operating system (OS) can worry about where the data is stored internally on an actual device we just need to use the construct for internal storage. The same applies for the SD card. On the emulator we will use the SD card and the "external" code construct.

In Chapter 3, "Application Design," we covered how to configure an emulator in Eclipse. You can use any emulator you have created in your development environment; just go back and be sure that you have included the use of an SD card in your configuration. Figure 8.2 will remind you where to do this.

Under the Eclipse window menu, choose Android AVD and SDK Manager. Pick the emulator you wish to check and click the Edit button. If you have already configured the emulator for an SD card, it will be in the list on the left. If you cannot find it in

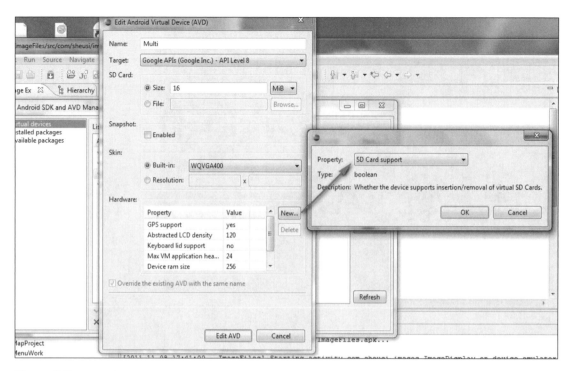

Figure 8.2
Emulator configuration panels in Eclipse.

the list, select the New button to the right of the list and find SD card in the picklist seen here on the right; then click OK. After that, close all the pop-ups and get back to Eclipse.

Now take a minute to find one or two small images you want to add to the SD card image in the emulator. As stated earlier, Android will work with JPG, BMP, GIF, or PNG formats. If you want to download them, do so and keep track of where they are stored on your development computer. Likewise, if you already have the images, just know where they are before you continue.

Before you can install images to the emulator, it must be running. You can either start it through the Android AVD and SDK Manager screens or just start an application in a project. When the emulator of choice is running, open the Window menu on Eclipse and choose Open Perspective. You want to choose DDMS. DDMS stands for Dalvic Debug Monitor Server and is part of the Android plug-in for Eclipse; it's not part of the basic Eclipse configuration. If it is not on the list, open Other, and you should find it in the expanded list. When the perspective is open, find the tab named File Explorer. It will list the contents of the emulator just like the File Explorer does on your development machine. See Figure 8.3.

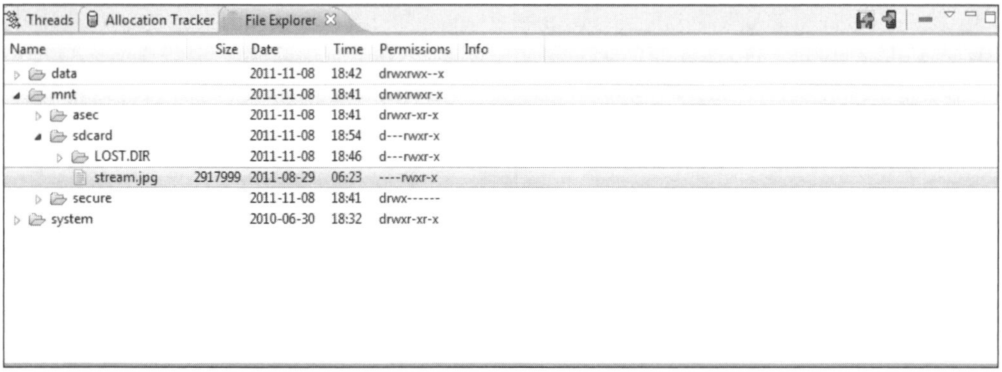

Figure 8.3
DDMS perspective in Eclipse.

As you move in on the `mnt` folder, eventually you will arrive at the `sdcard` folder. Open the `sdcard` folder as you see in the figure. (You will notice that I have added a file called `stream.JPG` to my emulator.) At the upper-right corner of the illustration, you will see two icons. One is an orange arrow pointing left on a floppy disk; the other is an arrow pointing right on a cell phone. The icon on the right is used to move files from an external source to the emulator. Select the latter, and it will open a File Explorer on your development machine. Find the file(s) you want to transfer and load them to the emulator. Note that once you do this, those files will stay tied to the chosen emulator as long as it exists on your development system; they will not disappear when the emulator is closed or even when Eclipse is closed; they are part of the emulator's configuration now. To get back to the Eclipse development screen, just pick the Java perspective as you did the DDMS perspective.

Now let's begin to design our image retrieving and viewing application. We need a simple `main.xml` file, which includes only a button to summon the image picker activity, and an `ImageView` element in which to load a chosen image. It could look like the example here:

```
<?xml version="1.0" encoding="utf-8"?>
<LinearLayout xmlns:android="http://schemas.android.com/apk/res/android"
  android:orientation="vertical"
  android:layout_width="fill_parent"
  android:layout_height="fill_parent"
  >
<TextView
  android:layout_width="fill_parent"
  android:layout_height="wrap_content"
  android:text="My Image Viewer"
/>
```

```
<Button
  android:layout_width="fill_parent"
  android:layout_height="wrap_content"
  android:text="Touch to view gallery"
  android:id="@+id/gallerybutton"
/>
<ImageView
  android:layout_width="fill_parent"
  android:layout_height="wrap_content"
  android:id="@+id/imageview"
/>
</LinearLayout>
```

The corresponding Java code isn't complicated because we have seen bits and pieces in previous exercises. As always, be sure to check your import statements. Examine this code:

```
package com.sheusi.ImageViewer;

import android.app.Activity;
import android.content.Intent;
import android.os.Bundle;
import android.widget.*;
import android.view.*;
import android.net.Uri;
public class ImageViewerActivity extends Activity {
  /** Called when the activity is first created. */
  Button b=null;
  ImageView iv=null;
  @Override
  public void onCreate(Bundle savedInstanceState) {
    super.onCreate(savedInstanceState);
    setContentView(R.layout.main);
    b=(Button)findViewById(R.id.gallerybutton);
    iv=(ImageView)findViewById(R.id.imageview);
    b.setOnClickListener(new View.OnClickListener(){
      public void onClick(View v){
        Intent myIntent=new Intent(Intent.ACTION_PICK,
android.provider.MediaStore.Images.Media.EXTERNAL_CONTENT_URI);
        startActivityForResult(myIntent,2);
      }
    });
  }
  @Override
  public void onActivityResult(int requestID, int resultID, Intent i){
```

```
  super.onActivityResult(requestID,resultID, i);
  if(resultID==Activity.RESULT_OK){
   Uri selectedImage=i.getData();
    iv.setImageURI(selectedImage);
   }
 }
}
```

The lines that follow are the construct I discussed earlier as choosing the SD card instead of internal storage:

```
   Intent myIntent=new Intent(Intent.ACTION_PICK,
 android.provider.MediaStore.Images.Media.EXTERNAL_CONTENT_URI);
 startActivityForResult(myIntent,2);
```

Notice the symbolic constant, EXTERNAL_CONTENT_URI. The number two (2) in the third line of the previous code, the second argument for the startActivityFor-Result( ) method, is an arbitrary but unique number assigned to this Intent. In Chapter 7, "Multiscreen Applications," we considered the possibility that there could be additional Intents associated with other data bundles in our application, and we need to keep them straight. Some programmers will associate this integer with a descriptive symbolic constant declaration at the top of the program.

Figures 8.4 through 8.6 show a succession of images showing how the application should look through its various states at run-time.

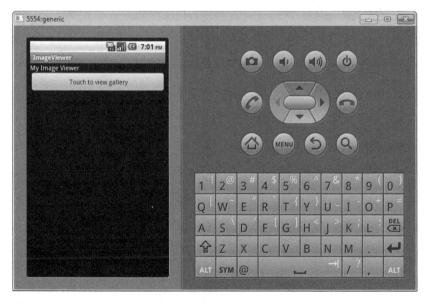

Figure 8.4
Emulator showing ImageViewer application.

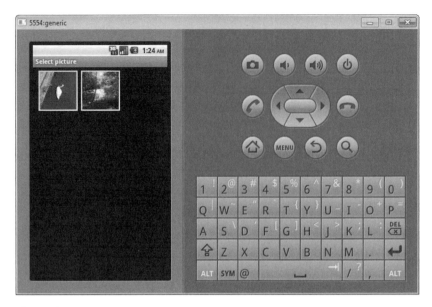

Figure 8.5
ImageViewer application with gallery on screen.

Figure 8.6
ImageViewer application showing image chosen from gallery.

Follow-Up

Go to http://developer.android.com/guide/developing/debugging/ddms.html and review the features of the DDMS perspective.

Key Classes Used in This Chapter

ImageView

Class	`ImageView`
Package	`android.view`
Extends	`java.view.View`
Overview	Displays an arbitrary image such as an icon. The `Image-View` class can load images from various sources, take care of computing its measurement from the image to properly display it, and show options such as scaling and tinting.

Methods used in this chapter:

`void setImageResource( int resid)`	Sets a `Drawable` object as this `Image-View`'s content
`void setImageURI(Uri uri )`	Sets the content for this `ImageView` to the specified uniform resource identifier (URI)

Other commonly used methods:

`int getBaseline()`	Returns the offset of the widget's text baseline from the widget's top
`boundary.void invalidate Drawable(Drawable dr)`	Invalidates the specified `Drawable` object
`void setBaseline(int baseline)`	Sets the offset of the widget's text baseline from the widget's top boundary
`void setImageBitmap(Bitmap map)`	Sets a `Bitmap` object as the content of this `ImageView`
`void setImageDrawable (Drawable drawable)`	Sets a `Drawable` object as the content of this `ImageView`
`final void setColorFilter (int color)`	Sets a tinting option for the image to be displayed
`void setMaxHeight ( int maxHeight)`	Sets the maximum height for this `ImageView`
`void setMaxWidth ( int maxWidth)`	Sets the maximum width for this `ImageView`

READER'S NOTES

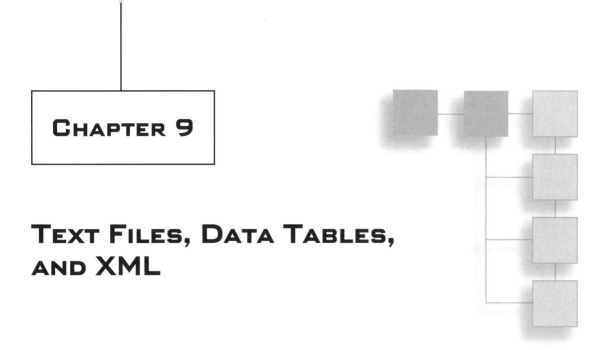

CHAPTER 9

TEXT FILES, DATA TABLES, AND XML

WORKING WITH TEXT FILES

Occasionally your application design requires the ability to store and retrieve persistent data. Normally you can do this in either a freeform text file, such as text notes, or organized data such as a data table. You can accomplish both within an Android application. Regarding text files, there are two choices for the application designer. A text file can be built as part of an application and delivered with the application, but these text files will be read-only. The alternative is to build the application so the user can create, modify, and delete his own files. Both are addressed in this chapter.

To create a text file that the application will use, create a new folder in the res folder by right-clicking the res folder in the Package Explorer and choosing New, Folder. Call the folder raw, which indicates to Eclipse and the Android software development kit (SDK) that it will contain media and plain text files. Right-click on your new folder name and select New, File. Name the file params.txt and place a few words of text in it. The file will serve to simulate some purpose, such as initial setting or information for the user of the application. The first run-through of the application will create an R.java file similar to the following code. Note the class called raw, which came from your folder creation of the same name, and the field called params, based on your naming of the text file. An example is shown here:

```
/* AUTO-GENERATED FILE.  DO NOT MODIFY.
 *
 * This class was automatically generated by the
 * aapt tool from the resource data it found.  It
```

```
 * should not be modified by hand.
 */

package com.sheusi.FileWerx;

public final class R {
   public static final class attr {
   }
   public static final class drawable {
      public static final int icon=0x7f020000;
   }
   public static final class id {
      public static final int FileViewer=0x7f060000;
   }
   public static final class layout {
      public static final int main=0x7f030000;
   }
   public static final class raw {
      public static final int params=0x7f040000;
   }
   public static final class string {
      public static final int app_name=0x7f050001;
      public static final int hello=0x7f050000;
   }
}
```

Next, we modify the main.xml file and add a TextView to display the contents of the text file. In a real application the text file would not necessarily be displayed, and it doesn't have to contain readable text; instead, it may contain data that is only important to the application. However, in this tutorial we will read it just to prove it exists as we are expecting. I added parameters to the TextView element for emphasis. Study this:

```
<?xml version="1.0" encoding="utf-8"?>
<LinearLayout xmlns:android="http://schemas.android.com/apk/res/android"
   android:orientation="vertical"
   android:layout_width="fill_parent"
   android:layout_height="fill_parent"
   >
<TextView
   android:layout_width="fill_parent"
   android:layout_height="wrap_content"
   android:text="@string/hello"
   />
   <TextView
```

```
    android:layout_width="fill_parent"
    android:layout_height="wrap_content"
    android:minLines="3"
    android:maxLines="3"
    android:textColor="#000000"
    android:textSize="12px"
    android:background="#ff0000"
    android:text=""
    android:id="@+id/FileViewer"
    />
</LinearLayout>
```

Finally, we can take a look at the Java file. First, you will notice that we cannot simply link to a raw resource, in this case the text file, by using findViewByID( ), because a file is not an object of the View class. Instead, we use the openRaw-Resource( ) method of the Resources class. The getResources( ) method of the Activity class assigns the Resourses class variable. The openRawResource( ) call returns an InputStream from the file, and we wrap that in a DataInput-Stream object to make the file contents retrievable. Finally, we assign the contents to a String and display it in the TextView we created for that purpose. Study this source code:

```
package com.sheusi.FileWerx;

import android.app.Activity;
import android.os.Bundle;
import android.widget.*;
import java.io.*;
import android.content.res.Resources;
public class FileWerx extends Activity {
  /** Called when the activity is first created. */
  InputStream is=null;
  DataInputStream dis=null;
  Resources myResources=null;
  TextView tv=null;
  @Override
  public void onCreate(Bundle savedInstanceState) {
    super.onCreate(savedInstanceState);
    setContentView(R.layout.main);
    myResources=this.getResources();
    tv=(TextView)findViewById(R.id.FileViewer);
    is=myResources.openRawResource(R.raw.params);
    dis=new DataInputStream(is);
    String someText=null;
```

```
  try{
    someText=dis.readLine();
  }catch(IOException ioe){
   someText="Couldn't read the file";
  }
  tv.setText(someText);
 }
}
```

Media files can be used through a similar process. Remember that "static" resources, or resources that are added at compile time, cannot be written to; they are read-only. However, Android allows users to create, read, modify, and write their own text files through a slightly different process. To illustrate this, we will create a simple text editor by converting our TextView widget to an EditText widget and add three buttons to retrieve, clear, and save the EditText contents to and from a text file called mystuff.txt. For convenience sake, we will hard-code the filename, but it would be just as easy to allow the user to choose a filename through another EditText control. Because we are using an EditText that is only three lines long, this is a small notepad, but it's functional nonetheless. Modify the previous main.xml file to match the following:

```
<?xml version="1.0" encoding="utf-8"?>
<LinearLayout xmlns:android="http://schemas.android.com/apk/res/android"
   android:orientation="vertical"
   android:layout_width="fill_parent"
   android:layout_height="fill_parent"
   >
<TextView
   android:layout_width="fill_parent"
   android:layout_height="wrap_content"
   android:text="@string/hello"
   />
   <EditText
   android:layout_width="fill_parent"
   android:layout_height="wrap_content"
   android:minLines="3"
   android:maxLines="3"
   android:textColor="#000000"
   android:textSize="12px"
   android:background="#ffffff"
   android:text=""
   android:id="@+id/FileViewer"
   />
   <TableLayout
```

```
  android:layout_width="fill_parent"
    android:layout_height="wrap_content"
>
<TableRow
 android:layout_width="wrap_content"
   android:layout_height="wrap_content" >
   <Button
   android:layout_width="wrap_content"
   android:layout_height="wrap_content"
   android:layout_weight=".5"
   android:text="Load File"
   android:id="@+id/loadbutton"/>
    <Button
   android:layout_width="wrap_content"
   android:layout_height="wrap_content"
   android:layout_weight=".5"
   android:text="Clear Viewer"
   android:id="@+id/clearbutton"/>
    <Button
   android:layout_width="wrap_content"
   android:layout_height="wrap_content"
   android:layout_weight=".5"
   android:text="Save File"
   android:id="@+id/savebutton"/>

   </TableRow>
   </TableLayout>
</LinearLayout>
```

The Java code should be written to match the following:

```
package com.sheusi.FileWerx;

import android.app.Activity;
import android.os.Bundle;
import android.widget.*;
import java.io.*;
import android.content.*;
import android.view.*;
public class FileWerx extends Activity {
   /** Called when the activity is first created. */
  Context myContext=null;
  EditText tv=null;
  Button load=null;
  Button clear=null;
  Button save=null;
```

```java
  @Override
  public void onCreate(Bundle savedInstanceState) {
    super.onCreate(savedInstanceState);
    setContentView(R.layout.main);
    myContext=this.getApplicationContext();
    tv=(EditText)findViewById(R.id.FileViewer);
    load=(Button)findViewById(R.id.loadbutton);
    clear=(Button)findViewById(R.id.clearbutton);
    save=(Button)findViewById(R.id.savebutton);
    load.setOnClickListener(new View.OnClickListener(){
      public void onClick(View v){
        try{
          StringBuffer sBuffer=new StringBuffer();
        FileInputStream fis=myContext.openFileInput("mystuff.txt");
        DataInputStream dis=new DataInputStream(fis);
        String someText=null;
        while((someText=dis.readLine())!=null)
          sBuffer.append(someText+"\n");
          dis.close();
          tv.setText(sBuffer.toString());
         }catch(IOException ioe){
          Toast.makeText(myContext,"Couldn't open the
file.",Toast.LENGTH_LONG).show();
         }
       }
    });
    clear.setOnClickListener(new View.OnClickListener(){
      public void onClick(View v){
        tv.setText(null);
      }
    });
    save.setOnClickListener(new View.OnClickListener(){
      public void onClick(View v){
        try{
          FileOutputStream
fos=myContext.openFileOutput("mystuff.txt",MODE_PRIVATE);
          DataOutputStream dos=new DataOutputStream(fos);
          String someText=null;
          someText=tv.getText().toString();
          dos.write(someText.getBytes());
          dos.close();
         }catch(IOException ioe){
        Toast.makeText(myContext,"Couldn't save the file.",Toast.LENGTH_LONG).show();
      }
```

```
      }
    });
  }
}
```

Just as in Java applications for the personal computer, input-output errors are trapped in `try-catch` blocks. If an input/output (I/O) error is encountered, a `Toast` message appears on the screen. You may want to note that files the user creates are stored in the Android device at `/data/data/<package name of application>/files/` in the file system, and each application on the system is treated as its own user account by the operating system. The `Context` class has several file management methods, such as the `.openFileInput( )` and `.openFileOutput( )` methods used in our code. The others are as follows:

```
Context.deleteFile( )
Context.fileList( )
Context.getFilesDir( )
Context.getCacheDir( )
Context.getDir( )
```

WORKING WITH DATA TABLES USING SQLITE

If a freeform text file doesn't seem appropriate to handle data and a more structured, organized solution is required, a SQL-style database may be the solution. Android uses the SQLite database management system. The application programmer has the option of creating the database on the first run of the application or bundling it with the application and activating it on the first run. In this chapter we will create our data table on the first run of the application. A tutorial on how to bundle a database with an application can be found at www.reigndesign.com/blog/using-your-own-sqlite-database-in-android-applications/. The following application is a basic example of using SQLite to manage data; it consists of only a few fields in a single table with a primary key. The example application will allow the user to add records, retrieve and edit records, and delete records based on the primary key. You can find more sophisticated implementations of SQLite databases using iterators and data-binding elsewhere. As simple as this example is, there is a fair amount of code involved, so for clarity sake we will create a new application consisting solely of the SQLite implementation.

In our example, we will keep track of checks written on a checking account using the check number as the primary key. The fields and data types we will use are as follows:

```
number  integer primary key
date    text
payee   text
```

```
amount   real
notes    text
```

Our interface will include an EditText field where we will enter a key value to
search, a button to start the search and retrieve a record, five EditText fields for
our values to be displayed, a button to delete a record, and a button to save a new
or edited record. The reader should realize that this is a stripped-down example,
made as brief as possible to emphasize the database functionality. No effort has been
made to validate appropriate field entries or to format dollar values correctly. These
things would require more code and would tend to obscure the lesson at hand.

Start a new project, and modify the main.xml to look like this:

```xml
<?xml version="1.0" encoding="utf-8"?>
<LinearLayout xmlns:android="http://schemas.android.com/apk/res/android"
   android:orientation="vertical"
   android:layout_width="fill_parent"
   android:layout_height="fill_parent"
>
<TextView
   android:layout_width="fill_parent"
   android:layout_height="wrap_content"
   android:text="Check Register"
/>
<TableLayout
   android:layout_width="fill_parent"
   android:layout_height="wrap_content"
>
<TableRow
   android:layout_width="wrap_content"
   android:layout_height="wrap_content" >
<TextView
   android:layout_width="wrap_content"
   android:layout_height="wrap_content"
   android:layout_weight=".5"
   android:text="Check Number:"/>
<EditText
   android:layout_width="wrap_content"
   android:layout_height="wrap_content"
   android:layout_weight=".5"
   android:text=""
   android:inputType="numberDecimal"
   android:id="@+id/checkno"/>
</TableRow>
<TableRow
```

```
   android:layout_width="wrap_content"
   android:layout_height="wrap_content" >
<Button
   android:layout_width="wrap_content"
   android:layout_height="wrap_content"
   android:layout_weight=".5"
   android:text="Retrieve"
   android:id="@+id/retrievebutton"/>
</TableRow>
<TableRow
   android:layout_width="wrap_content"
   android:layout_height="wrap_content" >
<TextView
   android:layout_width="wrap_content"
   android:layout_height="wrap_content"
   android:layout_weight=".5"
   android:text="Date:"/>
<EditText
   android:layout_width="wrap_content"
   android:layout_height="wrap_content"
   android:layout_weight=".5"
   android:text=""
   android:id="@+id/date"/>
   </TableRow>
   <TableRow
   android:layout_width="wrap_content"
   android:layout_height="wrap_content" >
<TextView
   android:layout_width="wrap_content"
   android:layout_height="wrap_content"
   android:layout_weight=".5"
   android:text="Payee:"/>
<EditText
   android:layout_width="wrap_content"
   android:layout_height="wrap_content"
   android:layout_weight=".5"
   android:text=""
   android:id="@+id/payee"/>
</TableRow>
<TableRow
   android:layout_width="wrap_content"
   android:layout_height="wrap_content" >
<TextView
   android:layout_width="wrap_content"
```

```xml
        android:layout_height="wrap_content"
        android:layout_weight=".5"
        android:text="Amount:"/>
  <EditText
        android:layout_width="wrap_content"
        android:layout_height="wrap_content"
        android:layout_weight=".5"
        android:text=""
        android:inputType="numberDecimal"
        android:id="@+id/amount"/>
  </TableRow>
  <TableRow
        android:layout_width="wrap_content"
        android:layout_height="wrap_content" >
  <TextView
        android:layout_width="wrap_content"
        android:layout_height="wrap_content"
        android:layout_weight=".5"
        android:text="Notes:"/>
  <EditText
        android:layout_width="wrap_content"
        android:layout_height="wrap_content"
        android:layout_weight=".5"
        android:text=""
        android:id="@+id/notes"/>
  </TableRow>
  <TableRow
        android:layout_width="wrap_content"
        android:layout_height="wrap_content" >
  <Button
        android:layout_width="wrap_content"
        android:layout_height="wrap_content"
        android:layout_weight=".5"
        android:text="Save"
        android:id="@+id/savebutton" />
  <Button
        android:layout_width="wrap_content"
        android:layout_height="wrap_content"
        android:layout_weight=".5"
        android:text="Delete from Table"
        android:id="@+id/deletebutton"/>
  </TableRow>
  </TableLayout>
  </LinearLayout>
```

The Java code for the application contains many new classes and methods, so we will address it one or two functions at a time before looking at the full code. First, you will notice a couple of new packages that must be imported: `android.database` and `android.database.sqlite`. For SQLite, the syntax of queries is tightly defined, and the queries have a fixed structure as a method with a specific number of arguments. For example, the actual creation of the database and tables is done with the following code:

```
Checkbook=openOrCreateDatabase("checkbook.db",SQLiteDatabase.CREATE_IF_NECESSARY,
null);
checkbook.setLockingEnabled(true);
  if(checkForTable()!=true)
    checkbook.execSQL("create table checks(number integer primary key not null,
date text,payee text, amount real, notes text)");
```

The `openOrCreateDatabase( )` method is a method of the `Context` class. It takes three arguments: a database name, a mode, and a `SQLiteDatabase.Cursor Factory` (`null` in our case.) This is a convenient construct because the application will create the database on the first run and doesn't need to do it again. Also, there's no intervention from the application user. The need to create the database is managed by a separate testing method in the code, as follows:

```
public boolean checkForTable(){
    Cursor c=checkbook.query("sqlite_master",null,"type=? and name=?",new String[]
{"table","checks"},null,null,null);
  if(c.getCount()>0)
    return true;
  else
    return false;
  }
```

This is the first use of the `query( )` method belonging to the `SQLiteDatabase` class. It takes seven specific arguments:

- Database name
- String array of columns
- Selection
- Selection criteria
- Group by specification
- Having specification
- Order by specification

The second query( ) method has an eighth argument: the "limit" or number of records desired. The use of the keyword null essentially indicates that the field is irrelevant. For instance, the second null in our query means, "just give me all the columns," and the last three in our query mean, "we don't care which order the records are in, how they are grouped, and so on." Literally, the query means, "tell me if there is a table with the name checks. Next, the method examines the list of returned values using a Cursor object. If the Cursor has a count of zero, there is no such table, and if the count is greater than zero, there is such a table. This answer, conveyed back as a true or false value, determines whether the application must create a table.

SQLite data tables have a limited number of data types. For example, there is no "date" data type; we can interpret the date as text or an integer. Our data table consists of a check number as an integer, which is the primary key (we assume that check numbers are unique); an amount as a "real" or floating point number; and the payee, date, and notes as text fields.

Our first button, labeled Retrieve, will search the primary key field called number for a match and populate the EditText controls on the screen with the fields from the matching record. If a record for the entered check number hasn't been created yet, a Toast message informs the user. The user can then search the data table for another record or fill in the fields and append a new record to the table. The following code handles the search:

```
retrieve.setOnClickListener(new View.OnClickListener(){
  public void onClick(View v){
     //if record exists retrieve it; if not, give Toast message
    String key=number.getText().toString();
    Cursor c=checkbook.query("checks",null,"number=?",new
String[]{key},null,null,null,null);
    if(c.getCount()==0)
      Toast.makeText(myContext,"no record exists",Toast.LENGTH_SHORT).show();
    else{
      c.moveToFirst();
      checkdate.setText(c.getString(1));
      payee.setText(c.getString(2));
      amount.setText(String.valueOf(c.getDouble(3)));
      notes.setText(c.getString(4));
    }
  }
});
```

The database code is written into an in-line class definition of an `OnClickListener` for the Retrieve button. You will notice that this time the .query( ) method is the eight-argument version described earlier. Again, the `null` in the second argument position requests all fields from the table. Written in standard SQL, this query would look like the following:

```
select * from checks where number = key;
```

Coders familiar with SQL in the J2SE will see that the `Cursor` class behaves much as the `ResultSet` class in the J2SDK. If a record is found, we enter the fields in the appropriate `EditText` fields.

The next button allows the user to either complete the fields for a new record or edit the fields on a retrieved record, and then save the new or changed record back to the table. The following code does these actions:

```
save.setOnClickListener(new View.OnClickListener(){
  public void onClick(View v){
  // if record exists, update it; if not, insert it
    String key=number.getText().toString();
    Cursor c=checkbook.query("checks",null,"number=?",new
String[]{key},null,null,null,null);
    if(c.getCount()>0){ // it exists, so update
      ContentValues cv=new ContentValues();
      cv.put("date",checkdate.getText().toString());
      cv.put("payee", payee.getText().toString());
      cv.put("amount",Double.parseDouble(amount.getText().toString()));
      cv.put("notes", notes.getText().toString());
      checkbook.update("checks",cv,"number=?",new String[]{key});
    }else{ //doesn't exist so insert
      ContentValues cv=new ContentValues();
      cv.put("number",key);
      cv.put("date",checkdate.getText().toString());
      cv.put("payee", payee.getText().toString());
      cv.put("amount",Double.parseDouble(amount.getText().toString()));
      cv.put("notes", notes.getText().toString());
      checkbook.insert("checks",null,cv);
    }
  }
});
```

The code again queries the data table to see if a record for the given check number exists. If it does, the returned record count is greater than zero, and we use an instance of the `ContentValues` class to store name-value pairs for all the fields we want to save; then we run an `update( )` to store the values. The `update( )` method takes four arguments: the table name, the ContentValues instance, the search field, and the search parameter. If the record count is equal to zero, which means no record currently exists for this check number, we run an insert( ) method to add the new record. The insert( ) method takes three arguments: the table name, the null column hack, and the name-value pairs for the fields. The null column hack field is used to prevent an error if someone attempts to insert a new record with no field-value pairs. In SQL, it might look like this:

```
insert into checks (number,date,payee,amount, notes) values ( mNumber,
mDate,mPayee,mAmount, mNotes);
```

Finally, you need the code for the button that deletes a record. I chose to write a delete query, but I also wanted to clear all the onscreen EditTexts to convey to the user that all trace of the record is deleted. If the fields are clear, the user cannot accidentally save a new record with the same information he just deleted. A Toast message is included to confirm the deletion. The code for the Delete button looks like this:

```
delete.setOnClickListener(new View.OnClickListener(){
  public void onClick(View v){
    String key=number.getText().toString();
    checkbook.delete("checks","number=?",new String[]{key});
    number.setText(null);
    checkdate.setText(null);
    amount.setText(null);
    payee.setText(null);
    notes.setText(null);
    Toast.makeText(myContext,"Record was deleted.",Toast.LENGTH_SHORT).show();
  }
});
```

The delete( ) method accepts three parameters: the table name, the search field, and the search parameter. In SQL, it might look like this:

```
delete from checks where number = mNumber;
```

The Java code in its entirety looks like this.

```
package com.sheusi.CheckBook;

import android.app.Activity;
import android.os.Bundle;
import android.database.*;
import android.database.sqlite.*;
import android.view.*;
import android.widget.*;
```

```java
import android.content.*;

public class CheckBook extends Activity {
    /** Called when the activity is first created. */
    SQLiteDatabase checkbook=null;
    Button retrieve=null;
    Button save=null;
    Button delete=null;
    EditText number=null;
    EditText checkdate=null;
    EditText payee=null;
    EditText amount=null;
    EditText notes=null;
    Context myContext=null;
    @Override
    public void onCreate(Bundle savedInstanceState) {
        super.onCreate(savedInstanceState);
        setContentView(R.layout.main);
        myContext=this.getApplicationContext();
        // build table if it doesn't exist already
checkbook=openOrCreateDatabase("checkbook.db",SQLiteDatabase.CREATE_IF_NECESSARY,
null);
        checkbook.setLockingEnabled(true);
        if(checkForTable()!=true)
            checkbook.execSQL("create table checks(number integer primary key not null,date
text,payee text, amount real, notes text)");
        retrieve=(Button)findViewById(R.id.retrievebutton);
        save=(Button)findViewById(R.id.savebutton);
        delete=(Button)findViewById(R.id.deletebutton);
        number=(EditText)findViewById(R.id.checkno);
        checkdate=(EditText)findViewById(R.id.date);
        payee=(EditText)findViewById(R.id.payee);
        amount=(EditText)findViewById(R.id.amount);
        notes=(EditText)findViewById(R.id.notes);
        retrieve.setOnClickListener(new View.OnClickListener(){
            public void onClick(View v){
        //if record exists, retrieve it; if not, give Toast message
            String key=number.getText().toString();
            Cursor c=checkbook.query("checks",null,"number=?",new
String[]{key},null,null,null,null);
            if(c.getCount()==0)
                Toast.makeText(myContext,"no record exists",Toast.LENGTH_SHORT).show();
            else{
                c.moveToFirst();
```

```
            checkdate.setText(c.getString(1));
            payee.setText(c.getString(2));
            amount.setText(String.valueOf(c.getDouble(3)));
          notes.setText(c.getString(4));
           }
        }
    });
    save.setOnClickListener(new View.OnClickListener(){
      public void onClick(View v){
      // if record exists, update it; if not, insert it
        String key=number.getText().toString();
      Cursor c=checkbook.query("checks",null,"number=?",new
String[]{key},null,null,null,null);
      if(c.getCount()>0){ // it exists, so update
        ContentValues cv=new ContentValues();
          cv.put("date",checkdate.getText().toString());
          cv.put("payee", payee.getText().toString());
          cv.put("amount",Double.parseDouble(amount.getText().toString()));
          cv.put("notes", notes.getText().toString());
          checkbook.update("checks",cv,"number=?",new String[]{key});
      }else{ //doesn't exist, so insert
        ContentValues cv=new ContentValues();
        cv.put("number",key);
          cv.put("date",checkdate.getText().toString());
          cv.put("payee", payee.getText().toString());
          cv.put("amount",Double.parseDouble(amount.getText().toString()));
          cv.put("notes", notes.getText().toString());
          checkbook.insert("checks",null,cv);
      }
       }
    });
    delete.setOnClickListener(new View.OnClickListener(){
      public void onClick(View v){
        String key=number.getText().toString();
        checkbook.delete("checks","number=?",new String[]{key});
        number.setText(null);
         checkdate.setText(null);
        amount.setText(null);
        payee.setText(null);
        notes.setText(null);
        Toast.makeText(myContext,"Record was deleted.",Toast.LENGTH_SHORT).show();
      }
    });
   }
```

```
public boolean checkForTable(){
   Cursor c=checkbook.query("sqlite_master",null,"type=? and name=?",new
String[]{"table","checks"},null,null,null);
   if(c.getCount()>0)
     return true;
   else
     return false;
 }
}
```

When the application runs, the screen should look like Figure 9.1.

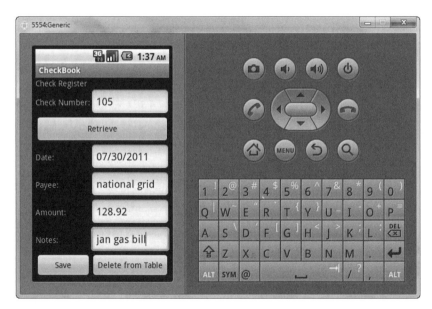

Figure 9.1
Emulator showing CheckBook application.

USING XML FOR DATA EXCHANGE

Having looked at plain text files as a way to manage freeform, unorganized data and SQLite as a way to manage the most structured data, we can turn our attention to a third alternative: XML files. XML, Extensible Markup Language, is a way to manage organized data while allowing us to create our own structure to suit our purpose. For instance, anything from a document to an RSS feed to a web commerce site is structured with XML. What separates XML from an SQL data table is that the XML file is plain text. No database management overhead is needed. Because of this, we don't have to worry about exchanging data between incompatible database management systems; we can convert data from one system to XML, and convert back at the other end. The catch to using XML format is that the documents have to be structurally perfect, or as they say in XML-ese, well-formed. That means that all the tags have to be in perfect pairs, with perfect placement. Whole textbooks are written on XML alone; it is not my intent to teach XML coding here. I will, however, give you examples of how to process XML files you encounter.

XML does not display data. Indeed, there is no inherent manager of XML-coded documents. Because they are simply text files, they need no special handling. They just organize data so the target application can make sense of what is being delivered. This is why formatting of these files must be done correctly. A reasonably competent programmer can write a utility that extracts data from an XML file (we call such a utility a *parser*), but that utility might only be useful for the particular XML format at hand, not XML documents in general. To avoid the burden of custom-coding for every XML file, a programmer can use one of many prewritten utilities that are designed to handle the basic structure of an XML document and not be concerned with the specific tag names and document tag levels. An Android programmer can use packages that are written into the Java Development Kit (JDK), the Android Development Kit (ADK), or even utilities written by third parties.

There are two essential sides to using XML files: assembling and exporting a file, and then disassembling and displaying its contents. The most important to the Android programmer, one might argue, is how to receive and pull the key elements out of the file. This is because the mobile device is more likely to be used to receive and present the contents of an XML file than it is to build one and send it out. As mentioned, several packages are available to handle all the operations necessary to process an XML file. One of the easiest to use is the `org.xmlpull.v1` package. You can learn more about it at www.xmlpull.org. Although the package name does not include "android," it does ship with the ADK, so you don't have to worry about acquiring it before using it in an application.

The example we will look at parses a simple XML file and displays its contents with a small amount of formatting. The XML file, aptly called `book.xml`, is a simple file consisting of two "book" elements with title and author elements in them, surrounded by a root tag called "inventory." Following is a listing of `book.xml`:

```
<?xml version="1.0" encoding="utf-8"?>
<inventory>
<book>
<title>android tutorial</title>
<author>jim sheusi</author>
</book>
```

```
<book>
<title>info security</title>
<author>tom calabrese</author>
</book>
</inventory>
```

As you can see, there is only one instance of the `inventory` tag pair: the root element. However, there are as many or as few `book` pairs as we choose to include. In a SQL data table, there might be an inventory database with a book table. There would be a record in the book table for each book in the inventory. Each book's record would have values for the title and the author. Likewise, we would have two tag pairs, `title` and `author`, within each book pair. Notice that none of the tag pairs overlaps. Each pair opens and closes within another open-close pair. This is what being well-formed means.

The simplest way to look at how an XML file is processed, although it's probably not the most practical, is to include an XML file in the application, similar to what we did with the text file we viewed in an earlier example. To do this, we create a subfolder in the resources (`res`) folder in the Package Explorer of Eclipse. Just right-click on the `res` folder, choose New from the menu, and pick Folder. Name the new folder `xml`, in lowercase. Remember that the structure of your projects directory tree will impact how the `R.java` file will be formed, thus impacting how we use `R.java` in our application source code. You need to be consistent.

When that is done, right-click on the new `xml` folder and choose New, then File, and you will get a clean editing window. Name the file `book.xml` and type in the previous example.

The application itself only needs an `EditText` field, so your `main.xml` file can look like the following example:

```
<?xml version="1.0" encoding="utf-8"?>
<LinearLayout xmlns:android="http://schemas.android.com/apk/res/android"
   android:orientation="vertical"
   android:layout_width="fill_parent"
   android:layout_height="fill_parent"
   >
<TextView
   android:layout_width="fill_parent"
   android:layout_height="wrap_content"
   android:text="XML Parser"
/>
<EditText
   android:layout_width="fill_parent"
```

```
      android:layout_height="wrap_content"
      android:id="@+id/et1"
/>
</LinearLayout>
```

Eclipse includes a `TextView` in all generated `main.xml` files for new projects, so I left it and just changed the `text` element to `XML Parser` as an application label.

The `main.xml` file is straightforward enough. Let's turn our attention to the Java code. As usual, pay attention to the import statements:

```java
package com.sheusi.XMLWork;

import android.app.Activity;
import android.content.res.Resources;
import android.os.Bundle;
import java.io.*;
import android.widget.*;
import android.util.Log;
import org.xmlpull.v1.*;
import android.content.res.*;

public class XMLWorkActivity extends Activity {
  /** Called when the activity is first created. */
  EditText et1=null;
  InputStream is=null;

  Resources myRes=null;
  @Override
  public void onCreate(Bundle savedInstanceState){
    super.onCreate(savedInstanceState);
    setContentView(R.layout.main);
    et1=(EditText)findViewById(R.id.et1);
    this.getRecordsFromXML(this);
  }
  private void getRecordsFromXML(Activity activity){
    try{

      Resources res=activity.getResources();
      XmlResourceParser xrp=res.getXml(R.xml.book);
      xrp.next();// skips descriptor line in XML file
      int eventType=xrp.getEventType();
      while(eventType!=XmlPullParser.END_DOCUMENT){
      //while we haven't reached the end of the xml file
        if(eventType==XmlPullParser.START_DOCUMENT){
          et1.append("My Library:\n");
```

```
      }
    if(eventType==XmlPullParser.START_TAG){
      if(xrp.getName().equals("book "))
    et1.append("\n"+xrp.getName()+":");
      if(xrp.getName().equals("author"))
        et1.append(" by ");
      if(xrp.getName().equals("title"))
      et1.append("\n");
      }
    if(eventType==XmlPullParser.END_TAG){}
    if(eventType==XmlPullParser.TEXT){
      et1.append(xrp.getText());
      }
    eventType=xrp.next();
    }
  }catch(Exception e){
    et1.append("App Error");
  Log.e("xml_error",e.getMessage());
  }
 }
}
```

There is a try-catch block in the code. In this case, I chose to use the all-inclusive Exception class, rather than one or more of the more specific child classes. Java programmers are familiar with these; for the novice, they're a graceful way to deal with exceptions, which usually manifest themselves as run-time errors, or as problems in the code that will crash the application at run-time. If the exception is a "checked" one, Eclipse will usually notify you of the potential run-time error and flag it in the editor, but that isn't always the case. This sometimes happens with I/O errors. At any rate, Java programmers usually use the associated method, .print-StackTrace( ), in the catch block to display exception information in the console of the development machine. Unfortunately, there is no console for the emulator itself or the actual Android device for that matter, at least for the average user. The alternative is to send a message to the LogCat in the Eclipse Debug perspective or to an EditText, TextView, or Toast in the application. Of course, you want to write your code so that a run-time error never occurs, at least to the extent that you can control it. Such displays are only ideal for the development stage. The whole run-time-error effort takes practice on the part of the developer. No matter how careful you are as a developer, Murphy's Law dictates that some user will find some way to cause an error in a running application. He may have the GPS service shut off when it is essential to the application, network access may not be present, or the SD card may not be present, just to name a few possibilities. Exception handling was made for these cases. But let's continue with the matter at hand. Let's look at the actual XML processing portion of the application.

```
Resources res=activity.getResources();
XmlResourceParser xrp=res.getXml(R.xml.junk);
xrp.next();// skips descriptor line in XML file
int eventType=xrp.getEventType();
  while(eventType!=XmlPullParser.END_DOCUMENT){
  //while we haven't reached the end of the xml file
  if(eventType==XmlPullParser.START_DOCUMENT){
    et1.append("My Library:\n");
  }
  if(eventType==XmlPullParser.START_TAG){
    if(xrp.getName().equals("book "))
      et1.append("\n"+xrp.getName()+":");
    if(xrp.getName().equals("author"))
      et1.append(" by ");
    if(xrp.getName().equals("title"))
      et1.append("\n");
  }
  if(eventType==XmlPullParser.END_TAG){ }
  if(eventType==XmlPullParser.TEXT){
    et1.append(xrp.getText());
  }
  eventType=xrp.next();
}
```

Remember that `activity` is the parameter passed to the XML processing method. It represents the main activity of the application here. We create an instance of the `XmlResourceParser` class and assign it the file that we put in the `xml` subfolder of the `res` folder.

The rest is a matter of matching tags with various operations in the application. The only "unmatched" tag is the XML descriptor line displayed here:

```
<?xml version="1.0" encoding="utf-8"?>
```

The line `xrp.next();` causes the code to skip this line in processing. For the rest of the XML file, if it is structured correctly, or well-formed, the built-in methods of the `XmlResourceParser` class will handle the rest of the XML file. In general, the `getName( )` method refers to what's in the tags, and `getText( )` refers to the values between the tags.

The `XmlPullParser` class has several symbolic constants that represent integer variables. The symbolic constants have names that adequately describe the events that can be encountered when processing the incoming XML document stream. The START_DOCUMENT and END_DOCUMENT are associated with the outermost and innermost tags in the document, and the START_TAG and END_TAG events are associated with other pairs as they are encountered. The parser uses the TEXT symbolic constant to represent the encounter with data between tags.

We use the getName( ) method to match the tags encountered with the various tags we are interested in using (the assumption is that the programmer knows the tag names he is expecting at coding time), and then we pull the data value from between the tags with the getText( ) method. If your intent is to display data as it is encountered as I do in this example, then base formatting of data on the various tags, such as adding a tab or carriage return to offset certain fields or records, or putting certain values in certain text-based widgets. On the other hand, if you are loading an ArrayList or appending to a SQLite data table, you would match text between certain tags with corresponding members or fields in your list or table.

Processing XML tables takes practice. There is no way around it. However, if you pick an XML processing package to stick with and learn the classes and methods in it, XML processing will become second nature. Figure 9.2 shows a screen shot of how the application code renders the book.xml file.

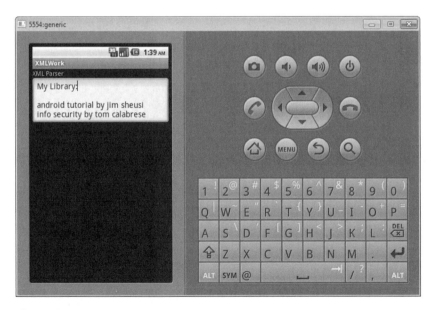

Figure 9.2
Emulator displaying the rendering of an XML file.

Follow-Up

1. Research and study the fundamentals of XML from the web page at www.w3. org/XML and similar resources.

2. Research and study the fundamentals of SQLite DBMS from the web page at www.sqlite.org and similar resources.

3. Review the file management methods of the Context class.

4. CRUD is an acronym for the database record management processes of Create, Read, Update, and Delete. Fill in the following chart with the appropriate methods and parameter lists for these operations using the SQLiteDatabase class for Android.

CRUD Operation	Appropriate Method's Name	Method's Parameter List
Create		
Read		
Update		
Delete		

5. Complete the following table with the four query( ) methods used by the SQLiteDatabase class.

Parameter List	Description of Parameters

KEY CLASSES USED IN THIS CHAPTER

Resources

Class	`Resources`
Package	`android.content.res`
Extends	`java.lang.Object`
Overview	This is a class used for accessing the application's resources. It essentially allows program access to the contents of the `res` folder of the project. The programmer can acquire access to the application's resources by using the `getResources( )` method of the application's `Activity` class.

Methods used in this chapter:

`XmlResourceParser getXml( int id)`	Returns an `XmlResourceParser` through which you can read a generic XML resource

Other commonly used methods:

`CharSequence getText( int id)`	Returns a string value associated with the particular ID
`Drawable getDrawable( int id)`	Returns a `Drawable` object associated with the particular ID
`String getResourceName(int id)`	Returns the name of the resource associated with the particular ID
`int getColor( )`	Returns a color integer associated with a particular resource ID
`DisplayMetrics getDisplay Metrics( )`	Returns the current display metrics that are in effect for this resource object
`InputStream openRawResource (int id)`	Open a data stream for reading a raw resource
`void parseBundleExtras(Xml ResourceParser parser, Bundle outBundle)`	Parses a series of <extra> tags from the XML file specified
`Configuration get Configuration( )`	Returns the current configuration that is in effect for this resource object

SQLiteDatabase

Class	SQLiteDatabase
Package	android.database.sqlite
Extends	android.database.sqlite.SQLiteClosable
Overview	This class exposes methods used to manage a SQLite database.

Methods used in this chapter:

void setImageResource LockingEnabled(boolean lockingEnabled)	Controls whether the database is made thread-safe
void execSQL(String sql)	Executes a single SQL statement that is not a SELECT statement or any other statement that returns data
Cursor query(String table, String[] columns, String selection, String[ ] selection args, String having, String groupBy, String orderBy)	Returns a result set of using the given query parameters
long insert(String table, String nullColumnHack, ContentValues values)	Inserts a row into a database table
int delete(String table, String whereClause, String[ ] whereArgs)	Method for deleting rows in a database table
int update(String table, ContentValues values, String whereClause, String[ ] whereArgs)	Method for updating rows in a database table

Other commonly used methods:

void close( )	Closes the database
void beginTransaction()	Begins a transaction in EXCLUSIVE mode
void endTransaction()	Ends the transaction

`void execSQL(String sqlStatement)`	Executes a single SQL statement that is not a `SELECT` statement or any other statement that returns data
`boolean isOpen()`	Returns whether the database is open
`boolean isReadOnly()`	Returns whether the database is opened as read-only
`void setLockingEnabled (boolean lockingEnabled)`	Controls whether or not the database is made thread-safe by using locks around critical sections
Multiple `query( )` methods not listed above	

Cursor

Class	`Cursor` (interface)
Package	`android.database`
Extends	n/a
Overview	The interface provides random access to the result set returned by a query.

Methods used in this chapter:

`abstract int getCount( )`	Returns the number of rows in the `Cursor` (result set)
`abstract boolean moveToFirst( )`	Moves the `Cursor` to the first row

Other commonly used methods:

`abstract boolean moveToNext( )`	Moves the `Cursor` to the next row
`abstract boolean moveToLast( )`	Moves the `Cursor` to the last row
`abstract boolean moveTo Position(int position)`	Moves the `Cursor` to an absolute position
`abstract int getColumnCount( )`	Returns the number of columns in the `Cursor` (result set)
`abstract int getInt ( int columnIndex)`	Returns the `int` value from the column specified by `columnIndex`
`abstract double getDouble ( int columnIndex)`	Returns the double value from the column specified by `columnIndex`
`abstract void close()`	Closes the cursor, releasing all of its resources and making it invalid
`abstract double getDouble(int columnIndex)`	Returns the value of the requested column as a `Double`
`abstract float getFloat (int columnIndex)`	Returns the value of the requested column index as a `Float`
`abstract long getLong (int columnIndex)`	Returns the value of the requested column as a `Long`
`abstract String getString (int columnIndex)`	Returns the value of the requested column as a `String`
`abstract boolean isFirst()`	Returns whether the cursor is pointing to the first row
`abstract boolean isLast()`	Returns whether the cursor is pointing to the last row

ContentValues

Class	`ContentValues`
Package	`android.content`
Extends	`java.lang.Object`
Overview	This class is used to store a set of values that the `Content Resolver` can process.

Methods used in this chapter:

`void put(String key, String value)`	Adds a value of `String` type to the set
`void put(String key, Integer value)`	Adds a value of `Integer` type to the set
`void put(String key, Double value)`	Adds a value of `Double` type to the set

Other commonly used methods:

`void put(String key, Long value)`	Adds a value of `Long` type to the set
`Void put(String key, Float value)`	Adds a value of `Float` type to the set
`Void put(String key, Boolean value)`	Adds a value of `Boolean` type to the set
`Double getAsDouble(String key)`	Retrieves a value and converts it to the `Double` type
`Float getAsFloat(String key)`	Retrieves a value and converts it to the `Float` type
`Integer getAsInteger(String key)`	Retrieves a value and converts it to the `Integer` type
`Long getAsLong(String key)`	Retrieves a value and converts it to the `Long` type
`String getAsString(String key)`	Retrieves a value and converts it to the `String` type
`void remove(String key)`	Removes a single value
`int size()`	Returns the number of values

XMLPullParser

Class	XMLPullParser (interface)
Package	xmlpull.v1
Extends	n/a
Overview	An interface that defines parsing functionality

Methods used in this chapter:

None; provides various symbolic constants

Other commonly used methods:

abstract int getAttribute Count( )	Returns the number of attributes for the current start tag.
abstract String getAttribute Name(int index)	Returns the local name of the attribute specified by the index parameter if namespaces are enabled, or just the attribute name if namespaces are disabled.
abstract String getAttribute Value(int index)	Returns the given attribute's value.
abstract String getAttribute Type(int index)	Returns the type of the specified attribute. If the parser is nonvalidating it must return CDATA.
abstract int getDepth()	Returns the current depth of the element.
abstract int getEventType()	Returns the type of the current event (START_TAG, END_TAG, and so on).
abstract String getInput Encoding()	Returns the input encoding, if known; null otherwise.
abstract int getLineNumber()	Returns the current line number starting at 1.
abstract String getText()	Returns the text content of the current event as a String.

XMLResourceParser

Class	XMLResourceParser (interface)
Package	android.content.res
Extends	Implements AttributeSet, XmlPullParser
Overview	The XML parsing interface returned for an XML resource. This is the standard XmlPullParser interface.

Methods used in this chapter: (inherited from XmlPullParser)

abstract int getAttribute Count( )	Returns the number of attributes for the current start tag
abstract String getAttribute Name(int index)	Returns the local name of the attribute specified by the index parameter if namespaces are enabled, or just the attribute name if namespaces are disabled
abstract String getAttribute Value(int index)	Returns the given attribute's value
abstract int next()	Gets next parsing event

Other commonly used methods:

abstract void close( )	Closes this interface to the resource

READER'S NOTES

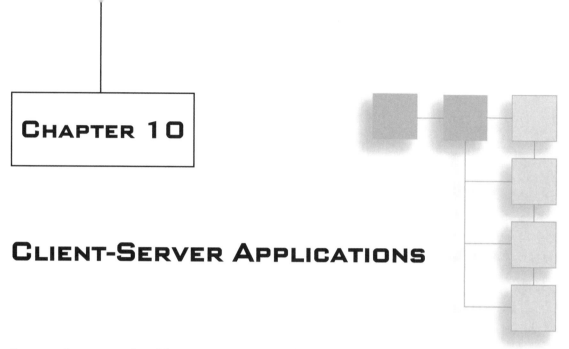

CHAPTER 10

CLIENT-SERVER APPLICATIONS

Smart phones and tablets are amazing devices, capable of most things that a typical personal computer is capable of. But like personal computers in the modern world, they are limited without access to a network. With the proliferation of software as a service (SaaS), cloud computing, and email, it's getting harder and harder to be productive with a stand-alone device. John Gage, cofounder of SUN Microsystems, said it best: "The network is the computer." The same can be said for mobile devices.

Some view mobile devices as a source of entertainment, and they certainly are, but I concentrate on development of information-providing applications, many using a network or the Internet as a source. Mobile devices make convenient client-side devices for client-server applications. Developing client-server applications for the mobile device is no more difficult than developing for personal computers. In fact, the `java.net` package works nicely on Android devices. The example application we will build sends a text string to a server and receives the text string back with an added confirmation. As you probably assume, you can build both the client side and the server side on the same Eclipse platform. However, you will probably want to run the server-side application on another machine with another IP address on the same local area network. If you have written any client-server applications, you are likely familiar with IP addresses and port numbers; this application uses port 8888, an arbitrary choice. You can use just about any port number you want; just stay away from the numbers zero through 1023. Because port numbers are 16-bit values, there are 65,536 choices. However, they are broken into the groups shown here:

0 to 1023	Well-known port numbers
1024 to 49151	Registered ports
49152 to 65536	Dynamic or private ports

Because you are likely to be doing this project on a local area network using unroutable IP addresses, the port choice isn't critical. For convenience sake, the server-side source code for this experiment is listed here:

```java
import java.io.*;
import java.net.*;
import java.util.*;
public class SimpleJavaServer {
   public static final int PORT=8888;
   public static void main(String args[]){
     new SimpleJavaServer().doIt();
   }
   public void doIt(){
     String received="";
     try{
       ServerSocket ss = new ServerSocket( PORT );
       while( true ){
         Socket sock = ss.accept();
         BufferedReader in =
new BufferedReader(new InputStreamReader(
sock.getInputStream() ) );
         received=in.readLine();
         System.out.println(received);
         OutputStreamWriter out =
new OutputStreamWriter(
sock.getOutputStream() );
         BufferedWriter bw=new BufferedWriter(out);
         bw.write(received +" received by server \n");
           bw.flush();
       }
     } catch( Exception e ){
         e.printStackTrace();
     }
   }
}
```

On the client side, there are some preliminary steps we need to take before getting into code. First, we have to be sure the device's networking capability is available to the application, so we need to add a permission line in the manifest file. The complete file is listed next. Look for the line that starts with <uses-permission.

```xml
<?xml version="1.0" encoding="utf-8"?>
<manifest xmlns:android="http://schemas.android.com/apk/res/android"
    package="com.sheusi.SimpleAndroidClient"
    android:versionCode="1"
    android:versionName="1.0">
  <uses-sdk android:minSdkVersion="8" />
  <uses-permission android:name="android.permission.INTERNET"></uses-permission>

  <application android:icon="@drawable/icon" android:label="@string/app_name">
    <activity android:name=".SimpleAndroidClientActivity"
            android:label="@string/app_name">
      <intent-filter>
        <action android:name="android.intent.action.MAIN" />
        <category android:name="android.intent.category.LAUNCHER" />
      </intent-filter>
    </activity>

  </application>
</manifest>
```

The user interface will simply be two EditText widgets: one for the text going out to the server, and the other to display the message that comes back. There's also a Button widget between the two EditText widgets to start the transmission to the server. The server's IP address is hard-coded in this example, as is the port number. That certainly restricts the utility of the application, but after all it is just an experiment. You could modify that application to accept a target IP address and port number from the user through an additional EditText or two if you so desire. If you stay with the hard-coded values, you must obtain the IP of the server-side machine. That is simple enough using the ipconfig console command on a Windows machine or the ifconfig command on a Linux machine. There are plenty of other ways to find a machine's IP address.

Following is the listing for the Java file:

```java
package com.sheusi.SimpleAndroidClient;

import android.app.Activity;
import android.os.Bundle;
import android.widget.*;
import android.view.*;
import java.net.*;
import java.io.*;
```

```
import android.util.*;
public class SimpleAndroidClientActivity extends Activity {
   /** Called when the activity is first created. */
   EditText etsend=null;
   EditText etreceive=null;
   Button b1=null;
   @Override
   public void onCreate(Bundle savedInstanceState) {
      super.onCreate(savedInstanceState);
      setContentView(R.layout.main);
      etsend=(EditText)findViewById(R.id.sendString);
      etreceive=(EditText)findViewById(R.id.receiveString);
      b1=(Button)findViewById(R.id.connect);
      b1.setOnClickListener(new View.OnClickListener(){
        public void onClick(View v){
           Socket s=null;
         String response="";
         try{
             InetSocketAddress sa=new InetSocketAddress("192.168.1.231",8888);
           s=new Socket();
           s.connect(sa,2000);
       OutputStreamWriter osw=new OutputStreamWriter(s.getOutputStream());
           osw.write(etsend.getText().toString()+"\n");
              osw.flush();
InputStreamReader isr =new InputStreamReader(s.getInputStream());
        BufferedReader br=new BufferedReader(isr);
         response=br.readLine();
            etreceive.append(response+"\n");
            s.close();
         }catch(IOException ioe){
            Log.e("Code Error",ioe.getMessage());
            etreceive.setText("Couldn't connect with server");
          }
        }
     });
   }
}
```

You will notice that we use the java.net and java.io packages to do most of the work. In fact, the code in the listener for the Button object is almost a mirror image of what is in the server-side code. The connect( ) method used here takes two parameters. One is the InetSocketAddress variable, and the other is a timeout value. The number 2000 represents 2000 milliseconds, or 2 seconds. After 2 seconds, the application will give up trying to reach the server and print an error message in the second EditText field. Otherwise, the application would hang trying to connect to a nonexistent server. Don't forget to change the IP address in the previous listing to the IP address on your server machine, and be sure to start the server application before you try the client-side application in the emulator. Figure 10.1 shows a screen shot of the application as it would appear if the server is found and has responded to the client.

Figure 10.1
Emulator showing successful client-server connection.

We have looked at how to parse an XML file delivered with an application and just finished looking at a simple client-server model. These two skills when combined open a world of possibilities for the application programmer. There is an infinite source of data on the Internet that is transferred in XML format, from government data that is open to the public to craigslist postings. The universality of XML makes data available to almost any platform, including Android!

The example we will build will allow us to submit an address to Google and retrieve the geocodes for the location. Although the Android appliance may be able to deliver the codes for its current location, we may want to know the location of some other address or landmark, and if desired calculate the distance as the crow flies. We might also want to catalog specific locations and their geocodes and display them on a map.

Google has a specific web address and query format we will use to request location data. Google also has restrictions on how many queries can be made in a given period, but the restriction is well beyond the needs of a casual user. You can find details on the process, formats used for returned data, and explanations of the data at http://code.google.com/apis/maps/documentation/geocoding/.

We are concerned with XML. Essentially what we need to supply to Google is a prefix, a correctly formatted address, and a sensor setting. The sensor setting tells Google whether or not the requesting device is able to detect its own location. The prefix looks like the following:

http://maps.googleapis.com/maps/api/geocode/xml?address=

This is followed immediately by the address we are interested in, formatted properly as we will see a little later. Finally, the sensor setting is set to either `true` or `false`. For the emulator, `true` works fine. The entry will look like this:

&sensor = true

All strung together with a correctly formatted address, the query string would look like this:

http://maps.googleapis.com/maps/api/geocode/xml?address=30+n+main+st+
providence,+ri&sensor=true

Notice that all the spaces in the location description are replaced with +, commas are allowed, and a zip code is not necessary. In fact, the XML file returned will include the zip code for the address.

If you place the string listed previously in the address bar of your favorite browser, it will return the following XML file. Try it now if you would like:

```
<GeocodeResponse>
<status>OK</status>
<result>
<type>street_address</type>
<formatted_address>30 N Main St, Providence, RI 02903, USA</formatted_address>
<address_component>
<long_name>30</long_name>
<short_name>30</short_name>
<type>street_number</type>
</address_component>
<address_component>
<long_name>N Main St</long_name>
<short_name>N Main St</short_name>
```

```
<type>route</type>
</address_component>
<address_component>
<long_name>Downtown Providence</long_name>
<short_name>Downtown Providence</short_name>
<type>neighborhood</type>
<type>political</type>
</address_component>
<address_component>
<long_name>Providence</long_name>
<short_name>Providence</short_name>
<type>locality</type>
<type>political</type>
</address_component>
<address_component>
<long_name>Providence</long_name>
<short_name>Providence</short_name>
<type>administrative_area_level_2</type>
<type>political</type>
</address_component>
<address_component>
<long_name>Rhode Island</long_name>
<short_name>RI</short_name>
<type>administrative_area_level_1</type>
<type>political</type>
</address_component>
<address_component>
<long_name>United States</long_name>
<short_name>US</short_name>
<type>country</type>
<type>political</type>
</address_component>
<address_component>
<long_name>02903</long_name>
<short_name>02903</short_name>
<type>postal_code</type>
</address_component>
<geometry>
<location>
<lat>41.8264179</lat>
<lng>-71.4085410</lng>
</location>
<location_type>ROOFTOP</location_type>
<viewport>
```

```
<southwest>
<lat>41.8250689</lat>
<lng>-71.4098900</lng>
</southwest>
<northeast>
<lat>41.8277669</lat>
<lng>-71.4071920</lng>
</northeast>
</viewport>
</geometry>
</result>
</GeocodeResponse>
```

There is a wealth of information here. You may also notice that there are several levels of nested tag pairs, a possibility we must address whenever we parse an XML file. Also, there are three latitude and longitude pairs. We will be interested in the first one only, because the second two are what Google considers to be the northeast and southwest corners of the location. For a complete description of all the tags, read the complete document at http://code.google.com/apis/maps/documentation/geocoding/.

Our application is concerned with two processes: dealing with an XML file as it streams into the Android device, and extracting only the fields we are interested in. In this case, the fields are lat and lng, but again, you will notice that there are three pairs of these. How will the application decide which pair to use? Upon close scrutiny, you will notice that the first pair is different from the other two by how far the tags are nested. The first pair is five levels deep, after <GeocodeResponse>, <result>, <geometry>, and <location>. The other two are six levels deep.

The XMLPullParser class has a method, .getDepth( ), that allows us to determine and use as a condition the level of nesting for particular tags that interest us. This method along with others we saw in the previous XML example will allow us to collect geocodes for a given address.

Before we look at any code or screen design, we must remember to add the Internet permission to our manifest file. Here is an example:

```
<?xml version="1.0" encoding="utf-8"?>
<manifest xmlns:android="http://schemas.android.com/apk/res/android"
    package="com.sheusi.AddressData"
    android:versionCode="1"
    android:versionName="1.0">
    <uses-sdk android:minSdkVersion="8" />
    <uses-permission android:name="android.permission.INTERNET"></uses-permission>
    <application android:icon="@drawable/icon" android:label="@string/app_name">
```

```
        <activity android:name=".AddressDataActivity"
                android:label="@string/app_name">
            <intent-filter>
                <action android:name="android.intent.action.MAIN" />
                <category android:name="android.intent.category.LAUNCHER" />
            </intent-filter>
        </activity>
    </application>
</manifest>
```

For this experiment, we merely need two EditText fields to collect the address, city, and state for which the user wants to retrieve geocodes; a Button to start the process; and a third EditText field to display the results. We need to substitute plus signs (+) for all the spaces in the address before they are built into the query string to be sent to Google, so you as the designer may use one, two, or three EditText fields for data entry; it's your call. I chose two. You will also want to put descriptive labels above each field using TextViews to make your application more user friendly. Following is the XML file used in this sample application:

```
<?xml version="1.0" encoding="utf-8"?>
<LinearLayout xmlns:android="http://schemas.android.com/apk/res/android"
    android:orientation="vertical"
    android:layout_width="fill_parent"
    android:layout_height="fill_parent"
    >
<TextView
    android:layout_width="fill_parent"
    android:layout_height="wrap_content"
    android:text="Street Address"
/>
<EditText
    android:layout_width="fill_parent"
    android:layout_height="wrap_content"
    android:text=""
    android:id="@+id/requestAddress"
    android:textSize="15pt"
    />
<TextView
    android:layout_width="fill_parent"
    android:layout_height="wrap_content"
    android:text="City, State"
/>
<EditText
    android:layout_width="fill_parent"
```

```
      android:layout_height="wrap_content"
      android:text=""
      android:id="@+id/requestCityState"
      android:textSize="15pt"
      />
<Button
 android:layout_width="fill_parent"
      android:layout_height="wrap_content"
      android:text="Click to send request"
      android:id="@+id/makeRequest"
       android:textSize="15pt"
      />
<EditText
      android:layout_width="fill_parent"
      android:layout_height="wrap_content"
      android:text=""
       android:textSize="15pt"
      android:id="@+id/responseInfo"
      />
</LinearLayout>
```

The Java code for the example is fairly standard for an HTTP connection and uses Java packages and classes for networking. However, you should pay particular attention to how the stream is connected to the XMLPullParser object. Most of all, take note of the use of the tag, text, and depth detection methods and their related code. In this example, we used the onStop( ) method to close the application. This will clear the application to prevent it from being brought back with old data. This technique could be used for any application if it seems appropriate. Following is the Java code for the application:

```
package com.sheusi.AddressData;

import android.app.Activity;
import android.os.Bundle;
import java.io.*;
import android.view.*;
import android.widget.*;
import android.util.Log;
import org.xmlpull.v1.*;
import java.net.*;

public class AddressDataActivity extends Activity {
   Button b=null;
```

```
EditText addr=null;
EditText citst=null;
EditText info=null;
/** Called when the activity is first created. */
@Override
public void onCreate(Bundle savedInstanceState) {
   super.onCreate(savedInstanceState);
   setContentView(R.layout.main);
   b=(Button)findViewById(R.id.makeRequest);
   addr=(EditText)findViewById(R.id.requestAddress);
   citst=(EditText)findViewById(R.id.requestCityState);
   info=(EditText)findViewById(R.id.responseInfo);
   b.setOnClickListener(new View.OnClickListener(){
      public void onClick(View v){
         googleIt();
      }
   });


 }
public void googleIt(){
   XmlPullParserFactory factory=null;
   try{
      String maddr=addr.getText().toString();
      String mcitst=citst.getText().toString();
      maddr=maddr.replace(" ","+");
      mcitst=mcitst.replace(" ","+");
      final String querystring=

"http://maps.googleapis.com/maps/api/geocode/xml?address="+maddr+"+"+mcitst
+"&sensor=true";
      URL myUrl = new URL(querystring);
      HttpURLConnection myConnection = (HttpURLConnection)myUrl.openConnection();
      InputStreamReader isr = new InputStreamReader(
      myConnection.getInputStream());
      BufferedReader br=new BufferedReader(isr);
      try{
         factory = XmlPullParserFactory.newInstance();
         factory.setNamespaceAware(true);
         XmlPullParser xpp = factory.newPullParser();
         xpp.setInput(isr);
         String curtag="";
         xpp.next();// skips descriptor line in XML file
         int eventType=xpp.getEventType();
         while(eventType!=XmlPullParser.END_DOCUMENT){
            //while we haven't reached the end of the xml file
```

```
                  if(eventType==XmlPullParser.START_DOCUMENT){ }
                  // do nothing for start document tag
                  if(eventType==XmlPullParser.START_TAG & xpp.getDepth()==5){
                    if(xpp.getName().equals("lng"))
                      curtag="lng";
                    if(xpp.getName().equals("lat"))
                      curtag="lat";
                  }
                  if(eventType==XmlPullParser.END_TAG){ }
                  // do nothing for end tags
                  if(eventType==XmlPullParser.TEXT ){
                    if (curtag=="lat")
                      info.append("\nlat: "+xpp.getText());
                    if (curtag=="lng")
                      info.append("\nlong: "+xpp.getText());
                    curtag="";
                  }
                  eventType=xpp.next();
              }// end while loop when end is reached
        br.close();
      }catch(XmlPullParserException xppe){
        Log.e("Code Error",xppe.getMessage());
        info.setText("Couldn't parse the XML stream");
      }
  }catch(IOException ioe){
        Log.e("Code Error",ioe.getMessage());
            info.setText("Couldn't connect with server");
  }
      } //ends googleIt

@Override
    public void onStop(){
      super.onStop();
      this.finish();
    }
}
```

You should realize that collected data from an XML stream doesn't need to be displayed on the screen, and the query parameters don't need to be entered on the screen. The process could be adapted to run in the background when an application starts to complete, update, or rebuild a data table, for example. Figure 10.2 shows the running application with results displayed in the third EditText field.

Figure 10.2
Emulator showing AddressData application.

FOLLOW-UP

1. Research IP address classes and complete the following chart.

Class	Address Range	Nonroutable Addresses in This Class (Used for Local Area Networks)
A		
B		
C		
D		
E		

2. Fill in the following chart of possible port numbers. (You can find them in this chapter.)

Range	Description

3. Research uniform resource locators (URLs) at http://archive.ncsa.uiuc.edu/SDG/software/Mosaic/Demo/url-primer.html.

KEY CLASSES USED IN THIS CHAPTER

Socket

Class	`Socket`
Package	`java.net`
Extends	`java.lang.Object`
Overview	Please review http://docs.oracle.com/javase/1.4.2/docs/ api/java/net/Socket.html for details on the Java `Socket` class.

Methods used in this chapter:

```
InputStream getInputStream( )
OutputStream getOutputStream( )
void connect(socketAddress address, int timeout)
```

Other commonly used methods:

```
int getLocalPort( )
InetAddress getInetAddress( )
void close( )
boolean getKeepAlive()
int getPort()
SocketAddress getRemoteSocketAddress()
int getSoTimeout()
boolean isBound()
boolean isConnected()
void setKeepAlive(boolean on)
void setSoTimeOut()
```

ServerSocket

Class	`ServerSocket`
Package	`java.net`
Extends	`java.lang.Object`
Overview	Please review http://docs.oracle.com/javase/1.4.2/docs/ api/java/net/ServerSocket.html for details on the Java `ServerSocket` class.

Methods used in this chapter:

```
Socket accept( )
```

Other commonly used methods:

```
int getLocalPort()
InetAddress getInetAddress()
void close()
int getSoTimeout()
boolean isBound()
boolean isClosed()
void bind(SocketAddress endpoint)
```

HttpURLConnection

Class	`HttpURLConnection`
Package	`java.net`
Extends	`java.lang.Object`
Overview	Please review http://docs.oracle.com/javase/1.3/docs/api/ java/net/HttpURLConnection.html for details on the Java `HttpURLConnection` class.

Methods used in this chapter:

```
InputStream getInputStream( )
```

Other commonly used methods:

```
String getRequestMethod( )
abstract void disconnect( )
abstract boolean usingProxy( )
abstract void disconnect()
Permission getPermission()
String getResponseMessage()
int getResponseCode()
```

URL

Class	`URL`
Package	`java.net`
Extends	`java.lang.Object`
Overview	Please review http://docs.oracle.com/javase/1.4.2/docs/api/ java/net/URL.html for details on the Java `URL` class.

Methods used in this chapter:

```
URLConnection openConnection( )
```

Other commonly used methods:

```
InputStream openStream( )
Uri toUri( )
int getPort( )
String getHost()
String getFile()
String getPath()
int getPort()
Object getContent()
```

READER'S NOTES

CHAPTER 11

PUBLISHING YOUR APPLICATION

The real gratification in writing an Android application comes with publishing it. However, there is plenty of prep work necessary before the author can do that. One of the first things a prospective publisher should consider is what graphics are necessary for the application. Even if there are no graphics in the application, which is the case for all the examples in this tutorial except the map marker, graphics should be included for launch icons at least. The address http://developer.android.com/guide/practices/ui_guidelines/icon_design.html will give you information on the size requirements for graphics for specific purposes such as launch icons, and acceptable formats as well. On this page you will also find a link to a set of templates to work with. A little experience with Photoshop or Gimp is helpful here.

The following is a guide to publishing an application in general: http://developer.android.com/guide/publishing/publishing.html

One thing that is ideal about publishing Android applications is that there are many markets, only one of which is the official market, market.android.com. Publishing here costs the publisher $25 for a publishing account (at the time of this writing) and allows the author to publish any number of applications. The number of Android markets is growing all the time.

After the author has built the entire application—including placing all support files such as media files, necessary graphics, text files, and so on in their appropriate directories—and has read the publication guide, it's time to build the deliverable application. This exists as a single file with the extension .apk.

You can think of the `.apk` file for Android as you would the `.jar` file for a personal computer.

No Android device will install an unsigned application. When you are developing your application, Eclipse will give it a debug key. If you intend to publish an application, it will need a production key. A production-signed application will not install over a debug-signed application, and upgrades to an application must be signed with the same production key or the upgrade will not install. The Java Development Kit (JDK) that you are using contains a program called `keytool` that allows you to generate a production key you can use to sign your application. It is in the `/bin` directory of your JDK directory. You can learn about the `keytool` utility and its sister utility, `jarsigner`, and the switches that go with them at http://download.oracle.com/javase/1.5.0/docs/tooldocs/windows/keytool.html.

A sample `keytool` command used in a console screen might be as follows. Note that `myandroid.keystore` is a fictitious name; your keystore file will have a different name.

```
keytool -genkey -v -keystore myandroid.keystore -alias myandroid -keyalg RSA -validity
10000 (enter)
```

You will then be asked a series of questions that will be used to develop the key. Finally, you will be asked for a password. When you enter the password, you will receive a confirmation that a key was created and stored, such as

```
[Storing myandroid.keystore]
```

It is a good idea to note the password you used and the location of the keystore on your development computer. If you wish, record them here:

Password: _____

Location of keystore: _____

You will need them both in the future.

To create an unsigned `.apk` file, right-click on your project in the Package Explorer in Eclipse, choose Android Tools in the menu, and then choose Export Unsigned Package. You will be asked where to store the unsigned `.apk` file. Make a note of your choice. Next, you will need to sign your application package with your newly generated key.

You will use the Jarsigner program to sign your application with your key. Jarsigner is located in the same directory as the keystore program. An example of the command-line string follows:

```
jarsigner -verbose -keystore <path>/myandroid.keystore
<path>/myApplicationName.apk myandroid (enter)
```

You will be prompted for the password you used to create the key (hopefully you saved it), and you will receive several confirmations that components of your application are being signed. We use the -verbose switch in the command line to receive these confirmations; they are a visible verification that the signing is taking place.

Remember in Chapter 6, "Find a Location with Google Maps," that I mentioned you would need a production key for Google Maps? Now you are able to obtain the fingerprint. While you are in the correct directory and have a console screen, type this:

```
keytool -list -alias myandroid -keystore myandroid.keystore (enter)
```

This will give you a new set of hex values. For safekeeping, write them on the line that follows:

Carry out the same procedure you used in Chapter 6, only this time use the new production hex values. The website will give you a new key string. You can note that string here:

Be sure to change the string in any XML file that contains a map element when it comes time to publish.

You may have noticed that when you created the unsigned .apk file, Eclipse warned you that you still needed to sign it and to zipalign it. The zipalign process aids in the installation of the .apk file to a device. The zipalign tool is part of the Android development software that you downloaded, found in the /tools subdirectory of the android-sdk directory. A typical command-line string for using zipalign follows:

```
zipalign -v 4 <path>/sourcename.apk <path>/targetname.apk (enter)
```

where the sourcename.apk represents your signed .apk file and the targetname.apk is the name of your signed and zipaligned .apk file. Note that these names should be different, or the target file should be in another directory. Also, be sure to add the .apk extension to these entries; it isn't automatic.

Your application is now ready for market. If you later modify your application and intend to upload the upgrade to the market, be sure to change the version number in the Android Manifest file according to Android guidelines.

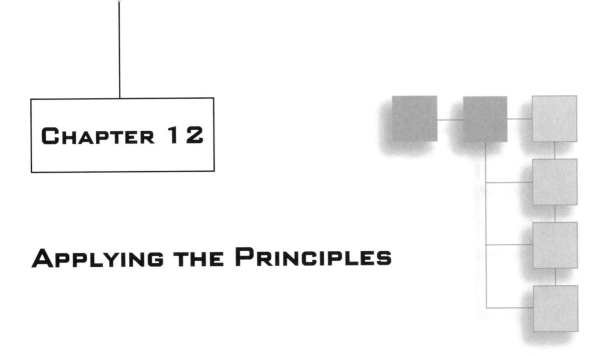

CHAPTER 12

APPLYING THE PRINCIPLES

PROJECT 1: A PHOTO-DIALER

Up to this point we have concentrated on specific aspects of application building, such as screen design, Google maps, multiscreen applications, and so on. Let's combine several of those principles to build an interesting and fun-to-use application. Anyone with a smart phone has probably used the on-board contact list to make a call. On the Android, it looks something like Figure 12.1.

The user could add a tiny icon or thumbnail for a person on the contact list, but that is still a little impersonal. To make a call, the user must start the contact list app, scroll the contact list until the target is reached, click the name, and then click again for the call. Wouldn't it be fun to bring up a picture of your family or favorite people and be able to start a call by touching a face? Well, we know how to display a photograph, we know how to save files, and we know how to use built-in services on the device, so let's give this a try.

The new concept presented here is how to detect a touch on the screen and record the coordinates. The coordinates will make the location the face of a particular person in the image, and that location will be associated with a particular phone number. The application will need two parts. First, we will have to load the image, detect the coordinates of the faces, and associate those coordinates with a phone number. Then we have to save all these items together, either in a text file or in a data table. For our small proof-of-concept exercise, we will use a text file and delimit (separate) the different data items with a colon. Likewise, for the proof-of-concept application, we will take one image and store it with the application at development time. Later

245

245

Figure 12.1
Android mobile phone's built-in phone directory.

on you might want to figure out how to take images stored in the gallery from photographs taken by the device's camera or from uploads and associate them with a set of phone numbers.

The second part of the application will require us to retrieve all the coordinate and phone number match-ups from persistent storage and display the saved image at start-up. When the application user touches a face, we will detect the coordinates and match them to the sets we saved to determine the correct phone number to call; then we will dial the number.

Note

If we use two different activities for configuring and dialing and two different screens, the image must be displayed in the same place all the time. This is because the coordinates of the touch spot will be based on the device's screen, not the image. We may want to think about locking the orientation of the device as well.

We must make some changes to the manifest file for this application. First, the application requests permission to use the phone component of the device. Obviously, this application is intended for a smart phone, not a tablet or other device without phone service, so we must be sure to assign an emulator that offers phone service. Next, the manifest must include a line to add the second activity—namely, the configuration screen. Here is the manifest file:

```xml
<?xml version="1.0" encoding="utf-8"?>
<manifest xmlns:android="http://schemas.android.com/apk/res/android"
    package="com.sheusi.familyDialer"
    android:versionCode="1"
    android:versionName="1.0">
  <uses-sdk android:minSdkVersion="8" />
  <uses-permission android:name="android.permission.CALL_PHONE"></uses-permission>
  <application android:icon="@drawable/icon" android:label="@string/app_name">
    <activity android:name=".FamDialer"
            android:label="@string/app_name">
      <intent-filter>
        <action android:name="android.intent.action.MAIN" />
        <category android:name="android.intent.category.LAUNCHER" />
      </intent-filter>
    </activity>
    <activity android:name=".ConfigScreen"></activity>
  </application>
</manifest>
```

Before we get too far, let's take care of our family photo. Find a suitable photo in digital form that you want to use on your dialer. Ideally, it should be in portrait mode, not landscape, because we will be freezing our application to stay in portrait mode in the Java code. Files should be named in all lowercase and have no spaces in the name (for example, family.jpg works well), so you may need to rename your photo. You can find general details on external resources at http://developer.android.com/guide/topics/resources/providing-resources.html.

To build the image into your application, create a folder called drawable inside the res folder, and copy the image into that folder. Now it will be ready to use in your application.

This application has two XML files used to configure the different screens: one to configure the coordinate phone number sets, and the other to dial the phone. (Incidentally, you can reuse the configure screen if one of the phone numbers changes, but you must reconfigure the entire screen at that time. If you choose to pursue improvements on this application and move to a SQLite table, you only need to change one particular coordinate: phone number record.) As stated previously, the controls must match exactly in terms of size because the coordinates of touch spots must remain consistent between the screens. They belong to the screen, not the image. As you look at the two XML files, you will notice that the component list is the same; only the text in the controls is different. What follows are the two XML files. The `main.xml` file is listed first, followed by the `configure.xml` file. Remember: both belong in the `layout` subdirectory of the `res` directory.

main.xml

```
<?xml version="1.0" encoding="utf-8"?>
<LinearLayout xmlns:android="http://schemas.android.com/apk/res/android"
   android:orientation="vertical"
   android:layout_width="fill_parent"
   android:layout_height="fill_parent"
   >
<TextView
   android:layout_width="fill_parent"
   android:layout_height="wrap_content"
   android:text="Dial Screen"
   android:textColor="#ffffff"
/>
<Button
   android:layout_width="fill_parent"
   android:layout_height="wrap_content"
   android:id="@+id/config"
   android:textColor="#00BB00"
   android:text="Go to configuration screen.">
</Button>
<ImageView
   android:layout_width="fill_parent"
   android:layout_height="fill_parent"
   android:id="@+id/family"
   android:src="@drawable/dadnbro"
/>
</LinearLayout>
```

configure.xml

```
<?xml version="1.0" encoding="utf-8"?>
<LinearLayout xmlns:android="http://schemas.android.com/apk/res/android"
   android:orientation="vertical"
   android:layout_width="fill_parent"
   android:layout_height="fill_parent"
   >
<TextView
   android:layout_width="fill_parent"
   android:layout_height="wrap_content"
```

```
    android:text="Configuration Screen"
    android:textColor="#ffffff"
/>
<Button
    android:layout_width="fill_parent"
    android:layout_height="wrap_content"
    android:id="@+id/saver"
    android:text="Save New Configuration"
    android:textColor="#FF0000">
</Button>

  <ImageView
    android:layout_width="fill_parent"
    android:layout_height="fill_parent"
    android:id="@+id/family"
    android:src="@drawable/dadnbro"
/>

</LinearLayout>
```

Notice that we add some colors to the text on the buttons. In the main.xml (dial screen), we use a subtle shade of green that is easier on the eyes than the full green; on the configuration screen, we use red. We also specify bright white on the text in the TextViews to make the labels a little more prominent.

In this application, there is actually a third class that defines a touch spot phone number set, simply called dialspot. It holds upper and lower bounds for the touched spot's horizontal and vertical touch locations (X and Y values) and the phone number that goes with them. The class is shared by both activities, so it makes sense to write it just once. The upper and lower bounds for the horizontal and vertical coordinates are calculated on the configuration screen when a spot is touched to allow subsequent touches of the dial screen to be slightly off the mark. In other words, instead of the user having to touch the *exact* coordinate spot to dial the phone, she can touch a 20 × 20 pixel square surrounding the exact spot. See Figure 12.2.

The size of the touch area, specified by the +10 and −10 in the configuration code, are arbitrary. You can make them bigger or smaller as you see fit, considering the picture you want to use, how many faces are in it, how big the faces are, and so on. You can fine-tune this aspect of the application by trying a certain setting, running the application in the emulator, and clicking areas with the mouse to see if they are detectable. If they are, the dialer will start when the click is made.

Figure 12.2
Illustration of defined touch area for family photograph.

The class is simple. It contains the necessary fields, a constructor, and several get methods to return values when necessary. The dialspot is listed here:

```
package com.sheusi.familyDialer;

class dialspot{
private float upperx;
private float uppery;
private float lowerx;
private float lowery;
private String pnumber;
public dialspot(float ux, float uy, float lx, float ly, String pn){
  upperx=ux;
  uppery=uy;
  lowerx=lx;
  lowery=ly;
  pnumber=pn;
}

public float getUx(){
  return upperx;
  }
```

```
public float getUy(){
  return uppery;
}
public float getLx(){
  return lowerx;
}
public float getLy(){
  return lowery;
}
public String getPnumber(){
  return pnumber;
}
}
```

The Java code for the configuration screen uses the `config.xml` file listed earlier. It associates an `OnTouchListener` with the `ImageView` that holds the family portrait and uses a `Button` object to save the configuration data to a text file on the device. When the user touches the image, the listener will save the coordinate of the touch it detected, calculate the bounds for the "sweet spot," and trigger an `AlertDialog` to collect the phone number to be associated with the spot that was touched. Creation of `AlertDialog` objects was covered in Chapter 7, "Multiscreen Applications." The code used to create the `AlertDialog` appears here:

```
AlertDialog.Builder alert= new AlertDialog.Builder(this);
alert.setTitle("Phone Number for this photo spot.");
alert.setMessage("Enter phone number here");
// Set an EditText view to get user input
final EditText input = new EditText(myContext);
alert.setView(input);
alert.setPositiveButton("OK", new DialogInterface.OnClickListener() {
  public void onClick(DialogInterface dialog, int whichButton) {
    String value = input.getText().toString();
  pn=value.replace("-","");
  spots.add(new dialspot(ux,uy,lx,ly,pn));
  }
});
phonodialog=alert.create();
```

Clicking the OK button on the dialog removes the hyphens from the phone number entered and adds a new instance of a `dialspot` to the `ArrayList` defined in the main code. Normally, an `AlertDialog` includes a No button, but this button and its listener can be eliminated if the designer chooses.

Finally, when all the spots are marked and the phone numbers are associated, the Button widget when clicked, converts all the ArrayList elements to lines of colon-delimited text and saves the text file on the system. On an Android device, the operating system creates a user for each process and allocates each its own storage space. Files are stored in subdirectories named for the package containing the application. The text created in this process will be stored at /data/data/com.sheusi.familyDialer/files.

Using the adb utility from a command line on the development machine, we can use the shell command to attach to a running emulator. After navigating to the appropriate directory, we can get a listing of the files, and if desired read the file using the cat command (a Linux command similar to the DOS/Windows type command). Figure 12.3 is a screen shot of a terminal screen using adb shell. The pwd command lists the path to our current location (the Linux command for Print Working Directory), and the ls command lists the files in the directory. (ls is short for *list*.)

Figure 12.3
Illustration of shell screen on development machine attached to the emulator using the adb utility.

Keeping in mind that phone numbers can change, the user can "reconfigure" the portrait at any time. A provision is made in the code so that any time the user reconfigures the application, the old configuration file is deleted and a new file is saved in its place. Unless the file is opened with the MODE_APPEND parameter, the file is overwritten automatically, but I added a line to specifically delete the file for instruction purposes. The MODE_PRIVATE parameter restricts access to this file to the application that created it: technically this application's user ID on the system. Following is the code used to configure the image:

```
package com.sheusi.familyDialer;

import android.app.Activity;
import android.os.Bundle;
import android.widget.*;
import android.view.*;
import android.app.AlertDialog;
import android.content.DialogInterface;
```

```java
import android.content.Context;
import java.io.*;
import java.util.ArrayList;
import android.content.pm.ActivityInfo;
public class ConfigScreen extends Activity {
/** Called when the activity is first created. */
  Button b=null;
  ArrayList<dialspot> spots=new ArrayList<dialspot>();
  private float ux;
  private float uy;
  private float lx;
  private float ly;
  private String pn;
  ImageView iv=null;
  Context myContext=null;
  AlertDialog phonodialog=null;
  @Override
    public void onCreate(Bundle savedInstanceState) {
      super.onCreate(savedInstanceState);
      this.setRequestedOrientation(
      ActivityInfo.SCREEN_ORIENTATION_PORTRAIT);
      setContentView(R.layout.configure);
      myContext=this.getApplicationContext();
      iv=(ImageView)findViewById(R.id.family);
      b=(Button)findViewById(R.id.saver);
      b.setOnClickListener(new View.OnClickListener(){
      public void onClick(View v){
        saveConfigFile();
       //return from this activity
        finish();
      }
    });
    iv.setOnTouchListener(new View.OnTouchListener(){
      public boolean onTouch(View v,MotionEvent me){
        ux=me.getX()+10.0f;
        lx=me.getX()-10.0f;
        uy=me.getY()+10.0f;
        ly=me.getY()-10.0f;
        phonodialog.show();
        return true;
      }
    });
```

```
        Toast.makeText(this.getApplicationContext(),"Touch each face and enter phone
number, touch SAVE button when finished.",Toast.LENGTH_LONG).show();
      //begin dialog box design
      AlertDialog.Builder alert= new AlertDialog.Builder(this);
      alert.setTitle("Phone Number for this photo spot.");
      alert.setMessage("Enter phone number here");
      // Set an EditText view to get user input
      final EditText input = new EditText(myContext);
      alert.setView(input);
      alert.setPositiveButton("Ok", new DialogInterface.OnClickListener() {
        public void onClick(DialogInterface dialog, int whichButton) {
          String value = input.getText().toString();
          pn=value.replace("-","");
          spots.add(new dialspot(ux,uy,lx,ly,pn));
        }
      });
      phonodialog=alert.create();
      }
  public void saveConfigFile(){
    try{
    //delete previous config file if there is one
      this.getApplicationContext().deleteFile("config.txt");
      FileOutputStream
fos=this.getApplicationContext().openFileOutput("config.txt",MODE_PRIVATE);
      DataOutputStream dos=new DataOutputStream(fos);
      dialspot currentspot=null;
      for(int ct=0;ct<spots.size();++ct){
        currentspot=spots.get(ct);
        dos.writeBytes(String.valueOf(currentspot.getUx())+":"+
        String.valueOf(currentspot.getUy())+":"+
String.valueOf(currentspot.getLx())+":"+
String.valueOf(currentspot.getLy())+":"+
currentspot.getPnumber()+"\n");
      }
      dos.close();
    }catch(Exception e){
      Toast.makeText(this.getApplicationContext(),"Couldn't save file.",
Toast.LENGTH_LONG).show();
    }
  }
}
```

The actual family dialer screen uses the `main.xml` file for its screen design. Again, it is identical in layout to the `configure.xml` file to ensure that the appropriate touches occur in the correct spots on both screens. In place of the Save Configuration button, this screen has a button that switches the user to the configuration screen. When the application opens, it checks to see if the image has been configured by attempting to open the `config.txt` file. If the file is missing, it causes an exception, and the catch block pops up a `Toast` message to inform the user that she must run the configuration process.

If the file does in fact open, each line that contains a coordinate-phone number pairing is parsed at the colons and loaded back into an `ArrayList` object. When a face is touched, each list member's coordinates are checked against the touched spot's coordinates, and the appropriate phone number is sent to the dialer activity. The Java file for the dialer screen is listed here:

```
package com.sheusi.familyDialer;
import android.app.Activity;
import android.net.Uri;
import android.os.Bundle;
import android.widget.*;
import android.view.*;
import android.content.Intent;
import java.io.*;
import java.util.ArrayList;
import android.content.Context;
import android.content.pm.ActivityInfo;
public class FamDialer extends Activity {
  /** Called when the activity is first created. */
  ImageView iv=null;
  Button config=null;
  Context myContext;
  ArrayList<dialspot> spots=new ArrayList<dialspot>();
  @Override
  public void onCreate(Bundle savedInstanceState) {
    super.onCreate(savedInstanceState);
    setContentView(R.layout.main);
    this.setRequestedOrientation(ActivityInfo.SCREEN_ORIENTATION_PORTRAIT);
    myContext=this.getApplicationContext();
    iv=(ImageView)findViewById(R.id.family);
    config=(Button)findViewById(R.id.config);
    config.setOnClickListener(new View.OnClickListener(){
```

```java
    public void onClick(View v) {
    //switch activities here
    Intent myIntent=new Intent(myContext,ConfigScreen.class);
    startActivity(myIntent);
    }
  });
  iv.setOnTouchListener(new View.OnTouchListener(){
    public boolean onTouch(View v,MotionEvent me){
      dialspot currentspot=null;
      for(int ct=0;ct<spots.size();++ct){
        currentspot=spots.get(ct);
        if(currentspot.getLx()<=me.getX()& currentspot.getUx()>=me.getX()
& currentspot.getLy()<=me.getY() & currentspot.getUy()>=me.getY()){
          Uri theNumber=Uri.parse("tel:"+currentspot.getPnumber());
        Intent dialMe=new Intent(Intent.ACTION_CALL,theNumber);
          startActivity(dialMe);
          finish();
        }//end if
      }//end for
    return true;
    }
  });
  this.loadConfigFile();
  }
  public void loadConfigFile(){
   String[] coords=null;
   try{
     StringBuffer sbuffer=new StringBuffer();
     FileInputStream fis=
this.getApplicationContext().openFileInput("config.txt");
     DataInputStream dis=new DataInputStream(fis);
     String someText=null;
     while((someText=dis.readLine())!=null){
       coords=someText.split(":");
       spots.add(new dialspot(Float.parseFloat(coords[0]),Float.parseFloat(coords[1]),
Float.parseFloat(coords[2]),Float.parseFloat(coords[3]),coords[4]));
     }
     dis.close();
    }catch(IOException ioe){
       Toast.makeText(this.getApplicationContext(),"Photo not configured, switch to
config screen.",Toast.LENGTH_LONG).show();
    }
  }
}
```

Figure 12.4
Emulator running the Family Dialer application.

Finally, the running application should look like Figure 12.4.

The ImageDisplay application presented in Chapter 8, "Working with Images," showed how to pull and display images from the device's image gallery. Using the.getPath( ) method of the Uri class, the developer could add a field to the dialspot class to track the actual image by path and name. Using this method to identify different images, the developer could configure any number of images in the gallery for the application.

PROJECT 2: A FLASH MOB APPLICATION

Our second application to encompass several of the principles and techniques we have seen so far is to develop a "flash mob" application based on the client-server model. Wikipedia defines a flash mob as follows:

> *A flash mob is a group of people who assemble suddenly in a public place, perform an unusual and sometimes seemingly pointless act for a brief time, then disperse, often for the purposes of entertainment, satire, artistic expression or—in rare cases—violence. Flash mobs are organized via telecommunications, social media, or viral emails.*

> *—http://en.wikipedia.org/wiki/Flashmob*

The object of our application is to allow the mobile user to both post a location for meeting and be able to view meetings posted in her area. Posted "mob scene" locations will be visible on a map. Details associated with the location will also be available to the user. Because the nature of a flash mob is spontaneity, the application will only retrieve mob scenes for the current calendar day. The application will be as simple as possible in all respects, but the reader can modify it according to her wishes. For instance, no login or other authentication is built in to the demonstration. Likewise, there is no filtering of users; all users will have access to all mob scenes, and any mob scene posted by a user will be accessible to all other users. In the first version of the application, data is transferred between client and server as strings of plain text that is delimited by colons. In the second version, data will be transferred from the server to the client in XML format.

The server side of the application in this demonstration is based on the LAMP stack model. The server that this demonstration was built on is actually a rented virtual machine in the cloud running CentOS Linux with a MySQL data table to hold the posted mob scenes. For novices, the term LAMP is an acronym for the four opensource products: Linux (an operating system), Apache (web server), MySQL (database management system), and PHP. (The "P" could as easily represent Perl or Python, two other scripting languages.) LAMP is a popular platform for prototyping; Facebook and many other successful websites and services were and are developed on LAMP stacks.

The Server Side

The server side of the application could be handled many different ways, but because we are concentrating on Java in this book, I chose Java to make a server program. The server program needs to run two threads: one to receive queries from mobile devices, and the other to collect new "mob scenes" from the field. The threads post to and retrieve from a MySQL data table. Each thread also listens on its own port number; this code includes ports 6050 and 6060, but the reader can use any two she wants, just being careful to avoid conflicts with other applications or services. The port number 3306 is typically associated (default) with MySQL. The program could be run on any computer connected to a LAN for demonstration purposes, assuming MySQL is available. The reader can substitute any other database management system as long as the driver is available for Java. In the code, where the reader sees `myaccount` and `mypassword`, she should substitute the appropriate values. Also, although the data table could be named `flashmob` as it is here, the database will likely have a different name. Hence, substitute a valid database name where you see mydatabase.

The data table includes the fields shown in Table 12.1.

Table 12.1   Field Descriptions for the Flash Mob Application's Data Table

Field Name	Data Type	Details
id	integer	This field should be set to primary key, not null, auto-incrementing.
lat	integer (or floating point)	See the paragraph following this table.
lon	integer (or floating point)	See the paragraph following this table.
ts	timestamp	Unlike a regular time or date field, this field automatically saves the date and time at which this record was created.
details	char(255)	This field holds 255 characters to describe the mob scene and could include a street address, times, and more.

The latitude and longitude fields could be an integer, string, or floating point data type; the necessary conversions just need to be done when they are used on the mobile application. The GPS service will retrieve them as floating point numbers on the device, but when they are ultimately mapped, they will be converted to integers representing microdegrees. I chose to convert the value to an integer before it is sent from the mobile device and stored.

Here is the Java code for the server side of the application:

```
import java.io.BufferedReader;
import java.io.BufferedWriter;
import java.io.IOException;
import java.io.InputStream;
import java.io.InputStreamReader;
import java.io.OutputStream;
import java.io.OutputStreamWriter;
import java.net.ServerSocket;
import java.net.Socket;
```

```java
import java.sql.*;
public class FlashMobServer{

public static void main(String[] args) {
  FlashMobServer fms= new FlashMobServer();
  Outgoing og=new Outgoing();
  Incoming ic=new Incoming();
  og.start();
  ic.start();
}
} //ends FlashMobServer class

class Outgoing extends Thread{
  ServerSocket ss;
  public void run(){
    try{
      ss=new ServerSocket(6060);
    }catch(IOException ioe){
      ioe.printStackTrace();
    }
    while(true){
     try{
        Socket s1=ss.accept();
        OutputStream os=s1.getOutputStream();
        OutputStreamWriter osr=new OutputStreamWriter(os);
        BufferedWriter bw=new BufferedWriter(osr);
        bw.write(queryTable());
        bw.flush();
        s1.close();
      }catch(Exception e){
        e.printStackTrace();
      }
    }//ends while
  }//ends run


  public String queryTable() {
    String returnData="";
    try{
      Class.forName("com.mysql.jdbc.Driver");
      Connection myConnection =
```

```
DriverManager.getConnection("jdbc:mysql://localhost:3306/mydatabase",
"myaccount","mypassword");
    Statement myStatement=myConnection.createStatement();
    ResultSet myResultSet=
myStatement.executeQuery("select lat,lon,details from flashmob where
date(ts)=curdate()");
    ResultSetMetaData rsmd=myResultSet.getMetaData();
    int colCount=rsmd.getColumnCount();
    myResultSet.beforeFirst();
    while(myResultSet.next()){

        for(int ii=1;ii<colCount;ii++){
        returnData=returnData+String.valueOf(myResultSet.getInt(ii))+":";
      } //ends for
       returnData=returnData+myResultSet.getString(colCount)+"\n";
    }//ends while
    myConnection.close();
    return returnData;
  }catch(Exception e){
    e.printStackTrace();
    return "Error";
    }
  }//ends method queryTable

}//ends Outgoing class

class Incoming extends Thread{
  ServerSocket ss=null;
  public void run(){
    try{
      ss=new ServerSocket(6050);
    }catch(IOException ioe){}
    while(true){
      try{
        Socket s1=ss.accept();
        InputStream is=s1.getInputStream();
        InputStreamReader isr=new InputStreamReader(is);
        BufferedReader br=new BufferedReader(isr);
        String greeting=br.readLine();
        String[] newrecord;
        newrecord=greeting.split(":");
        Class.forName("com.mysql.jdbc.Driver");
        Connection myConnection =
```

```
    riverManager.getConnection("jdbc:mysql://localhost:3306/mydatabase","myaccount",
"mypassword");
        Statement myStatement=myConnection.createStatement();
        String fields= newrecord[0]+","+newrecord[1]+",'"+newrecord[2]+"'";
        boolean junk= myStatement.execute("insert into flashmob(lat,lon,details)
values ("+fields+")");
        myConnection.close();
        s1.close();
      }catch(Exception e){
        e.printStackTrace();
      }
    }
  }//ends run
} //ends class
```

If the reader wants to run the server application on a Linux machine, she can do so in the background and leave it running even after logging off by using the following command:

```
nohup java -cp ./ FlashMobServer & (enter)
```

The command `nohup` is an abbreviation for "no hangup," which instructs the Linux system to leave this process running after the user logs out. Normally, all processes started as children of the login process are terminated when the login session is terminated. The next piece, `java -cp ./ FlashMobServer`, instructs Linux to run the server program and reports that the class path for the application is in the current directory. The class path switch may not be necessary for the reader; it depends on the configuration of the server computer. Finally, the ampersand (&) is the Linux instruction to run the application in the background. This allows the Linux user to have access to the terminal again. Some experience with Linux is helpful here, but the reader can easily run the server application on a Windows machine if she desires. Occasionally you see the term "Logger" in the catch blocks of the server code. If you run the server programs in the background, you shouldn't try to print anything to the screen, because it defeats the "background" concept. Java has a class called `Logger` that simplifies writing to a log file. Pursue this if you really want to check for exceptions at some point.

The Client (Mobile Device) Side

The mobile client for the system allows a user to post a mob scene and retrieve all mob scenes from a single screen. The screen uses a `MapView` object to display the user's location on a map of the vicinity of the user's current location. This "current location" of the user is used as the site of the mob scene that the user might ultimately want to post, which complies with the flash mob's "get here now" theme. When the application is started on the mobile device, it assesses its location and immediately polls the flash mob server to see if any mob scenes have been posted for that given day. If so, they are added to the map on the screen. Details of the mob scene are available to the user through a touch on a marked location. If the user is interested in the mob scene and close by, she can attend.

Because the mobile application requires GPS services and use of the Internet to post to the server, permissions are required for the application and must be included in the application's manifest file. Pay close attention to the uses-permission elements in the manifest file. Also, notice that the Google Maps library is included. The manifest file for the application is listed here:

```
<?xml version="1.0" encoding="utf-8"?>
<manifest xmlns:android="http://schemas.android.com/apk/res/android"
    package="com.sheusi.FlashMob"
    android:versionCode="1"
    android:versionName="1.0">
  <uses-sdk android:minSdkVersion="8" />
  <uses-permission android:name="android.permission.INTERNET"></uses-permission>
  <uses-permission android:name="android.permission.ACCESS_FINE_LOCATION">
</uses-permission>
  <uses-permission android:name="android.permission.ACCESS_COARSE_LOCATION">
</uses-permission>

  <application android:icon="@drawable/icon" android:label="@string/app_name">
    <activity android:name=".FlashMobActivity"
          android:label="@string/app_name">
      <intent-filter>
        <action android:name="android.intent.action.MAIN" />
        <category android:name="android.intent.category.LAUNCHER" />
      </intent-filter>
    </activity>
    <uses-library android:name="com.google.android.maps"/>
  </application>
</manifest>
```

Because the application gets the job done with only one screen, we only need one XML file: main.xml. This XML file includes a map view with the debug key in it, as we saw in an earlier application. It also includes several buttons evenly spaced in a table row. What follows is the main.xml file for the application. You will notice that, again, I removed some of the debug key so it is rendered unusable. It is worth noting that each debug key is unique to the installation of the development toolkits, so if one reinstalls the development environment or changes machines, the key will no longer work, and the map will not show on the emulator. Notice that the

MapView control belongs to the Google Maps package, not the Android packages, so the actual fully qualified name for the control is listed in the XML file.

```xml
<?xml version="1.0" encoding="utf-8"?>
<LinearLayout
xmlns:android="http://schemas.android.com/apk/res/android"
xmlns:myapp="http://schemas.android.com/apk/res/com.sheusi.FlashMob"
    android:orientation="vertical"
    android:layout_width="fill_parent"
    android:layout_height="wrap_content">
<TextView android:layout_width="fill_parent"
    android:layout_height="wrap_content"
    android:textColor="#AA0000"
    android:textSize="9pt"
    android:background="#ffffff"
    android:text="Enter mobscene details below" />
<EditText android:id="@+id/et1"
    android:layout_width="fill_parent"
    android:layout_height="wrap_content"
    android:focusable="true"
    android:singleLine="false"
    android:text="" />
<TableLayout android:orientation="horizontal"
    android:layout_height="wrap_content"
    android:layout_width="fill_parent">
<TableRow>
<Button android:id="@+id/blast"
    android:layout_column="1"
    android:layout_width="wrap_content"
    android:layout_height="wrap_content"
    android:layout_weight=".5"
    android:singleLine="true"
    android:text="POST IT!" />
<Button android:id="@+id/refresh"
    android:layout_column="2"
    android:layout_width="wrap_content"
    android:layout_height="wrap_content"
    android:singleLine="true"
    android:text="REFRESH MAP"
    android:layout_weight=".5" />
<Button android:id="@+id/exit"
    android:layout_column="3"
    android:layout_width="wrap_content"
    android:layout_height="wrap_content"
```

```
    android:singleLine="true"
    android:layout_weight=".5"
    android:text="EXIT" />
</TableRow>
</TableLayout>
<com.google.android.maps.MapView
    android:id="@+id/map"
    android:clickable="true"
    android:apiKey="0GblCZOB21yK********dz7mUHMtB-Um2S8w_hg"
    android:layout_width="wrap_content"
    android:layout_height="wrap_content" />
</LinearLayout>
```

There are two markers used in this application. One marks the location of the device (and hopefully its user) on the map. The other is used in a layer that contains all the mob scenes to mark their locations on the map. These two image files should be stored in a subdirectory under the res directory called drawable. The programmer needs to create that directory. The icon images themselves can be made by the developer using Gimp or a similar image editor, and ideally should have a transparent background. Another alternative is to find desirable icons on the Internet.

The actual Java code for the application is more complicated than most seen so far in the book. Therefore, it will be displayed first, and parts of it will be discussed individually. The Java code follows:

```
package com.sheusi.FlashMob;

import java.io.*;
import java.net.*;
import java.util.ArrayList;
import android.app.AlertDialog;
import android.os.Bundle;
import android.view.View.OnClickListener;
import android.view.*;
import android.widget.*;
import android.content.*;
import android.location.*;
import android.view.ViewGroup.*;
import android.graphics.drawable.*;
import android.util.Log;
import java.text.*;
import java.util.*;
import com.google.android.maps.*;
```

```
public class FlashMobActivity extends MapActivity implements OnClickListener {
  ArrayList<Record> locationlist = null;
  Location loc = null;
  Button blast;
  Button exit;
  Button refresh;
  EditText et1;
  String dts;
  String dlat;
  String dlon;
  String ddetails;
  MapView myMapView = null;
  Object points[];
  Drawable mobIcon = null;
  GeoPoint newPoint = null;
  MapView.LayoutParams mvlp = null;
  MapController myMapController = null;
  ImageView mapMarker = null;
  View mainview = null;
  Context myContext = null;
  // AdView adView=null;
  public double xpos;
  public double ypos;
  LocationListener mlocListener = new MyLocationListener();
  LocationManager lm = null;
  DateFormat df=new SimpleDateFormat();
  @Override
  public void onCreate(Bundle savedInstanceState) {
    super.onCreate(savedInstanceState);
    setContentView(R.layout.main);// must be the first statement
    locationlist = new ArrayList<Record>();
    myContext = this.getApplicationContext();
    lm =
(LocationManager) getSystemService(Context.LOCATION_SERVICE);
    mainview = (View) findViewById(R.layout.main);
    et1 = (EditText) findViewById(R.id.et1);
    blast = (Button) findViewById(R.id.blast);
    exit = (Button) findViewById(R.id.exit);
    refresh = (Button) findViewById(R.id.refresh);
    refresh.setOnClickListener(this);
    blast.setOnClickListener(this);
    exit.setOnClickListener(this);
    mapMe(); //finds my current location from GPS service on device
    refreshMe();
  } // ends onCreate
```

```
public void mapMe() {
  try {
    lm.requestLocationUpdates(LocationManager.GPS_PROVIDER, 0, 0,mlocListener);
    Criteria cri = new Criteria();
    cri.setAccuracy(Criteria.ACCURACY_FINE);
    String gps = lm.getBestProvider(cri, true);
    loc = lm.getLastKnownLocation(gps);
    myMapView = (MapView) findViewById(R.id.map);
    myMapView.removeView(mapMarker);
    myMapView.setSatellite(false);
    myMapController = myMapView.getController();
    myMapController.setZoom(13);
    myMapView.setBuiltInZoomControls(true);
    newPoint = new GeoPoint((int) (loc.getLatitude() * 1e6),
 (int) (loc.getLongitude() * 1e6));

    mvlp=new MapView.LayoutParams(LayoutParams.WRAP_CONTENT,
LayoutParams.WRAP_CONTENT, newPoint,
MapView.LayoutParams.CENTER);
    mapMarker = new ImageView(this);
    mapMarker.setImageResource(R.drawable.me);

    myMapView.addView(mapmaker, mvlp);

    myMapController.animateTo(newPoint);
  }catch (Exception e) {
    Toast.makeText(myContext, "Cannot determine your current location. Exiting…",
Toast.LENGTH_LONG).show();
    this.finish();
  }// ends exception
}// ends mapMe


protected boolean isRouteDisplayed() {
  return false;
}

public void onClick(View v) {
  if (v == blast) {
    Toast.makeText(myContext, "Repositioning and posting .....",
Toast.LENGTH_SHORT).show();
    mapMe(); //this is to get current coordinates
    postScene();
  }
```

```java
   if (v == refresh) {
       Toast.makeText(myContext, "Repositioning and loading mobscenes.....",Toast.
LENGTH_SHORT).show();
     refreshMe();
   }

   if (v == exit) {
     this.finish();
   }
   }// ends onClick
 public void refreshMe(){
   Socket client = null;
   mapMe(); //reposition to current position
   mobIcon = getResources().getDrawable(R.drawable.g_pin);
   mobsoverlay mo = new mobsoverlay(mobIcon, this);
   List<GeoPoint> geopoints = new ArrayList<GeoPoint>();
   locationlist.clear();
   try {
     int linecount = 0;
     String inputString="";
     String inputFields[];
     Integer ilat=null;
     Integer ilon=null;
     String idetails="";
     InetSocketAddress isa=new InetSocketAddress("aaa.bbb.ccc.ddd", 6060);
     client = new Socket();
     client.connect(isa,2000); // allow two seconds to connect
     InputStreamReader isr = new       InputStreamReader(client.getInputStream());
     BufferedReader br=new BufferedReader(isr);
     while((inputString=br.readLine())!=null){
       inputFields=inputString.split(":");
       ilat=Integer.parseInt(inputFields[0]);
       ilon=Integer.parseInt(inputFields[1]);
       idetails=inputFields[2];
       locationlist.add(new Record(ilat,ilon,idetails));
     }
     isr.close();
   }catch(IOException ioe){
     Log.e("some error",ioe.getMessage());
   }catch(NumberFormatException nfe){
     Log.i("number format error",nfe.getMessage());
   }
// now post all the collected points on the map
   GeoPoint points[] = new GeoPoint[locationlist.size()];
```

```
    int tlat;
    int tlon;
    Record rtemp;
    for (int x = 0; x < locationlist.size(); ++x) {
      rtemp=(Record)(locationlist.get(x));
      tlat=rtemp.getLat();
      tlon=rtemp.getLon();
      points[x] = (new GeoPoint(tlat, tlon));
    }
    mobIcon.setBounds(0, 0, mobIcon.getIntrinsicWidth(),
    mobIcon.getIntrinsicHeight());
    for (int x = 0; x < points.length; ++x) {
      OverlayItem overlayitem = new OverlayItem(points[x],"Mobscene",
((Record) locationlist.get(x)).details);
      mo.addOverlay(overlayitem);
    }
    if (locationlist.size() > 0) {
      mapOverlays.add(mo);
      View junk = new View(this);
      myMapView.addView(junk); // gets markers to show
      Toast.makeText(myContext, "Touch map markers for details.",
Toast.LENGTH_SHORT).show();
    }
    Toast.makeText(myContext,
    String.valueOf(locationlist.size()) + " mobscenes near you today.",
Toast.LENGTH_SHORT).show();
    }//ends method

  public void postScene() {
    String datastring = "";
    String detail = et1.getText().toString();
    String templat = String.valueOf((int)(loc.getLatitude()*1e6));
    String templon = String.valueOf((int)(loc.getLongitude()*1e6));
    datastring =   templat + ":"+ templon+ ":" + detail;
    RecordProcessor rp = new RecordProcessor(datastring);
    rp.processIt(myContext);
  }
class MyLocationListener implements LocationListener {
  public void onLocationChanged(Location l) {}
  public void onProviderDisabled(String provider) {}
  public void onProviderEnabled(String provider) {}
  public void onStatusChanged(String provider, int status, Bundle   extras) {}
}// ends mylocationlistener
```

```java
class mobsoverlay extends ItemizedOverlay {
  private ArrayList<OverlayItem> mOverlays = new    ArrayList<OverlayItem>();
  Context mContext;
  public mobsoverlay(Drawable pin) {
    super(boundCenterBottom(pin));
  }

  public mobsoverlay(Drawable pin, Context context) {
    super(boundCenterBottom(pin));
    mContext = context;
  }

  public void addOverlay(OverlayItem overlayitem) {
    mOverlays.add(overlayitem);
    populate();
  }
  protected OverlayItem createItem(int i) {
    return mOverlays.get(i);
  }

  protected boolean onTap(int index) {
    OverlayItem item = mOverlays.get(index);
    AlertDialog.Builder dialog = new AlertDialog.Builder(mContext);
    dialog.setTitle(item.getTitle());
    dialog.setMessage(item.getSnippet());
    dialog.show();
    return true;
  }

  public int size() {
    return mOverlays.size();
  }
}
class RecordProcessor {
  String datastring;

  public RecordProcessor(String ds) {
    this.datastring = ds;
  }

public void processIt(Context myContext) {
  try {
    InetSocketAddress isa=new InetSocketAddress("aaa.bbb.ccc.ddd", 6050);
    Socket client = new Socket();
```

```
        client.connect(isa,2000); // allow two seconds to connect
        OutputStreamWriter osw = new OutputStreamWriter(client.getOutputStream());
        BufferedWriter bw = new BufferedWriter(osw);
        datastring = datastring.replace(",", ";");
        Toast.makeText(myContext, datastring, Toast.LENGTH_SHORT).show();
        bw.write(datastring + "\n");
        bw.flush();
        client.close();
        Toast.makeText(myContext, "Submitted! Your mobscene was posted! ",
Toast.LENGTH_SHORT).show();
        } catch (IOException ioe) {
          Log.e("send error",ioe.getMessage());
          Toast.makeText(myContext,
"Submission failed! Please try again in a few minutes.",
Toast.LENGTH_LONG).show();
        } //ends catch block
      }//ends processIt method
    }//ends RecordProcessor class

}// ends main class
class Record {
  public Integer lat;
  public Integer lon;
  public String details;
  public Record(Integer a, Integer b, String c) {
    this.lat = a;
    this.lon = b;
    this.details = c;
  }
  public int getLat(){
    return (lat.intValue());
  }
  public int getLon(){
    return (lon.intValue());
  }
}//ends Record Class
```

Starting at the top, notice all the import statements, the last of which is the Google maps package, com.google.android.maps. This is a good place to check your project's application programming interface (API) to be sure it is correct. Under the Project menu in Eclipse, choose Properties and then select Android in the list on the left. Be sure you selected one of the Google APIs under the Build Target list. Next, notice that our application's main activity class extends the MapActivity class rather than the Activity class. This class is actually in the com.google.android.maps package, not in the standard Android packages. If you look at the following web page, http://code.google.com/android/add-ons/google-apis/reference/com/google/android/maps/MapActivity.html, you will see that use of this class requires the `<uses-library>` element in the manifest file.

Let us take a look at the mapMe( ) method that appears early in the code. This method determines the position on the map of the device using the GPS service, moves the map in the MapView to center the location, and places the appropriate marker on the position. The following code creates a set of parameters similar to those we use in the main.xml files and them applies them to the tiny ImageView object that holds our map marker:

```
mvlp=new MapView.LayoutParams(LayoutParams.WRAP_CONTENT,
LayoutParams.WRAP_CONTENT, newPoint,
MapView.LayoutParams.CENTER);
```

The lines that follow select the graphic for the marker, apply the parameter set, and add the marker to the map. Finally, the map controller moves the map to center the marker:

```
mapMarker = new ImageView(this);
mapMarker.setImageResource(R.drawable.me);

myMapView.addView(mapMarker,mvlp);
myMapController.animateTo(newPoint);
```

The MapActivity interface requires the following method. Java programmers run into methods required by interfaces quite often, and many end up doing nothing in a given application; they just have to be there.

```
protected boolean isRouteDisplayed() {
  return false;
}
```

The refreshMe( ) method polls the server machine to check for new mob scenes. It runs once when the application is started and again whenever the user wants the map refreshed. First, you will notice that the IP address of the server is stated as aaa.bbb.ccc.ddd. Remember, you need to insert your server's IP address. In this method there is a reference to a class called Record. This is a class created for this application; it is not part of Android or Google. It is designed to hold data on mob scenes extracted from the server's data table.

Imagine that the MapView is a paper map and that it can have multiple layers of cellophane or glass laid on it, each having a series of marks on them. The marks correspond to locations so when they fall over the map, they land in the right positions.

The `MapView` on the device works this way with a series of overlays. We take just one of these overlays and attach markers for our mob scenes to it. That is the next job of the `refreshMe( )` method. The method takes the list of `Record` objects it retrieved from the server, gives them each a marker specified by `R.drawable.g_pin`, adds them to an overlay layer, and then displays the layer. The `mobsoverlay` class extends the `ItemizedOverlay` class, and the essential abstract methods of `ItemizedOverlay` are added to the code. Likewise, the `MyLocationListener` class extends the `LocationListener` class and must implement the abstract methods.

The `postScene( )` method responds to the Post button on the screen. It grabs the current location based on the GPS service in the device, combines it with the description of the mob scene the user entered, and passes it to the `RecordProcessor` object. The `RecordProcessor` class is designed to contact the server and submit a mob scene.

When the application is running, it should look like Figure 12.5. Here, the user has begun to post a mob scene. The description is in the `EditText` field on the top of the screen.

Figure 12.5
Emulator showing Flash Mob application.

Assume that another user, not too far away, opens the application on her mobile device. She might see what appears in Figure 12.6.

Figure 12.6
Emulator showing flash mob location in upper-left corner.

Notice that along with the dark shaded pin in the middle of the screen, which marks the user's location, there is a lighter pin with an exclamation mark in the upper left. This is a mob scene marker. Figure 12.7 shows what the user would see if she touched the mob scene marker.

Figure 12.7
Emulator showing details associated with a flash mob site.

The XML Version

On the server side, the program must take the data from the database and create an instance of the Document class. The Document creates a framework for the data, which can be many records long. It can be rendered in many forms later; in our case we need to render it as XML. To do this, we pass the Document object to another method called renderAsXML( ). This method specifies the encoding and some other specifications and ultimately yields a String variable that contains the whole data set. That String is fed to the output stream so it arrives at the mobile device as an XML file.

On the mobile device (client) side, the stream is read by an instance of XmlPull-Parser, similar to the XML example in Chapter 9, "Text Files, Data Tables, and XML." Note that we also specify US-ASCII encoding on the receiving side. The revised server-side application, this time called FlashMobXMLServer.java, is listed here:

```java
import java.io.BufferedReader;
import java.io.BufferedWriter;
import java.io.IOException;
import java.io.InputStream;
import java.io.InputStreamReader;
import java.io.OutputStream;
import java.io.OutputStreamWriter;
import java.io.StringWriter;
import java.net.ServerSocket;
import java.net.Socket;
import java.sql.*;
import javax.xml.parsers.*;
import javax.xml.transform.*;
import javax.xml.transform.stream.*;
import javax.xml.transform.dom.*;
import org.w3c.dom.*;

public class FlashMobXMLServer {
  public static void main(String[] args) {
    FlashMobXMLServer fms = new FlashMobXMLServer();
    Outgoing og = new Outgoing();
    Incoming ic = new Incoming();
    og.start();
    ic.start();
  }
} // ends FlashMobServer class

class Outgoing extends Thread {
```

```
  ServerSocket ss;
  public void run() {
    try {
      ss = new ServerSocket(6060);
    } catch (IOException ioe) {
   // Logger entry if desired
    }
    while (true) {
      try {
        Socket s1 = ss.accept();
        OutputStream os = s1.getOutputStream();
        OutputStreamWriter osr = new OutputStreamWriter(os);
        BufferedWriter bw = new BufferedWriter(osr);
        DocumentBuilderFactory myDBF = DocumentBuilderFactory
.newInstance();
        DocumentBuilder db = myDBF.newDocumentBuilder();
        Document doc = db.newDocument();
        Element results = doc.createElement("Results");
        doc.appendChild(results);
        Class.forName("com.mysql.jdbc.Driver");
        Connection myConnection = DriverManager.getConnection(
"jdbc:mysql://localhost:3306/mydatabase","myaccount", "mypassword");
        Statement myStatement = myConnection.createStatement();
        ResultSet myResultSet = myStatement
.executeQuery("select lat,lon,details from flashmob where date(ts)=curdate()");
        ResultSetMetaData rsmd = myResultSet.getMetaData();
        int colCount = rsmd.getColumnCount();
        myResultSet.beforeFirst();
        while (myResultSet.next()) {
          Element row = doc.createElement("Row");
          results.appendChild(row);
          for (int c = 1; c <= colCount; ++c) {
            try {
              String columnName = rsmd.getColumnName(c);
              Object value = myResultSet.getObject(c);
              Element node = doc.createElement(columnName);
              node.appendChild(doc.createTextNode(value
.toString()));
              row.appendChild(node);
            } catch (Exception e) { }
          }
        }
        myConnection.close();
        bw.write(renderAsXML(doc));
```

```
        bw.flush();
        s1.close();
        } catch (Exception e) {
// Logger entry if desired
        }
      }
    }

  public static String renderAsXML(Document doc) {
// throws TransformerConfigurationException, TransformerException{
    try {
      DOMSource domSource = new DOMSource(doc);
      TransformerFactory tf = TransformerFactory.newInstance();
      Transformer transformer = tf.newTransformer();
      transformer.setOutputProperty(OutputKeys.METHOD, "xml");
      transformer.setOutputProperty(OutputKeys.ENCODING, "US-ASCII");
      transformer.setOutputProperty(OutputKeys.INDENT, "yes");
      StringWriter sw = new StringWriter();
      StreamResult sr = new StreamResult(sw);
      transformer.transform(domSource, sr);
      return sw.toString();
    }catch (Exception e) {
// Logger entry if desired
      return "Error";
    }
  }// ends method
}// ends Outgoing class

class Incoming extends Thread {
  ServerSocket ss = null;

  public void run() {
    try {
      ss = new ServerSocket(6050);
    } catch (IOException ioe) {}
    while (true) {
      try {
        Socket s1 = ss.accept();
        InputStream is = s1.getInputStream();
        InputStreamReader isr = new InputStreamReader(is);
        BufferedReader br = new BufferedReader(isr);
        String greeting = br.readLine();
        String[] newrecord;
        newrecord = greeting.split(":");
```

```
        Class.forName("com.mysql.jdbc.Driver");
        Connection myConnection = DriverManager.getConnection(
"jdbc:mysql://localhost:3306/mydatabase", "myaccount", "mypassword");
        Statement myStatement = myConnection.createStatement();
        String fields = newrecord[0] + "," + newrecord[1] + ",'"
+ newrecord[2] + "'";
        boolean okay = myStatement
.execute("insert into flashmob(lat,lon,details) values ("
+ fields + ")");
        myConnection.close();
        s1.close();
      } catch (Exception e) {
    // Logger entry if desired
      }
    }
  }
} // ends incoming class
```

On the mobile device side, we can just add a method to interpret the incoming stream as XML instead of colon-delimited text. It will replace the functionality of the refreshMe( ) method, so we call it refreshMeXML( ). No changes are necessary to the manifest file or the main.xml file, but there many additional import statements to be aware of. Also, remember to change the method calls to refreshMe( ) with method calls to refreshMeXML( ). There is one at the end of the onCreate( ) method and one in the listener for the Refresh button. The new Java code containing the XML changes is listed here:

```
package com.sheusi.FlashMob;


import java.io.*;
import java.net.*;
import java.util.ArrayList;
import android.app.AlertDialog;
import android.os.Bundle;
import android.view.View.OnClickListener;
import android.view.*;
import android.widget.*;
import android.content.*;
import android.location.*;
import android.view.ViewGroup.*;
import android.graphics.drawable.*;
import android.util.Log;
import java.text.*;
import java.util.*;
```

```java
import com.google.android.maps.*;
import org.xmlpull.v1.*;


public class FlashMobActivity extends MapActivity implements OnClickListener {
  ArrayList<Record> locationlist = null;
  Location loc = null;
  Button blast;
  Button exit;
  Button refresh;
  EditText et1;
  String dts;
  String dlat;
  String dlon;
  String ddetails;
  MapView myMapView = null;
  Object points[];
  Drawable mobIcon = null;
  GeoPoint newPoint = null;
  MapView.LayoutParams mmp = null;
  MapController myMapController = null;
  ImageView mapMarker = null;
  View mainview = null;
  Context myContext = null;
// AdView adView=null;
  public double xpos;
  public double ypos;
  LocationListener mlocListener = new MyLocationListener();
  LocationManager lm = null;
  DateFormat df=new SimpleDateFormat();
  @Override
  public void onCreate(Bundle savedInstanceState) {
    super.onCreate(savedInstanceState);
    setContentView(R.layout.main);// must be the first statement
    locationlist = new ArrayList<Record>();
    myContext = this.getApplicationContext();
    lm = (LocationManager) getSystemService(Context.LOCATION_SERVICE);
    mainview = (View) findViewById(R.layout.main);
    et1 = (EditText) findViewById(R.id.et1);
    blast = (Button) findViewById(R.id.blast);
    exit = (Button) findViewById(R.id.exit);
    refresh = (Button) findViewById(R.id.refresh);
    refresh.setOnClickListener(this);
    blast.setOnClickListener(this);
```

```
      exit.setOnClickListener(this);
      mapMe(); //finds my current location from GPS service on device
      refreshMeXML();
  } // ends onCreate


  public void mapMe() {
    try {
      lm.requestLocationUpdates(LocationManager.GPS_PROVIDER, 0, 0,mlocListener);
      Criteria cri = new Criteria();
      cri.setAccuracy(Criteria.ACCURACY_FINE);
      String gps = lm.getBestProvider(cri, true);
      loc = lm.getLastKnownLocation(gps);
// end copied code
      myMapView = (MapView) findViewById(R.id.map);
      myMapView.removeView(mapMarker);
      myMapView.setSatellite(false);
      myMapController = myMapView.getController();
      myMapController.setZoom(13);
      myMapView.setBuiltInZoomControls(true);
      newPoint = new GeoPoint((int) (loc.getLatitude() * 1e6), (int)
(loc.getLongitude()* 1e6));
      mmp = new MapView.LayoutParams(LayoutParams.WRAP_CONTENT,
LayoutParams.WRAP_CONTENT, newPoint,
MapView.LayoutParams.BOTTOM);
      myMapController.animateTo(newPoint);
      mapMarker = new ImageView(this);
      mapMarker.setImageResource(R.drawable.me);
      myMapView.addView(mapMarker, mmp);
    }catch (Exception e) {
      Toast.makeText(myContext, "Cannot determine your current location.
Exiting...",Toast.LENGTH_LONG).show();
      this.finish();
    }// ends exception
  }// ends mapMe
  protected boolean isRouteDisplayed() {
    return false;
  }
  public void onClick(View v) {
    if (v == blast) {
      Toast.makeText(myContext, "Repositioning and posting .....",
Toast.LENGTH_SHORT).show();
      mapMe(); //this is to get current coordinates
      postScene();
```

```
   }
   if (v == refresh) {
     Toast.makeText(myContext, "Repositioning and loading
mobscenes.....",Toast.LENGTH_SHORT).show();
     refreshMeXML();
   }
   if (v == exit) {
     this.finish();
   }
 }// ends onClick

 public void refreshMeXML(){
   Socket client = null;
   mapMe(); //reposition to current position
   mobIcon = getResources().getDrawable(R.drawable.g_pin);
   mobsoverlay mo = new mobsoverlay(mobIcon, this);
   List<Overlay> mapOverlays = myMapView.getOverlays();
   locationlist.clear();
   try {
     int ilat=0;
     int ilon=0;
     String idetails="";
     InetSocketAddress isa=new InetSocketAddress("aaa.bbb.ccc.ddd", 6060);
     client = new Socket();
     client.connect(isa,2000); // allow two seconds to connect
     InputStream is=client.getInputStream();
     try{
     XmlPullParserFactory factory=XmlPullParserFactory.newInstance();
     factory.setNamespaceAware(true);
     XmlPullParser xpp=factory.newPullParser();
     xpp.setInput(is,"US-ASCII");
     xpp.next();
     String curtag="";
     int eventType=xpp.getEventType();
     while (eventType!=XmlPullParser.END_DOCUMENT){
       if(eventType==XmlPullParser.START_DOCUMENT){}
       if (eventType==XmlPullParser.START_TAG){
         curtag=xpp.getName();
       }
       if(eventType==XmlPullParser.TEXT){
         if(curtag.equals("lat")){
           ilat=Integer.parseInt(xpp.getText());
         }
```

```
      if(curtag.equals("lon")){
        ilon=Integer.parseInt(xpp.getText());
      }
      if(curtag.equals("details")){
        idetails=xpp.getText();
        locationlist.add(new Record(ilat,ilon,idetails));
      }
      Log.i("text",xpp.getText().toString());
      curtag="";
    }
    eventType=xpp.next();
  }//end while

}catch(XmlPullParserException xppe){
  Log.i("pp excep", xppe.getMessage());
}

client.close();
}catch(IOException ioe){
  Log.i("some error",ioe.getMessage());
}catch(NumberFormatException nfe){
  Log.i("number format error",nfe.getMessage());
}
// now post all the collected points on the map
GeoPoint points[] = new GeoPoint[locationlist.size()];
int tlat;
int tlon;
Record rtemp;
for (int x = 0; x < locationlist.size(); ++x) {
  rtemp=(Record)(locationlist.get(x));
  tlat=rtemp.getLat();
  tlon=rtemp.getLon();
  points[x] = (new GeoPoint(tlat, tlon));
}
mobIcon.setBounds(0, 0, mobIcon.getIntrinsicWidth(), mobIcon
.getIntrinsicHeight());
  for (int x = 0; x < points.length; ++x) {
    OverlayItem overlayitem = new OverlayItem(points[x],
"Mobscene",((Record) locationlist.get(x)).getDetails());
    mo.addOverlay(overlayitem);
  }
  if (locationlist.size() > 0) {
    mapOverlays.add(mo);
    View junk = new View(this);
```

```
      myMapView.addView(junk); // gets markers to show
      Toast.makeText(myContext, "Touch map markers for
details.",Toast.LENGTH_SHORT).show();
    }
    Toast.makeText(myContext,String.valueOf(locationlist.size()) + " mobscenes near
you today.", Toast.LENGTH_SHORT).show();
  }
  public void refreshMe(){
    Socket client = null;
    mapMe(); //reposition to current position
    mobIcon = getResources().getDrawable(R.drawable.g_pin);
    mobsoverlay mo = new mobsoverlay(mobIcon, this);
    List<Overlay> mapOverlays = myMapView.getOverlays();
    locationlist.clear();
    try {
      String inputString="";
      String inputFields[];
      Integer ilat=null;
      Integer ilon=null;
      String idetails="";
      InetSocketAddress isa=new InetSocketAddress("aaa.bbb.ccc.ddd", 6060);
      client = new Socket();
      client.connect(isa,2000); // allow two seconds to connect
      InputStreamReader isr = new InputStreamReader(client.getInputStream());
      BufferedReader br=new BufferedReader(isr);
      while((inputString=br.readLine())!=null){
        et1.setText(inputString);
        inputFields=inputString.split(":");
        ilat=Integer.parseInt(inputFields[0]);
        ilon=Integer.parseInt(inputFields[1]);
        idetails=inputFields[2];
        locationlist.add(new Record(ilat,ilon,idetails));
        et1.append("making a record\n");
      }
      isr.close();
    }catch(IOException ioe){
     Log.e("some error",ioe.getMessage());
    }catch(NumberFormatException nfe){
      Log.i("number format error",nfe.getMessage());
    }
    // now post all the collected points on the map
    GeoPoint points[] = new GeoPoint[locationlist.size()];
    int tlat;
```

```
    int tlon;
    int temp;
    Record rtemp;
    for (int x = 0; x < locationlist.size(); ++x) {
      rtemp=(Record)(locationlist.get(x));
      tlat=rtemp.getLat();
      tlon=rtemp.getLon();
      points[x] = (new GeoPoint(tlat, tlon));
    }
     mobIcon.setBounds(0, 0, mobIcon.getIntrinsicWidth(), mobIcon.getIntrinsicHeight
());
    for (int x = 0; x < points.length; ++x) {
      OverlayItem overlayitem = new OverlayItem(points[x],
"Mobscene",((Record) locationlist.get(x)).getDetails());
      mo.addOverlay(overlayitem);
    }
    if (locationlist.size() > 0) {
      mapOverlays.add(mo);
      View junk = new View(this);
      myMapView.addView(junk); // gets markers to show
      Toast.makeText(myContext, "Touch map markers for
details.",Toast.LENGTH_SHORT).show();
    }
    Toast.makeText(myContext,
String.valueOf(locationlist.size()) + " mobscenes near you today.",
Toast.LENGTH_SHORT).show();
  }//ends method

  public void postScene() {
    String datastring = "";
    String detail = et1.getText().toString();
    String templat = String.valueOf((int)(loc.getLatitude()*1e6));
    String templon = String.valueOf((int)(loc.getLongitude()*1e6));
    datastring =   templat + ":"+ templon+ ":" + detail;
    RecordProcessor rp = new RecordProcessor(datastring);
    rp.processIt(myContext);
  }
  class MyLocationListener implements LocationListener {
    public void onLocationChanged(Location l) {
    }

    public void onProviderDisabled(String provider) {}
    public void onProviderEnabled(String provider) {}
```

```java
    public void onStatusChanged(String provider, int status, Bundle extras) {}
}// ends mylocationlistener

class mobsoverlay extends ItemizedOverlay {
    private ArrayList<OverlayItem> mOverlays = new    ArrayList<OverlayItem>();
    Context mContext;
    public mobsoverlay(Drawable pin) {
        super(boundCenterBottom(pin));
    }
    public mobsoverlay(Drawable pin, Context context) {
        super(boundCenterBottom(pin));
        mContext = context;
    }
    public void addOverlay(OverlayItem overlayitem) {
        mOverlays.add(overlayitem);
        populate();
    }

    protected OverlayItem createItem(int i) {
        return mOverlays.get(i);
    }
    protected boolean onTap(int index) {
        OverlayItem item = mOverlays.get(index);
        AlertDialog.Builder dialog = new AlertDialog.Builder(mContext);
        dialog.setTitle(item.getTitle());
        dialog.setMessage(item.getSnippet());
        dialog.show();
        return true;
    }
    public int size() {
        return mOverlays.size();
    }
}class RecordProcessor {
    String datastring;
    public RecordProcessor(String ds) {
        this.datastring = ds;
    }
    public void processIt(Context myContext) {
        try {
            InetSocketAddress isa=new InetSocketAddress("aaa.bbb.ccc.ddd", 6050);
            Socket client = new Socket();
            client.connect(isa,2000); // allow two seconds to connect
            OutputStreamWriter osw = new OutputStreamWriter(client.getOutputStream());
            BufferedWriter bw = new BufferedWriter(osw);
```

```
            datastring = datastring.replace(",", ";");
            Toast.makeText(myContext, datastring, Toast.LENGTH_SHORT).show();
            bw.write(datastring + "\n");
            bw.flush();
            client.close();
            Toast.makeText(myContext, "Submitted! Your mobscene was posted!
",Toast.LENGTH_SHORT).show();
          }catch (IOException ioe) {
            Log.e("send error",ioe.getMessage());
            Toast.makeText(myContext,
"Submission failed! Please try again in a few minutes.",
Toast.LENGTH_LONG).show();
          } //ends catch block

          }// ends the processIt method
    }//ends RecordProcessor class

}// ends main class
class Record {
  private int lat;
  private int lon;
  private String details;
  public Record(int a, int b, String c) {
    this.lat = a;
    this.lon = b;
    this.details = c;
  }
  public int getLat(){
    return lat;
  }
  public int getLon(){
    return lon;
  }
  public String getDetails(){
    return details;
  }
}//ends Record
```

There is no visible change to the application, so additional screen shots aren't necessary. The application could be further modified to transmit data from the mobile
device as XML, but doing so would require changes to the "incoming" thread on
the server side.

INDEX

Symbols

& (ampersand), 262
// (double slash), 127
@ sign, 45
* (wildcard character), 49

A

AbsoluteLayout class, 34
ACTION_VIEW action, 144
Activity class
   description, 26
   methods, 28
   multiscreen application, 143, 146, 152–153, 164
   pop-up dialog box, 159
   state chart, 27
   subclass, 10
activity name, 10, 14
ADB (Android Debug Bridge), 57–59
adb command, 58–59, 252
addView() method, 94
ADK (Android Development Kit), 4–5, 7, 57, 94, 208
AlertDialog class, 156–159, 172
AlertDialog.Builder class, 158, 173
ampersand (&), 262
Android Debug Bridge (ADB), 57–59
Android Development Kit (ADK), 4–5, 7, 57, 94, 208
Android SDK and AVD Manager, 56
AndroidManifest.xml file, 13, 15
API (application programming interface), 9, 50, 118–119
.apk file, 241–243
application design
   component IDs, 45–46
   controls, 46–55

emulator communication, 57–59
emulator creation/configuration, 55–56
graphical user interface, 29
name, 9
screen layout and main.xml file, 30–44
text styles, 44
XML structure elements, 30
application programming interface
   (API), 9, 50, 118–119
array, image, 181
ArrayAdapter class, 78, 88
ArrayList class, 105, 213
arrays of string, 43, 75
assignment statements, 77
AVD Edit panel (Eclipse), 120

B

Back button, 182
back key, symbolic constant, 54
background color, 40–41
Bitmap class, 108, 113
bitmap graphics, 43
BMP file format, 179
BorderLayout class, 34
breakpoint, 24–25
Bundle class, 148, 169–170
Button class, 46, 60, 144–145
button controls, screen layout, 35
button events, 46, 50–55

C

Calendar class, 78, 81
Camera button key, symbolic constant, 54

287